The Times' Whistle.

DUBLIN: WILLIAM MᶜGEE, 18, NASSAU STREET.
EDINBURGH: T. G. STEVENSON, 22, SOUTH FREDERICK STREET.
GLASGOW: HUGH HOPKINS, ROYAL BANK PLACE.
BERLIN: ASHER & CO., UNTER DEN LINDEN, 11.
NEW YORK: C. SCRIBNER & CO.; LEYPOLDT & HOLT.
PHILADELPHIA: J. B. LIPPINCOTT & CO.

The Times' Whistle:

or

A Newe Daunce of Seven Satires, and other Poems:

Compiled by R. C., Gent.

———◇———

NOW FIRST EDITED FROM MS. Y. 8. 3. IN THE LIBRARY OF
CANTERBURY CATHEDRAL;

With Introduction, Notes, and Glossary,

BY

J. M. COWPER,

EDITOR OF 'ENGLAND IN THE REIGN OF KING HENRY THE EIGHTH,' ETC.

LONDON:

PUBLISHED FOR THE EARLY ENGLISH TEXT SOCIETY,
BY N. TRÜBNER & CO., 60, PATERNOSTER ROW.

——

MDCCCLXXI.

OXFORD
UNIVERSITY PRESS

Great Clarendon Street, Oxford OX2 6DP
United Kingdom

Oxford University Press is a department of the University of Oxford.
It furthers the University's objective of excellence in research, scholarship,
and education by publishing worldwide. Oxford is a registered trade mark of
Oxford University Press in the UK and in certain other countries

© The Early English Text Society 1973

The moral rights of the authors have been asserted

Database right Oxford University Press (maker)

First Edition published in 1973

Published in the United States of America by Oxford University Press
198 Madison Avenue, New York, NY 10016, United States of America

British Library Cataloguing in Publication Data
Data available

Library of Congress Cataloging in Publication Data
Data available

Original Series, 48

ISBN 978-0-85-991826-8

CONTENTS.

INTRODUCTION.

THE Prologue to Hall's Satires opens with these lines :—

"I first adventure, with fool-hardy might
To tread the steps of perilous despite.
I first adventure, follow me who list,
And be the second English Satirist."

But Hall was hardly correct in his assertion that he was the first to adventure in this perilous path, for Hake's *Newes out of Powles Churchyarde* had been given to the public eighteen years before, though without attracting the attention and obtaining the honour which befell Hall's "toothless satires."[1] His challenge, "who 'll be the second English Satirist," was not, however, long unaccepted. In the following year (1598) appeared Marston's *Scourge of Villanie* and *The Metamorphosis of Pigmalion's Image*. Samuel Rowlands also (as well as others) now began to write, and continued to add during

---

[1] Thomas Timme's *Discoverie of Ten Lepers* appeared in 1592. The "Ten Lepers" are :—

1. The Schismatique.	6. The Glutton.
2. The Church-robber.	7. The Adulterer or Fornicator.
3. The Simoniac.	8. The Couetous Man.
4. The Hypocrite.	9. The Murtherer.
5. The Proud Man.	10. The Murmurer.

The full title is :—

A plaine discouerie of ten English Lepers, verie noisome and hurtfull to the Church and common wealth : Setting before our eies the iniquitie of these latter dayes, and indusing vs to a due consideration of our selues. Published by Thomas Timme Minister. London, Printed by Peter Short, dwelling vpon Bredstreet hill, &c. 1592. 4to. A to M in fours. Dedicated to Sir William Brooke, Baron of Cobham (*Hazlitt*), Brit. Mus. 4103. e.

many years to the satiric literature of the time. It was in vain that
the authorities endeavoured to wrest the "Rhamnusian whip" from
the hands of these powerful writers ; it was in vain to enjoin "that
noe Satyres or Epigrams be printed hereafter." Whitgift and Ban-
croft might burn them, but they could not stay their re-appearance,
and the Satirist found not only materials for books in abundance,
but buyers also, and Satires continued to appear long after the
death of the "Virgin Queen," whose ministers condemned Hall's
Satires to the flames, but spared Harington's *Orlando Furioso*.[1]

The date at which the *Times' Whistle* was written is easily
ascertained. The Rev. H. J. Todd, who compiled the Canterbury
Catalogue, though acquainted with the MS., was incorrect in fixing
the date "near 1598." The internal evidence is satisfactory upon
this point. The reference to Faux and Ravaillac[2] gives the first
clue : the former died in 1605 and the latter in 1610. Other
allusions more to the point are to Coryate's *Crudities*, p. 26, which
appeared in 1611, and to Dr Carrier,[3] p. 52. Now Carrier died

---

[1] See *Notes and Queries*, 3rd S. xii. 436, and Dyce's *Marlowe*, p. xxxviii.
note.

[2] Ravaillac, a lay-Jesuit, had, it is said, watched a whole twelvemonth
for an opportunity to murder the king, Henry IV., and at last stabbed him as
he was on his way to the Bastile. The assassin was at once apprehended and
carefully guarded from the fury of the populace. Many consultations were
held how to punish him, some Italian physicians offering to prescribe a tor-
ment which should continue without intermission for three days. "But he
scaped only with this, his body was pulled between four horses, that one
might hear his bones crack, and after the dislocation, they were set again,
and so he was carried in a cart standing half naked, with a torch in that hand
which had committed the murder ; and in the place where the act was done,
it was cut off, and a gauntlet of hot oil was clapped upon the stump, to
stanch the blood, whereat he gave a doleful shriek. Then was he brought
upon a stage, where a new pair of boots was provided for him, half filled with
boiling oil. Then his body was pincered, and hot oil poured into the holes ;
in all the extremity of this torture he scarce showed any sense of pain, but
when the gauntlet was clapped upon his arms to stanch the flux, at which
time he was reeking with blood, he gave a shriek only. He bore up against
all these torments about three hours before he died."—Howel's *Familiar
Letters*, ed. 1678, p. 25.

John Taylor, in his *Complaint of Christmas* (1646) mentions, among
others, the following *Saints :* Saint *Raviliac*, Saint *Faux*, Saint *Garnet*.

[3] Benjamin Carrier, or Carier, D.D., was the son of Anthony Carrier, a learned
and devout preacher, who caused his son to be strictly educated in the Pro-
testant religion, and afterwards in academical literature at Cambridge, where
he became a fellow of C. C. Coll., and a noted scholar and preacher. About

" before Midsummer 1614," probably in May or the early part of June in that year, and hence it is evident that the *Satires* cannot have an earlier date than the middle of 1614 ; most probably they were not finished before the end of this or the beginning of the following year.

The *Poems* will help us to fix the later date. In 1616 Ben Jonson's *Works*, containing his Epigrams, appeared, and to these there is a reference in the Minor Poems.[1] If " R. C." did not see these Epigrams of Jonson's until they appeared in the "Works," then 1616 may be safely taken as the later date, and we are able to fix the Satires and Poems as having been written between Midsummer 1614 and the end of 1616, sufficiently near to answer every purpose. But we know that it was the fashion then for authors to hand about their writings in manuscript.[2] There is abundant evidence that Jonson did so, and presumptive evidence that " R. C." had seen those Epigrams before they were given to the world.

A reference to Jonson will show this. His Eighteenth Epigram, addressed " To my mere English Censurer," answers objections which had been made to his new style of epigrams, and their being unlike those of Weever and Davis. Epigram xlix. is addressed

" To PLAYWRIGHT.

Playwright me reades, and still my verses damnes ;
He sayes, I want the tongue of epigrammes ;
I have no salt ; no bawdrie he doth meane,
For wittie, in his language, is obscene.

the time when James I. came to the throne of England, Carrier published one or more sermons, was made a Royal Chaplain, and one of the first Fellows of Chelsea College, founded by Dr Matthew Sutcliff. Becoming very unsettled in his religious opinions, he abandoned the Church of England for the Church of Rome, and removed to Liege, where he wrote his *Missive* to the king, containing the motives which led him to renounce Protestantism. This appeared in October, 1614. He also published a Letter of the miserable Ends of such as impugn the Catholic Church, which appeared in 1615. He died, according to Anth. à Wood, before Midsummer-day, 1614, when he " concluded his last day, putting thereby a period to the great imaginations that men of learning had of him and his worth, and to the expectation of other books to be published." For further information the reader is referred to a valuable note in *Notes and Queries*, 4th S. vii. 130 ; Wood's *Fasti Oxon. ;* and Bohn's *Lowndes*, but the fullest account of Carrier which I have seen is that in Masters's History of C. C. C. Cambridge (Camb. 1753).

[1] p. 132. [2] Dyce's *Marlowe*, p. 65, note.

    Playwright, I loath to have thy manners knowne
    In my chaste booke : professe them in thine owne."
Jonson's Works, folio, 1616.

This reads very much like an answer to that of " R. C." The latter says :—

    " Peruse his booke, thou shalt not find a dram
      Of witt befitting a true Epigram " ;

and the retort is,

    " He sayes I want the tongue of epigrammes ;
      I have no salt ; no bawdrie he doth meane,
    For wittie, in his language, is obscene."[1]

One other point as to date. The poem *In Neandrem* refers, no doubt, to the visit of James I. to Cambridge. Now this visit took place in March, 1615, and gave rise to much good and ill-humoured banter. Francis (afterwards Sir Francis) Nethersole was Public Orator at the time, and, all are agreed, made something very much like a fool of himself. But it cannot be to him that the poem refers. Had he been " struck mute with fear " he would have been spared such taunts as

    " Now come we to the wonderment
      Of Christendom, and eke of Kent,
      The Trinity ; which to surpass,
      Doth deck her spokesman by a glass :
      Who, clad in gay and silken weeds,
      Thus opes his mouth, hark how he speeds.

    " I wonder what your grace doth here,
      Who have expected been twelve year,

---

[1] I am indebted to Mr Furnivall for the following :—
In the Sale Catalogue of Lilly's books is a copy (No. 1557) of the first edition of Ben Jonson's Workes, 1616, and
  On the fly-leaf are the following verses in a cotemporary handwriting :—
    " Jonson that whilome brought the guilty age
      To suffer for her misdeeds on ye stage,
      Ruin'd by age now cannot hold out play,
      And must bee forc'd to throw his cards away :
      For since he so ill keeps what hee earst wonne,
      Since that his reputation 's lost and gone,
      The age sweares she 'll no longer hold him play
      With her attention ; but without delay
      Will rise, if some fresh Gamester will not fitte,
      That 's furnished with a better stocke of witte."
Catalogue, p. 160.

> And this your son, fair *Carolus*,
> That is so *Jacobissimus:*
> Here's none, of all, your grace refuses,
> You are most welcome to our Muses";

and more to the same purpose.[1]

In *A New Quaint Ballad of Cambridge*, the author of which is unknown, we read—

> " Oxford she a Christ-church had,
>   To entertain the king ;
> And Cambridge had a Trinity,
>   And scarce one wise therein.
> ' Most Jacob'd Charles,' did Cambridge cry,
>   'Thou welcome art to us ;'
> An Oxford boy must have untruss'd,
>   If he had crièd thus."[2]

In *News out of Cambridge*[3] also the Trinity Oration is dwelt upon ; but we learn in addition that Cambridge not only was guilty of nonsense there, but of absolute failure at St Mary's, as we shall show further on. If, then, the poem *In Neandrem* refers to this event, we have another element in fixing the date, and the years 1614 to 1616 may be accepted as conclusive.

To the question, " Who was ' R. C.' ?" I am unable to give an answer. "There were," says Mr Corser,[4] " several poetical authors about this period who rejoiced in these initials, Robert Chamberlaine, Robert Chester, Roger Cocks, Robert Copland, Roger Cotton, Ralph Crane, Richard Crashaw, Robert Crowley, and Robert Croft," and to these may be added Richard Carew, Robert Carliell, and Richard Corbet, successively Bishop of Oxford and Norwich. Several of these may be dismissed at once—they were dead, or wrote later than when these Satires were written ; Carew, Carliell, Corbet, Crane, and others, were alive, but to few of these can this volume be attributed. One well-known scholar[5] thinks Richard Carew was the author ; another[6] suggests Ralph Crane. But after an examination of some of their writings I am reluctantly compelled to say I do not think either Carew or Crane wrote the *Times' Whistle*. If either

---

[1] *Corbet's Poems*, ed. Gilchrist, 1807, pp. 17, 18.
[2] Inedited Miscellanies. Privately printed, 1870.   [3] *Ibid.*
[4] *Collectanea Anglo-Poetica*, p. 231.
[5] J. Payne Collier, Esq.   [6] W. Carew Hazlitt, Esq.

did, then it must be confessed that their known writings are far inferior to these Satires. A few lines in *Crane's New Year's Gift* are all that can bear comparison with any portion of this volume :—

> ——" His great Prouidence (neuer forsaking)
> Did first excite thee to this vnder-taking :
> He bids thee write : rely on him, and send
> Thy prayers vp, and he will fairely end
> This thy desire."—*N. Y. Gift*, p. 2.

> " Euery one
> Moues by his power, liues by his permission,
> And can do nothing if the prohibition
> Of the Almighty doe oppugne ; it lies
> Only in him to end each enterprise."—*T. Whistle*, p. 3.

> ——" All such labours in his nostrils stinke,
> And therfore shall prove fruitlesse : men intend,
> But God it is that consummates the end."—*Ib.*, p. 17.

There is a writer, who, but for one difficulty, to be mentioned shortly, would meet all the requirements of the case, and that is Richard Corbet, who was at this time very active with his pen. He was born at Ewell, in Surrey, in 1582, received the rudiments of his education at Westminster School, and in 1598 was entered at Broadgate Hall, and in the following year was admitted a student of Christ-Church College, Oxford. In 1605 he graduated Master of Arts, and became celebrated as a wit and a poet.[1] A man who had the reputation of being a wit and a poet, and who was at one time found in a tavern with the jolly fellows of his day; who at another time, and after he was Doctor of Divinity, was seen putting off his Doctor's gown and putting on a leathern jacket, and singing ballads at Abingdon Cross, certainly would not be found among the ranks of the Puritans : and so we find him undisguisedly opposed to Abbott, at this time Archbishop of Canterbury, and siding with Laud, then rising into fame. In 1616 he was recommended by Convocation as a proper person to be elected to Chelsea College, of which, as we have already seen,[2] Benjamin Carrier had been a Fellow. Even when promoted to a bishopric, Corbet could not forget, and did not choose to abandon, some of his jovial habits, for it is said that he would sometimes take

---

[1] *The Poems of Richard Corbet*, edited by Octavius Gilchrist, 1807.
[2] p. x, *note* [3].

the key of the wine-cellar, and with his chaplain, Dr Lushington, would go and lock himself in and be merry. First of all the Bishop would lay down his hood, with "There lies the Doctor;" then he would put off his gown, with "There lies the Bishop;" and then it was "Here's to thee, Corbet," and, "Here's to thee, Lushington!" The man who could act thus would be the very man to write the lines

> "Then straight into the cellar he 'll them bring—
> 'Tis sweetest drinking at the very spring,"[1]

and to record such a journey as that to Islington to eat cream,[2] described on page 83, and to be credited with writing the song in praise of good ale, which is sometimes attributed to him.[3]

Corbet was certainly no "precisian." But in spite of the want of an austerity befitting his sacred calling, and his hatred of the go-to-meeting portion of Englishmen, it is gratifying to find that the merry bishop died beloved and honoured. "In no record of his life is there the slightest trace of malevolence or tyranny. 'He was,' says Fuller, 'of a courteous carriage, and no destructive nature to any who offended him, counting himself plentifully repaired with a jest upon him.' Benevolent, generous, and spirited in his public character; sincere, amiable, and affectionate in private life; correct, eloquent, and ingenious as a poet;[4] he appears to have deserved and enjoyed through life the patronage and friendship of the great, and the applause and estimation of the good."[5]

Such was the man; and his character seems perfectly consistent with the theory that he wrote these *Satires* and *Poems*. It now remains to present portions of Corbet's acknowledged writings, that the reader may compare them in style and sentiment with what we

---

[1] p. 60.

[2] Samuel Pepys visited Islington at various times. "My father," he says (ii. 111), "used to carry us to Islington, to the old man's, at the King's Head, to eat cakes and ale." "Back to Islington, and at the King's Head, where Pitts lived, we 'light, and eat and drunk for remembrance of the old house sake."—(*Ib.* 121.) "Thence to Islington, and there eate and drank at the house my father and we were wont of old to go."—(*Ib.* 183.) "Thence to Hackney. There light, and played at shuffle-board, eat cream and good cherries; and so with good refreshment home."—(ii. 133.) [3] See p. xxxvii.

[4] J. Payne Collier, Esq., writes to me, "It is seldom one meets with such measure and such meaning" as are found in the *Times' Whistle*.

[5] O. Gilchrist's *Corbet*, p. li.

have in this volume. King James visited Cambridge, as before
stated, in 1615. Many Oxford men were present, and among them
Corbet. Now, although Corbet declared "he had left his malice and
judgment at home, and came there only to commend," the oppor-
tunity to exercise his wit at the expense of Cambridge was too
strong for him to resist, and on his return to Oxford he composed a
ballad "To the Tune of Bonny Nell." This ballad, and others
which appeared at the same time, make reference to the failure of
one or more who were appointed to dispute before the king, but
broke down. Corbet, in the ballad, says,—

> "Now pass we to the civil law,
> And eke the doctors of the spaw,
> Who all performed their parts so well,
> Sir Edward Ratcliffe *bore the bell*,
> Who was, by the king's own appointment,
> To speak of spells, and magick oyntment."
>
> *Corbet's Poems*, p. 20.

With this compare the following :—

> "IN NEANDREM.
>
> Neander, held a great cevillian[1]
> (Let me not say a Machiavillian)
> Appointed to dispute before the king,
> Struck mute with fear, could not say anything
> Save twas ill luck; for if he had done well
> As we expected, he would *bear the bell*
> From the whole Academie for the test,
> Tis certaine he had been a knight at lest,
> And made his wife (what she hath lookt for long)
> A Madame. Fortune, thou hast done her wrong
> To hinder his once dubbing of his wife
> Which hath dubde him soe often in his life."
>
> *T. Whistle*, p. 134.

These extracts are given that the reader may have an opportunity
of comparing the known R. Corbet with the unknown "R. C." It
is probable that the poem *In Neandrem*, and the following lines
from *News from Cambridge*,[2] refer to Dr Richardson.[3]

[1] Cevillian, one versed in civil law.
[2] Inedited Miscellanies. Privately printed, 1870.
[3] The following extract is from Nichol's *Progresses, &c., of Jas. I.*, vol.
iii. p. 57 (4to, Lond. 1828). "An extraordinary Act in Divinity was kept at
Cambridge before King James, wherein Doctor John Davenant was Answerer,

" One morn they went unto St Mary's,
  Where one amongst the rest miscarries,
  For, thinking well for to dispute,
  Propounds the question and falls mute.
  Nor did he blush nor want excuse :
  He follow'd but the Cambridge use."

To quote all from Corbet's Poems which might fairly be quoted
would be to occupy more space than can be spared ; a few examples
must suffice. See how he treats the Puritans :—

" I needs must say 'tis a spirituall thing
  To raile against a bishopp, or the king ;
  Nor are they meane adventures wee have bin in,
  About the wearing of the churches linnen."

Corbet's Poems, ed. 1807, p. 106.

" Routes and wilde pleasures doe invite temptation,
  And this is dangerous for our damnation ;
  Wee must not move our selves, but if w' are mov'd
  Man is but man ; and therefore those that lov'd
  Still to seeme good, would evermore dispence
  With their own faults, so they give no offence.
  If the times sweete entising, and the blood
  That now begins to boyle, have thought it good
  To challenge Liberty and Recreation,
  Let it be done in holy contemplation :
  Brothers and Sisters in the fields may walke,
  Beginning of the Holy Word to talke,
  Of David, and Uriahs lovely wife,
  Of Thamar, and her lustfull brothers strife ;
  Then, underneath the hedge that woos them next,
  They may sitt doune, and there act out the text.
  Nor doe wee want, how ere we live austeere,
  In winter Sabbath-nights our lusty cheere ;

and Dr. Richardson amongst others the Opposers. The question was main-
tained in the negative concerning the Excommunicating of Kings. Dr. Rich-
ardson vigorously pressed the practice of St. Ambrose excommunicating the
Emperor Theodosius ; insomuch that the King in some passion returned :
'Prefecto fuit hoc Ambrosio insolentissime factum ! ' To whom Dr. Richard-
son rejoyned : 'Responsum verè Regium, et Alexandro dignum ! Hoc non
est argumenta dissolvere, sed dissecare ;' *and so, sitting down, desisted from
any further dispute.*"

I am indebted to the kindness of Mr Dennis Hall, of the Cambridge
Union Library, for this note, and also for pointing out the similarity of ex-
pression used by Corbet in reference to Sir E. Ratcliffe and by the writer of
In Neandrem. Mr Hall, without knowing that the same question had pre-
sented itself to me, asks, " Can the R. C. in question be Richard Corbet, Bp.
of Norwich ? "

And though the pastors grace, which oft doth hold
Halfe an howre long, make the provision cold,
Wee can be merry ; thinking 't nere the worse
To mend the matter at the second course.
Chapters are read, and hymnes are sweetly sung,
Joyntly commanded by the nose and tongue ;
Then on the Worde wee diversly dilate,
Wrangling indeed for heat of zeale, not hate :
When at the length an unappeased doubt
Feircely comes in, and then the light goes out ;
Darkness thus workes our peace, and wee containe
Our fyery spiritts till we see againe.
Till then, no voice is heard, no tongue doth goe,
Except—" &c., &c.—*Ib.*, pp. 108—110.

Another quotation from Corbet may be given here.

" Have I renounc't my faith, or basely sold
Salvation, and my loyalty, for gold ?
Have I some forreigne practice undertooke
By poyson, shott, sharp-knife, or sharper booke
To kill my king ? have I betrayd the state
To fire and fury, or some newer fate,
Which learned murderers, those grand destinies,
The Jesuites, have nurc'd ? if of all these
I guilty am, proceed ; I am content."—*Ib.* p. 47.

These quotations, and other passages to be found in Corbet's
writings, have the ring and the swing which characterize the whole
of the *Times' Whistle.* No other Satires which I have read, by any
one "rejoicing in these initials," allow of scarcely any comparison
being made ; but with the Bishop the case is altogether different.
The same smooth measure, the same frequent references to history,
the same intense scorn of Puritans and Puritanism, are found in
Corbet's poetry and in that of " R. C." I am aware of the difficulty
—there is, I think, but one—which besets this theory. " R. C.,
Gent.," is not the same as the " Rev. R. C.," or " R. C., Clerk."
But it must be remembered that Corbet published none of his
Poems during his lifetime, and that it was not till some twelve years
after his death that any of them were given to the public. The
Times' Whistle and the *Poems* were evidently written for pub-
lication ; but why the intention was not carried out there is no hint
to show. If Corbet wrote them, his elevation to high positions in
the Church may have led him to abandon the publication alto-

gether, judging that some of the scenes in which the writer took a part would but ill correspond with his ecclesiastical character.[1]

Our Poet, whoever he was, was well read in and made good use of the literature of his time, as well as of ancient classic authors. Shakespeare, Marston, Marlowe, Jonson, Hall, and others, appear to have been consulted to some purpose, but not to an extent to render the author liable to any grave charge of plagiarism. Only a few of these allusions to his contemporaries can be given; the reader will readily supply omissions. And first as to Shakespeare :

Gloucester. Suspicion always haunts the guilty mind ;
The thief doth fear each bush an officer.
K. Henry. The bird that hath been limèd in a bush,
With trembling wings misdoubteth every bush.—3 *K. Hen. VI.* v. 6.

---

[1] The MS. is not in the handwriting of Bp Corbet. I have compared it with an autograph letter of the Bishop's in the British Museum.

Another " R. C." appears in W. Bosworth's *The Chast and Lost Lovers.* Mr Furnivall referred to the book for me, and forwarded me the following, which seems worthy of attention :—

" The Chast and Lost Lovers, Lively shadowed in the persons of *Arcadius* and *Sepha*, and illustrated with the severall stories of *Hœmon* and *Antigone*, *Eramio* and *Amissa*, *Phaon* and *Sappho*, *Delithason* and *Verista :* Being a description of severall Lovers smiling with delight, and with hopes fresh as their youth, and fair as their beauties in the beginning of their Affections, and covered with Blood and Horror in the conclusion. To this is added the Contestation betwixt *Bacchus* and *Diana*, and certain Sonnets of the Author to *AVRORA.* Digested into three Poems, by *Will. Bosworth*, Gent.

——————— *Me quoque*
Impune volare, & sereno
Calliope dedit ire cælo.

London, Printed by F. L. for *Laurence Blaiklock*, and are to be sold at his shop at *Temple-Bar*, 1651."

8vo. A in 8 unpaged ; B, C, D, E, F, G, H, I, 127 pages, and last page blank (Brit. Mus. press-mark E. $\frac{1236}{2}$).

The prose Epistle Dedicatory ' To the true Lover of all good Learning, the Honourable *Iohn Finch*, Esq.' is signed R. C., and says that the Poems are 'the work of a young Gentleman of 19 years of Age, who, had he lived, might have been as well the Wonder as the Delight of the Arts, and been advanced by them amongst the highest in the Temple of Fame.'

The prose address ' To the Reader' is also signed R. C., and contains a hit at Ben Jonson, which may identify its writer with the author of *Times' Whistle*, and the Satire against Jonson. Speaking of Bosworth and his work, R. C. says :

" The strength of his fancy, and the shadowing of it in words, he taketh from Mr Marlow in his Hero and Leander, whose mighty lines Mr *Benjamin Johnson* (*a man sensible enough of his own abilities*) was often heard to say, that they were Examples fitter for admiration than for parallel, you shall find our Author every where in this imitation."

With this compare

> " He, though he had the murderous hand to spill
> Another's blood, himself yet durst not kill,
> And was afraid of others.   Whatever stirs
> He judgeth to be men and officers
> Come to attach him, and, his sight unstable,
> Takes every bush to be a constable."—*T. Whistle*, p. 108.

The same idea occurs on p. 94 :—

> " Each bush doth fright him, and each flying bird,
> Yea, his own shadow, maketh him afeard."

Marston's *Scourge of Villanie* was also familiar to our author :—

> " Infectious blood, ye gouty humours, quake,
> Whilst my sharp razor doth incision make."
> > *Marston's Works*, iii. 274, ed. J. O. Halliwell.

> " Let ulcer'd limbs and gouty humours quake
> Whilst with my pen I do incision make."—*T. W.* 2/19, 20.

Marston has

> > " Camphire and lettuce chaste
> Are clean cashier'd, now sophi ringoes eat,
> Candi'd potatoes are Athenians meat.
> Hence, holy thistle, come sweet marrow pie,
> Inflame our backs to itchin luxury.
> A crab's bak'd guts, a lobster's butter'd thigh,
> I hear them swear is blood of venery."—*Works*, iii. 257.[1]

Compare with the above,

> " Provocatives to stir up appetite
> To brutish lust and sensual delight
> Must not be wanting ; lobsters' butter'd thighs,
> Artichoke, marrow-bone, potato-pies,
> Anchovies, lambs' artificially drest stones,
> Fine jellies of decocted sparrows' bones.
> Or if these fail, th' apothecary's trade
> Must furnish them with rarest marmalade,
> Candi'd eringoes and rich marchpane stuff.
>
> . . . .
>
> With allegant, the blood of venery
> Which strengthens much the back's infirmity."[2]—*T. W.* p. 87.

---

[1] " Virginius vow'd to keep his maiden-head,
And eats chaste lettice, and drinks poppyseed,
And smells on camphor fasting."—Hall's *Satires*, iv. 4.
  " Letuce seede being often vsed to be eaten a long space, drieth vp the natural seede, and putteth away the desire to Lecherie."—Lyte's *Dodoens*, f. 573 (1578).

[2] Ben Jonson, *Every Man out of his Humour*, ii. 1, has " Diving into the

Marlowe was charged with holding atheistical opinions, and it would almost seem that "R. C." had him in view in the opening of the first Satire. The lines

"Which by religion dost not set a straw,
Devis'd, thou think'st, but to keep fools in awe" (*T. W.* p. 5)

seem to be another form of one of the opinions "of one Christofer Marlye," namely, "That the first beginning of religion was only to keep men in awe."[1] Marlowe's *Doctor Faustus* was published, in quarto, in 1604, and again in 1616. The *Times' Whistle*[2] contains a reference to the story of this Play, although it may be said the story was common enough for "R. C." to have got it elsewhere. The whole scene in which Faust cuts his arm, and writes the agreement with his blood, is too long for insertion here, an extract must suffice:—

> "*Faust.* Lo, Mephistophilis, for love of thee,
> I cut mine arm, and with my proper blood
> Assure my soul to be great Lucifer's,
> Chief lord and regent of perpetual night !
> View here the blood that trickles from mine arm,
> And let it be propitious for my wish.
>   *Meph.* But, Faustus, thou must
> Write it in a manner of a deed of gift.
>   *Faust.* Ay, so I will. [*Writes.*] But, Mephistophilis,
> My blood congeals, and I can write no more."

The mention of Tamburlaine[3] will at once call the reader's mind to Marlowe's *Tamburlaine the Great.*

fat capons, drinking your rich wines, feeding on larks, sparrows, potato-pies, and such good unctuous meats."

Howel, writing from Alicant, says : "I have bin here now these three months, and most of my food have bin grapes and bread, with other roots, which have made me so fat, that I think if you saw me you would hardly know me, such nourriture these deep sanguin Alicant grapes give."—*Fam. Let.* p. 35, ed. 1678.

And John Taylor, *Works,* folio, 1630 (Spenser Society's Reprint) : "The Taste plays the Bawd with both Art and Nature, and searcheth through the Earth, Seas, and Skies for variety of temptation ; poore and innocent Lamb-stones, Potatoes, Eringoes, Crabs, Scallops, Lobsters, Wilkes, Cockles, Oysters, Anchoues and Caucare [Qy. Caueare], Cock-sparrowes, Coxcome-pyes, ... doe waite upon the Taste."—f. 259.

> "[He] eates more Lobsters, Artichokes, and Crabs,
> Blew roasted Egges, Potatoes, Maskadine,
> Oysters, and pith that growes i' th' Oxes Chine."—*Ib.* f. 509.

See also Howel's *Familiar Letters,* p. 215.
[1] See Dyce's *Marlowe,* p. 389.   [2] p. 53.   [3] p. 25.

The Prologue to Hall's Satires has been partly quoted already, another portion of it may fitly come in here :—

> "Envy waits on my back, Truth on my side ;
> Envy will be my page, and Truth my guide.
> Envy the margent holds, and Truth the line :
> Truth doth approve, but Envy doth repine.
> For in this smoothing age who durst indite
> Hath made his pen an hired parasite,
> To claw the back of him that beastly lives,
> And pranck base men in proud superlatives.
> Whence damned Vice is shrouded quite from shame,
> And crown'd with Virtue's meed, immortal name !
> Infamy dispossess'd of native due,
> Ordain'd of old on looser life to sue :
> The world's eye-bleared with those shameless lies,
> Mask'd in the show of meal-mouth'd poesies.
> Go, daring Muse, on with thy thankless task,
> And do the ugly face of Vice unmask :
> And if thou canst not thine high flight remit,
> So as it might a lowly satire fit,
> Let lowly satires rise aloft to thee :
> Truth be thy speed, and Truth thy patron be."

That a similar spirit to this animated "R. C." may be seen by reading his introductory lines on the second page of this volume.

The references to Jonson's writings are numerous. Compare the Sordido in *Every Man out of his Humour*, with R. C.'s Sordido,[1] and especially Misotochus,[2] and the effect of fine clothes in the same Play,[3] with the character of Moros[4] and the closing lines of our author's second Satire,[5] and it will be seen at once how closely they coincide. Carlo in this Play[6] says, " Love no man ; trust no man ; speak ill of no man to his face ; nor well of any man behind his back. Salute fairly on the front, and wish them hanged upon turn. Spread yourself upon his bosom publicly, whose heart you would eat in private. These be principles, think on them."

And R. C.,

> " Another's mind by hate distempered is,
> Malicing whom in show he seems to kiss.
> This bare affection causeth dismal strife,
> Despoileth honour and destroyeth life.

---

[1] pp. 26, 27. [2] p. 99. [3] Act ii. 1; iii. 3. [4] p. 28.
[5] p. 30. [6] *Every Man*, &c., iii. 1.

> Yet in these days 'tis counted policy
> To use dissimulation ; villany
> Masked under friendship's title (worst of hate)
> Makes a man live secure and fortunate.
>
> . . . .
>
> These mankind haters, bloody-minded slaves,
> Which all the world with horrid murders fill,
> Laughing on those whom they intend to kill."[1]

There is evidence too that *The Puritan* had been seen by the author, but it is only necessary to mention the fact.

I do not think any apology will be required for putting these *Satires* before the few scholars who are interested in the literature of the Shakesperean age. Some casual readers there may be, who will fail to see any advantage in having such books within reach—"precisians," they are unwilling to have their senses polluted with the rough language and the pictures, drawn by contemporary hands, of the vices of their countrymen. For such these Satires are not published—they can pass by on the other side, and leave this book to its fate. It is too much the fashion now-a-days to shut our eyes to vice and crime and oppression ; to turn our faces from the dark and squalid portions of our cities, towns, and villages ; to endeavour to hide all the wickedness and misery under which so many groan, to drive them from the garish light of day, and, compelling them to lie in secret and avoid offending our eyes, to turn with self-righteous complacency to the world, and say, 'See how bright and holy all things are ! Vice and misery are not seen in our streets, they do not exist. We manage things better now. A man may walk on the village green, in the beautiful country lanes, in the great streets of our great cities, and see nothing to offend the eye, hear nothing to grate upon the ear. Our writers tell us of nothing but what is pleasant,—of our advances in education, of the improvements which are made on every side.' Yes, it is quite true. We don't like to see vice and misery, we prefer to walk blindfold, and to be ignorant of such things ; but is not the difference between the vices of men two hundred and fifty years ago and the vices of men now, simply a difference of dress ? Then vices were clothed in

[1] p. 94.

fustian, and were not always hidden from the light; now, we clothe them in broadcloths and silks, and indulge in them secretly.

I do not apprehend that any one reading these Satires will be the worse for the reading. They need no apology from me. If they do, then must all who have spent their talent on the Playwrights and Satirists of the time of Elizabeth, James I., and Charles I. have erred more deeply than I can have done. The whole Literature is tainted with a certain coarseness, and to condemn one writer is to condemn all. But let no man despise it and think it poor or bad because it is unlike our own. "It is refreshing to look out of ourselves sometimes, not always to be holding the glass to our own peerless perfections; and as there is a dead wall which always intercepts the prospect of the future from our view (all that we can see beyond it is the heavens), it is as well to direct our eyes now and then without scorn to the page of history, and repulsed in our attempts to penetrate the secrets of the next six thousand years, not to turn our backs on auld lang syne!"[1] I do not apologize for adding to this literature. The reader must judge whether I have done well or ill, and by his judgment willingly I abide.

In this volume there is much that is interesting historically, such as the drinking scenes, the tobacco-smoking customs, the alehouse haunting on Sundays, the manner in which the Puritan was spoken of by the orthodox Churchman. These, and the hints illustrative of the atheism, infidelity, and apostasy which were common then (as well as now), give a value to the book which each reader will estimate for himself. Of the moral and religious tone which runs through the whole of it I cannot speak too highly. In our Dramatists and others this is too often overlaid, or lost altogether. Not so here. Is there a sin, a vice, a crime described? the denunciation of its certain punishment is sure to follow, and that in terms so plain that they who run may read.

The preface to the minor poems in this volume is curious. What occurred to prevent the Satires "and this piece of poetry alsoe . . . . . soe sodainlie thrust into the presse" from being given to the world, at present is a mystery, and will probably remain one

[1] W. Hazlitt; Lectures, &c.

for some time to come. Whether the "subsequent endeavours" spoken of ever came to anything is also unknown. The "judicious Catoes" and barking Momists of the time had had their fling at R. C.,[1] and had planted a thorn in his side. His retort calls to mind Ben Jonson's lines :—

> " Perhaps, upon the rumour of their speeches,
>   Some grieved friend will whisper to me ; Crites,
>   Men speak ill of thee. So they be ill men,
>   If they spake worse, 'twere better : for of such
>   To be dispraised, is the most perfect praise.
>   What can his censure hurt me, whom the world
>   Hath censured vile before me ? " [2]

These poems display the fancies and beliefs which were common at the time they were written. Few of them are without interest of some kind, the best probably being that commencing on page 137.

Of the poetical merits of " R. C." nothing need be said. The book is in the reader's hands. Let it speak for its author. One extract must suffice here :—

> " Latro did act a damnèd villainy,
>   Adding black murder to his robbery,
>   Yet cause 'twas closely done he might conceal it,
>   For save himself none living could reveal it.
>   But see the just revenge for this offence ;—
>   After the deed, his guilty conscience
>   Torturing his soul, enforc'd him still to think
>   The act disclosed, and he in danger's brink.
>   He thought the birds still in their language said it ;
>   He thought the whistling of the wind bewrayed it ;
>   He called to mind that murder was forbidden,
>   And though a while it could not long be hidden.
>   Distract in mind, and fearfull in his place,
>   Having no power to call to God for grace,
>   The devil doth suborne him to despair,
>   Tells him 'tis pity he should breath this air
>   Which hath been such a villain ; thrusts him on
>   To work his own death and confusion.
>   He, though he had the murderous hand to spill
>   Another's blood, himself yet durst not kill,
>   And was afraid of others. What e'er stirs
>   He judgeth to be men, and officers

---

[1] See also the poem *In Momum*, p. 152.
[2] Cynthia's Revels, iii. 2.

Come to attach him, and his sight unstable
Takes every bush to be a constable.
Thus plagued and tortured with despair and fear,
Out must the fact, he can no more forbear;
For which, according to the course of law,
Death's heavy sentence on him he doth draw,
And being brought unto the place of death,
There in despair yields up his latest breath.
    Thus each affection like a tyrant reigns
Over man's soul, which letteth loose the reins
Unto selfe will, in which so slavish state,
Man's sense captived, his reason subjugate,
Makes the soul clogg'd, a massy lump of sin,
Which following his creation should have been,
Like his Creator, pure."—*T. W.* p. 108.

I have taken no liberties with my MS. other than those explained in the footnotes. For the punctuation and the use of the hyphen in some of the compound words, as well as the use of Capital letters, I am answerable. I hope it will be found that I have avoided mistakes as much as it is possible to do, and I believe the reader may rest assured that every reading, and every word, which bears a peculiar look is as it stands in my original. I should have preferred to modernize the spelling throughout, but the laws of the E. E. T. S. allow of no such tampering with texts, and it is right they should not. Once begin, and the reader is never sure that his author's *ipsissima verba* are before him.

I have added to this brief introduction a few notes illustrative of the text, and at the end of the volume a glossary of words and phrases, which is intended not only to assist the general reader, but to save any future Lexicographer the trouble of wading through the volume for an example of the use of any word, phrase, or proverb. Of the use of proverbs and phrases these Satires contain many examples.

The most pleasing of my duties remains to be done. To thank the Dean[1] (too late, alas! for him to hear) and Chapter of Canterbury for so generously placing the MS. in my hands to copy and use at my own home. And to express the many obligations under which I rest to the Rev. Canon Robertson, Librarian of the Canterbury

---

[1] Dr Alford.

Cathedral Library, to J. Payne Collier, J. O. Halliwell, W. Bodham Donne, F. J. Furnivall, W. Carew Hazlitt, and Dennis Hall, Esqrs., and my brother, B. Harris Cowper, who have been kind enough to read my proofs, and to afford me many valuable hints and suggestions, as well as to express their satisfaction that I had undertaken to see these Satires through the press.

JOSEPH M. COWPER.

Davington Hill, Faversham,
March 21, 1871.

NOTES.

Puritans and Puritanism. Page 4. At this day it is scarcely pos-
sible to conceive the amount of obloquy which was heaped upon these
men. No vice was deemed too horrible for them to commit—they were
in all things considered the very incarnation of hypocrisy. In spite of
the oppressions under which they bowed they became, as our author
says, so numerous that they encumbered the Church, and stuck as a dis-
ease within her bowels (p. 10). It is unnecessary to reproduce the
taunts and abuses which are scattered up and down the literature of this
period. The reader curious in such matters will find enough in the
works of Taylor the Water-Poet, Bp Corbet's *Poems*, *The Puritan*, and
elsewhere.
    As to their numbers we may quote Taylor: "*Item*, he told that
there were a great many Puritans in England, and that they did now so
disturb the quietness of the Commonwealth that it was now almost
turned topsy-turvy."—*The Liar*, 1641, p. 5.
    Brownism. p. 4. Robert Brown, the founder of the Sect of Brown-
ists, was born in 1549. He was educated at Cambridge, and, while a
young man, obtained the mastership of the Free-School of St Olave's,
Southwark, and became chaplain to the Duke of Norfolk. In 1571 he was
cited to appear before Parker to answer for his opinions. The influence
of Norfolk saved him for this time. Subsequently Brown abandoned
the views of the Puritans for those of the Separatists. For preaching
against bishops and church ceremonies he asserted that he was commit-
ted to thirty-two prisons. Soon after 1580 he found it prudent to go to
Holland, but in 1584 he was stirring up strife in Scotland. He returned
to the Church of England, but not much to his or her credit, as the re-
mainder of his life seems to have been spent at Achurch, near Oundle
(the living of which he accepted as the price of his conformity), in idle-
ness, occasionally varied by beating his wife, not " as his wife, but as a
curst old woman." For an almost contemporary account of him see
Taylor's *Cluster of Coxcombes*, 1642.
    Anabaptists. p. 9. (See Glossary.) The following is from Taylor's

account of *Anabaptists of these latter times* (pub. 1642): On the 29th April in the 32nd Henry VIII. one Mandeville and one Collins (both Anabaptists) were examined in St Margaret's Church at the Hill in Southwark, and there they were condemned and judged to be burnt as heretics, which was executed on them accordingly in the highway between Southwark and Newington.

In 1574 one man and ten women were judged to be burnt for being Anabaptists, but after much suit made, one woman recanted, and all the rest were banished. In the same year four carried faggots and did penance at Paul's Cross, and recanted, but two Dutchmen were burnt in Smithfield for being Anabaptists. "And in these our days the said Anabaptistical sect is exceeding rife, for they do swarm here and there without fear of either God or man, Law or order."—*A Cluster of Cox-combes* (1642), p. 4.

Howel "could be content to see an Anabaptist go to hell on a Brownist's back."—*Fam. Letters*, ed. 1678, p. 255a.

The Family of Love. p. 9. This sect, often called *Familists*, had its rise in Holland about the year 1550. Thirty years later the Familists appeared in England. They pretended to a more than ordinary sanctity. They asserted that none were of the number of the elect but such as were admitted into their family, and that all the rest were reprobate. They held that it was lawful for them to swear to an untruth before a magistrate or before any other person who was not of their society, for their own convenience. The originator of this sect was Henry Nicholas of Leyden, who made certain blasphemous pretensions that he partook of the Divinity of God. Their numerous books were ordered by Elizabeth to be burnt.[1]

The Familists are often referred to in language far from complimentary.

Those who care to know in what estimation they were held by the orthodox may refer to Taylor's *A Bawd, The Vertue of a Jayle, etc.*, and his *Apology for Private Preaching*.

In 1574, five Englishmen of the sweet sect called The Family of Love did penance at Paul's Cross, and there confessed and detested their wicked and damnable heresies.—*A Cluster of Coxcombes* (1642), p. 4.

Amsterdam. p. 11. No place seems to have been held in such vile repute as Amsterdam. Of course the gossiping Howel has something to say about it. Writing from Amsterdam, in 1617, he says: "The ground here, which is all for the most part twixt marsh and moorish, lies not only level but to the apparent sight of the eye far lower than the sea, which made the Duke of Alva say that the inhabitants of this country were the nearest to hell (the great Abyss) of any people on Earth. . . . . . . One of the chiefest parts of his [the native's] Litany is From the Sea, the Spaniard, and the Devil, the Lord deliver me."—*Fam. Letters*, ed. 1678, p. 8.

Two years later he writes, "I am lodged in a Frenchman's house

[1] See Hook's *Ch. Dict.*

(at Amsterdam) who is one of the deacons of our English Brownists here; 'tis not far from the Synagogue of the Jews, who have free and open exercise of their religion here. I believe in this street where I lodge there be well near as many religions as there be houses; for one neighbour knows not, nor cares not much, what religion the other is of, so that the number of conventicles exceeds the number of churches here. . . . . The dog and rag Market is hard by, where every Sunday morning there is a kind of public mart for those commodities, notwithstanding their precise observance of the Sabbath."—*Ib.* p. 10.

<blockquote>
" The pure reformed Amsterdammers,
Those faithful Friday feasting capon crammers."
Taylor, Works, folio, 1630, f. 402 (Spenser Society's Rep.).
</blockquote>

In his *Brood of Cormorants,* speaking of " A Separatist," he writes:

<blockquote>
" If in lesser room they may be cramm'd,
And live and die at *Amster* and be dam'd."—*Works,* f. 485.
</blockquote>

<blockquote>
" Let Amsterdam send forth her brats,
Her fugitives and runagates;
Let Bedlam, Newgate and the Clink
Disgorge themselves into this sink."
</blockquote>

A Poem on New England, *Ined. Misc.,* privately printed, 1870.

Sleeping in Church. p. 15.

<blockquote>
" Men sleep in church, sure their brains are addle,
Sly Satan lulls them, and doth rock the cradle:
When men thus do no ill, 'tis understood,
The devil hinders them from doing good."—*Taylor, Works,* f. 351.
</blockquote>

See also *News from Hell, Hull, and Hallifax, etc.,* p. 46, and Howel's *Fam. Let.,* p. 255.

Sabbath customs. pp. 16, 19.   See Crowley's Epigram of Alehouses (1550).

<blockquote>
" NEdes must we haue places for vitayls to be solde,
   for such as be sycke, pore, feble, and olde.
But, Lorde, to howe greate abuse they be growne!
In eche lyttle hamlet, vyllage, and towne,
They are become places of waste and excesse,
And herbour for such men as lyue in idlenes.
And lyghtly in the contrey they be placed so,
That they stande in mens waye when they shoulde to church go.
And then such as loue not to hear theyr fautes tolde,
By the minister that readeth the newe Testament and olde,
do turne into the alehouse, and let the church go;
Yea, and men accompted wyse and honeste do so.
But London (God be praysed) all men maye commende,
Whych doeth nowe this greate enormitie emende,
For in seruice tyme no dore standeth vp,
Where such men are wonte to fyll can and cuppe.
</blockquote>

Wolde God in the countrey they woulde do the same,
Either for Gods feare, or for worldly shame!
How hallow they the Saboth, that do the tyme spende
In drynkinge and idlenes tyll the daye be at an ende?
Not so well as he doeth, that goeth to the plowe,
Or pitcheth vp the sheues from the carte to the mowe.
But he doeth make holye the Sabothe in dede,
That heareth Goddes worde, and helpeth suche as nede."

And *Newes out of Powles Churchyarde* (1577), Satyr 5:—

> " Search Tauernes through, and typling bowres
>   eche Saboth day at morne:
> And you shall thinke this geare to be
>   ene too too much forborne.
>
> . . . .
> What else but gaine and Money gote
>   maintaines each Saboth day
> The bayting of the Beare and Bull?
>   What brings this brutish play?
> What is the cause that it is born,
>   and not controlled ought,
> Although the same of custome be
>   on holy Saboth wrought?"

Stubs (*Anatomie of Abuses*, p. 157, ed. 1836) thus writes of Sunday labour:—

" If he were stoned for gathering a fewe stickes vppon the Sabbaoth daie, which in some cases might be lawful for necessities sake, and yet did it but once, what shal they be who all the Sabbaoth dayes of their life giue themselues to nothing els but to wallowe in all kinde of wickednesse and sinne, to the great contempt bothe of the Lord and his Sabbaoth? And though thei haue played the lazie lurdens all the weeke before, yet that daie, of set purpose, they will toyle and labour, in contempt of the Lord and his Sabaoth."

The Mausolean Monument. p. 22.   See *Taylor, Works,* f. 553:—

> " The Tomb of Mausoll, King of Carea,
> Built by his Queen (kind Artemisia)
> So wondrous made by art and workmanship,
> That skill of man could never it outstrip:
> 'Twas long in building, and it doth appear
> The charges of it full two millions were." (!)

Fertile Kent. p. 26.

" When as the pliant Muse, straight turning her about,
And coming to the land as Medway goeth out,
Saluting the dear soil, O famous Kent, quoth she,
What country hath this isle that can compare with thee!
Which hast within thy self as much as thou canst wish,
Thy conies, venison, fruit, thy sorts of fowl and fish,

And what with strength comports, thy hay, thy corn, thy wood :
Nor any thing doth want that any where is good."
Drayton's Polyolbion, 1613.
  " Kent
    Is termed the civilest place of all this isle ;
    Sweet is the country, because full of riches ;
    The people liberal, valiant, active, wealthy."
2 K. Hen. VI. iv. 7.
Milk, a cosmetic. p. 36.

  " Some I have heard of that have been so fine
    To wash and bathe themselves in milk or wine,
    Or else with whites of eggs their faces garnish,
    Which makes them look like visors or new varnish."
Taylor, Works, f. 44.
Avarice. p. 41.

  " The Earth is rip'd and bowel'd, rent and torn,
    For gold and silver which by man is worn :
    And sea and land are rak'd and search't and sought,
    For jewels too far fetcht, and too dear bought."—*Ib.* f. 43.
Simony. pp. 43, 45.   On this subject see Hall's *Satires,* ii. 5 :—

  " Saw'st thou ever SI-QUIS patch'd on Paul's church door,
    To seek some vacant vicarage before ?
    Who wants a churchman, that can service say,
    Read fast and fair his monthly homily ?
    And wed and bury and make christen-souls ?
    Come to the left-side alley of Saint Pauls.
    Thou servile fool, why could'st thou not repair
    To buy a benefice at Steeple-fair ?
    There moghtest thou, for but a slender price,
    Advowson thee with some fat benefice :

  . . . .

    A thousand patrons thither ready bring
    Their new-fall'n churches to the chaffering ;
    Stake three years' stipend ; no man asketh more :
    Go take possession of the church-porch door,
    And ring thy bells."

Bribery—Lawyers. pp. 42, 45 — 49.
       " One here bewayles his wofull case
          and wisheth him vnborne,
       Another cryes with wringing handes,
          alas, I am forlorne.
       My sute thus long depended hath :
          The Lawe is on my syde,
       And yet in harde delayes I lye
          true Iudgement to abyde.

> Another thus be friended is,
>   The Iudge doth loue him well
> And me (as poore and needie) they
>   doo dayly thus depell
> Two hundreth myles and more I come :
>   My Wife at home (alas)
> Lyes with my Children halfe forepynde :
>   (O lamentable case.)
> My goods are spent, which labor brought,
>   through long and carefull toyle :
> The Lawe hath lyckt vp all my wealth
>   for which I dyd turmoyle."

Newes out of Powles, Sat. 2.

The whole Satire might be quoted. Hall (ii. 3) satirizes lawyers thus :—

> " The crouching client, with low-bended knee,
> And many worships, and fair flattery,
> Tells on his tale as smoothly as him list,
> But still the lawyers eye squints on his fist ;
> If that seem lined with a larger fee,
> Doubt not the suit, the law is plain for thee."

Well-drest fools. p. 43. "It is a scurvy fashion of your devising that wise men in russet must reverence and stand bare to silken fools." —*News from Hell, Hull, and Hallifax*, p. 51.

"Why, assure you, signior, rich apparel has strange virtues; it makes him that hath it without means, esteemed for an excellent wit: he that enjoys it with means, puts the world in remembrance of his means: it helps the deformities of nature, and gives lustre to her beauties."— *Every Man out of his Hu.* ii. 1.

> " Here, in the court, be a man ne'er so vile,
> In wit, in judgment, manners, or what else ;
> If he can purchase but a silken cover,
> He shall not only pass, but pass regarded :
> Whereas, let him be poor, and meanly clad,
> Though ne'er so richly parted, you shall have
> A fellow that knows nothing but his beef,
> Or how to rinse his clammy guts in beer
> Will take him by the shoulders, or the throat
> And kick him down the stairs. Such is the state
> Of virtue in bad clothes ! ha, ha, ha, ha !
> That raiment should be in such high request."—*Ib.* iii. 3.

Fairies. p. 53.

" *Gert.* Good Lord, that there are no fairies now-a-days, Syn.
Syn. Why, Madam ?
Gert. To do miracles and bring ladies money."

1605.   *Eastward Hoe*, v. i.

" Wash your pails and cleanse your dairies,
 Sluts are loathsome to the Fairies :
 Sweep your house, who doth not so
 Mab will pinch her by the toe."—Herrick's *Hesperides.*

" Grant that the sweet Fairies may nightly put money in your shoes,
and sweep your house clean."—Holiday's *Marriages of the Arts.*

" Farewell rewards and Faeries,
  Good houswives now may say,
 For now foule slutts in daries
  Doe fare as well as they.
And though they sweepe theyr hearths no less
  Then maydes were wont to doe,
 Yet who of late for cleaneliness,
  Finds sixe-pence in her shoe ? "—Corbet's *Poems*, p. 213.

For more information on the subject of Fairies the reader is referred
to Brand's *Pop. Antiq.*, edited by W. C. Hazlitt, 1870.

Gluttony. p. 55.

" This day, my Lorde his speciall friende
  must dyne with him (no naye)
 His Partners, Friendes and Aldermen :
  Wherfore he must puruaye
 Both Capon, Swan, and Hernshoe good,
  fat Bitture, Larcke and Quayle :
 Right Plouer, Snype, and Woodcock fine
  with Curlew, Wype and Rayle :
 Stonetiuets, Teale, and Pecteales good,
  with Busterd fat and plum,
 Fat Pheasaunt Powt, and Plouer base
  for them that after come.
 Stent, Stockard, Stampine, Tāterucale,
  and Wigeon of the best :
 Puyt, Partrich, Blackebirde and
  fat Shoueler with the rest.
 Two Warrants eke he must prouide
  To haue some Venson fat,
 And meanes héele make for red Déere too,
  (there is no nay to that.)
 And néedefully he must prouide
  (although we speake not ont)
 Both Peacock, Crane, and Turkicock,
  and (as such men are wont)
 He must foresee that he ne lacke
  colde bakemeates in the ende ;
 With Custards, Tarts, and Florentines,
  the bancquet to amende.

And (to be short and knit it vp)
  he must not wanting sée
Straunge kindes of fysh at second course
  to come in their degrée.
As Porpesse, Seale and Salmond good,
  with Sturgeon of the best
And Turbot, Lobster, with the lyke
  to furnish out the feast.
All this theyle haue, and else much more,
  sydes Marchpane and gréene chéese,
Stewde wardens, Prunes, & sweete conserues
  with spiced Wine like Lées:
Gréeneginger, Sucket, Suger Plate,
  and Marmaladie fine:
Blauncht Almonds, Peares and Ginger bread.
  But Peares should we assigne
And place before (as meete it is)
  at great mens boordes: for why,
Raw fruites are first in seruice styll,
  Else Seruing men doo lye."
         Newes out of Powles, Sat. 4.

To the above add the following:—"And nowadays if the table be not covered from the one end to the other, as thick as one dish can stand by another, with delicate meat of sundry sorts, one clean different from another, and to every dish a several sauce appropriate to his kind, it is thought there unworthy the name of a dinner. . . . . . And these many shall you have at the first course, as many at the second; and, peradventure, more at the third; besides other sweet condiments, and delicate confections of spiceries, and I cannot tell what. And to these dainties, all kinds of wines are not wanting, you may be sure."—*Anat. of Abuses*, p. 107.

Drunkenness. p. 57. Drunkenness "is a horrible vice and too too much used in Ailgna (Anglia); every county, city, town, village, and other places, hath abundance of ale-houses, taverns, and inns, which are so fraught with maltworms, night and day, that you would wonder to see them. You shall have them there sitting at the wine and good-ale all the day long, yea, all the night long too, peradventure a whole week together, so long as any money is left, swilling, gulling and carousing from one to another, till never a one can speak a ready word."—*Anat. of Abuses*, pp. 113, 114.

King Harries Gold. p. 61. The gold coins issued by Henry VIII. were sovereigns, half sovereigns, rose nobles, and George nobles, angels, crowns, and half-crowns. See Humphrey's *Coin Collector's Manual*, p. 451, ed. 1853.

Tobacco. pp. 70—72. Tobacco seems to have been a common road to ruin:

"Tobacco robs some men, if so it list,
    It steals their coin (as thieves do) in a mist."
Taylor, Works, f. 279.

"Too many there are that pass the bounds of liberality, and spend most prodigally . . . . . on (the devil of India) Tobacco."—*Ib.* f. 336.

"Mischief or mischances seldom come alone : and it is a doubtfull question, whether the devil brought *Tobacco* into England in a *Coach*, or else brought a coach in a fog or mist of Tobacco."—*Ib.* f. 378.

Every thing that can possibly be said against Tobacco may be seen in *A Proclamation* (*Taylor*, ff. 251—253). It is too long for insertion here. The phrase *to drink* (inhale) tobacco was common. "He *drank* colt's-foot among his tobacco." *Taylor*, f. 358. Is this a practice now? I remember my father was in the habit of mixing colt's-foot with his tobacco thirty years ago. In Davies's *Epigrams* which appeared about 1598, one (xxxvi.) is in *praise* of tobacco.

Pict-hatch, the Spitle and Turnboll street. p. 80.

"Old Bembus . . . . . of Pickt-hatch,
    That plunging through the Sea of Turnebull Street,
    He safely did arrive at Smithfield Bars."—*Taylor, Works*, f. 164.

"Sometimes [she] is in the full at Pickt-hatch and sometimes in the wane at Bridewell."—*Ib.* f. 257.

"Turnbull street poor bawds."—*Ib.* f. 253.

"Did ever any man ere heare him talke
    But of Pick-hatch, or of some Shoreditch baulke?"
Scourge of Villanie, iii. 305.

The *Spittle*, St Bartholomew's.

Dancing. p. 85. Stubs, in his *Anatomie of Abuses*, on 'The Horrible Vice of Pestiferous Dauncing used in Ailgna,' says: "Dauncing, as it is vsed (or rather abused) in these daies, is an introduction to whordome, a preparatiue to wantonnesse, a prouocatiue to vncleannesse, and an introite to all kinde of lewdnesse, rather then a pleasant exercise to the minde, or a wholesome practise for the bodie (as some list to calle it) : . . . . say they, it induceth loue : so say I also ; but what loue? truely a lustfull loue, a venerous loue, a concupiscencious, bawdie, and beastiall loue, such as proceedeth from the stinking pump and lothsome sinck of carnall affection and fleshly appetite" (pp. 179, 182, ed. 1585, reprint of 1836).

Bread made of Peas. p. 99. "Do we not see the poor man that eateth brown bread (whereof some is made of rye, barley, peason, beans, oats, and such other gross grains) and drinketh small drink, yea, sometimes water, [and] feedeth upon milk, butter, and cheese."—*Anat. of Abuses*, p. 112.

"My house and I can feed on peas and barley."
Every M. out of his Hu. i. 1.

Wapping. p. 118. Pirates were commonly executed at Wapping.

" I haue seene many of these Prowling fisher-men end their liues like Swans (in a manner singing) and sometimes making their wills at Wapping, or looking through a hempen window at St. Thomas Waterings." —*Taylor, Works*, f. 87.

" By Wapping, where as hang'd drown'd Pirats dye."—*Ib.* f. 181.

" Thus much I mildly write in hope 'twill mend thee ;
If not, the Thames or Wapping shore will end thee."—*Ib.* f. 316.

In Henry the VIII.'s time a place called " the Willows " was used for this purpose :—" And this yere was hongyd at the Wyllow by the Temse syde Woolfe and hys wyffe, for kyllynge of two Lumberttes in a bote on the Temse."—*Grey Friars Chron.* p. 37.

Corbet's Song. p. xv. I know not how this song came to be attributed to Corbet. It occurs in *Gammer Gurton's Needle*, Act ii., and may be found in Hawkins's *Origin of the English Drama*, vol. i. 1773 ; in Dodsley's *Old Plays*, vol. ii. 1825 ; and in Hazlitt's *Lectures on the English Drama*, p. 197, ed. 1840. The Comedy of *Gammer Gurton's Needle* has been attributed to John Still, who died Bishop of Bath and Wells in 1607 ; and to Nicholas Udal, who died in 1557. It is not likely that Corbet wrote the song, but I give it here notwithstanding.

> Back and syde go bare, go bare,
>   booth foote and hande go colde :
> But belley, God sende thee Good ale ynoughe,
>   whether it be newe or olde.
>
> I Can not eate, but lytle meat,
>   my stomacke is not good ;
> But sure I thinke, that I can drynk
>   with him that weares a hood.
> Thoughe I go bare, take ye no care,
>   I am nothinge a colde ;
> I stuffe my skyn so full within,
>   of joly good ale and olde.
> Back and syde go bare, go bare,
>   booth foote and hand go colde :
> But belly, God send the good ale inoughe,
>   whether it be new or olde.
>
> I love no rost, but a nut-brown toste,
>   and a crab layde in the fyre,
> A lytle bread shall do me stead,
>   much breade I not desyre.
> No froste nor snow, no winde, I trow,
>   can hurte mee, if I wolde,
> I am so wrapt, and throwly lapt
>   of joly good ale and olde.
>   Back and side go bare, &c.

And Tyb my wyfe, that as her life
 loveth well good ale to seeke,
Full ofte drinkes shee, tyll ye may see
 · the teares run down her cheekes ;
Then dooth she trowle to mee the bowle,
 even as a mault worme shuld ;
And sayth, sweet hart, I tooke my part
 of this joly good ale and olde.
  Back and side go bare, &c.

Now let them drynke, tyll they nod and winke,
 even as good felowes shoulde do,
They shall not mysse to have the blisse
 good ale doth bringe men to :
And all poor soules that have scowred boules,
 or have them lustely trolde,
God save the lyves of them and their wyves
 whether they be yonge or olde.
  Back and side go bare, &c.

¹𝔈𝔭𝔦𝔤𝔯𝔞𝔪𝔪𝔦 𝔖𝔞𝔱𝔦𝔯𝔬𝔫.

Septem compacta cicutis
Fistula.²

The Times Whistle ; or a newe Daunce³
of seven Satires : whervnto are annexed
divers other Poems comprising Things
naturall, morall, & theologicall. Compiled
by [R. C.] Gent.

Parturit, assiduo si non renovetur aratro,
Non nisi cum spinis, gramina mundus ager.

Ad Lectorem.

Reader, if thou expect to find in this booke either
affectation of poeticall stile, or roughnesse of vnhewen
invention, which amongst many is of moste estimation,
being
[*Remainder cut off.*]

---

¹ leaf 1.   ² Virg. Ecl. 2. 36.
³ Cf. " The Letting of Hvmovrs Blood in the Head-Vaine.
With a new Morissco, daunced by seauen Satyres," etc.
London, 1600.

Epigram*mi*satiron.

I am sent from Nemesis to punish the sins

From *the* Rhamnusian goddesse am I sent,
On sinne t' inflict deservèd punnishment
All-seeing sunne, lend me thy searching eye,
That I may finde and scourge impietie,   4
And pull from vice, w*hi*ch hath beguilèd sence,

and expose the vices of this age,

Disguisd' like vertue, brasse facd' impudence.
For now this age, this worse then iron age,
This sincke of synne, this map of hell, this stage   8
Of all vncleannesse, whose disease is ease,
Wallowing in worlds of pleasure, swallowing seas
Of sensuall delightes, is whollie growne

which is very corrupt, and needs severe remedies.

A huge impostume of corruption,   12
Whose swelling tumor (well I am assur'de)
Must needs be launcd', or ne'er will be recurde :
To the w*hi*ch act[1] my genius prompteth me,
Though it passe Æsculapian surgerie.   16
Be stout my heart, my hand be firm and steady,
Strike, and strike home, the vaine worlds veine is ready ;
Let vlcerd limbes and gowtie humo*u*rs quake,
Whilst w*i*th my pen I doe incision make.[2]   20

Ad Rithmum.

Fear not, my verse, the punishments which are pi e- pared for truth,

March forth, and boldly march, my tel troth rimes,
Disclose the lewdnesse of these looser times ;
Fear not the frowne of grim authority,
Or stab of truth-abhorring villanie ;   24
Fear not the olde accustomèd reward,
A loathsome prison still for truth preparde ;
Though many hundred (Argus hundred) eyes,

or the spies

View, and review, each line, each word, as spies,   28

---

[1] *art* crossed out, and *act* written over.
[2] A line is drawn here : the lower half of the leaf is cut off.

Your meaning to entrap[1] by wrong construction,
Vndaunted speake the truth ; let not detraction
Apall your courage ; spite of iniuries,
Tell to the world her base enormities.   32

*which will mis-
construe your
meaning.*

A Ioue principium Musæ.[2]

When first I did intend to write 'gainst sinne,
My Muse was in suspence how to beginne ;
What crime to put i' th' forefront of my booke,
Not through defect (let me not be mistooke)   36
Of number, for the world abounds in vice,
But 'cause 'twas somewhat hard to breake the ice
To any ; but at last methought 'twas fitt
First to inveigh 'gainst those that doe committ   40
The greatst offences ; whom I tooke to be
Our Ath[e]ists, which striue to roote vp the tree
Of true religion : by these reasons movd :—
First, that this sinne might be from vs remov'd ;   44
Without the which, it were in vaine to taxe
Other offences, of what note or sexe
Soever ; next, because this kinde of men
Doth most dishoner God ; and lastly, when   48
All that we are is his, from whom alone
We doe all good deriue, when every one
Moues by his power, lives by his permission,
And can doe nothing if the prohibition   52
Of the Almighty doe oppugne ; it lies
Only in him to end each enterprise.
These things concurring, I my selfe did fitt
To vse the inchoation of my witte   56
First in his cause, by whose direction
I hope to bring the rest vnto perfection.

*At first I knew
not on what
subject to
commence,*

*but I thought I
would begin with
atheists who
commit the worst
offences.*

*God only can
bring my enter-
prise to per-
fection.*

---

[1] *rap* not clear in MS.   [2] Virg. Ecl. 3. 60.

[leaf 2, back]

𝕾𝖆𝖙𝖎𝖗𝖆 1.

[AGAINST THE ATHEISTS, SABBATH-BREAKERS, ETC.]

———

ARGUMENTUM.

Regnat in humanis diuina potentia rebus,
Non ex naturæ vi generatur homo.
Quid deus, et cui fini animal ratione creatum
Est pietas, est in relligione scelus.

The atheist will
one day find a
God who can
punish sin.

Atheos! forbear to speake such blasphemie!
"There is noe God," O, damnd impiety!
Yes, wicked villaine, thou shalt one day finde,
With horror of a selfe-tormenting minde,   4
A God, though long it be ere he begin,
That can and will severely chastice sinne.
Thou execrable monster, hatchd in hell,

The atheist was
brought into the
world by the
devil.

Brought by a crew of devills heer to dwell   8
A plague one earth, why hast thou thus bewitcht
With thy contagion mindes that are enricht
With gifts of nature aboue common ranke?
Who with *the* poyson *that* from thee they dranke   12
Envenom'd, wound themselues, and others harme
With strange opinions, w*h*ich in heapes doe swarme
From their ill-iudging thoughts; for heresie,

Schism, Puritan-
ism, Brownism,
and Papistry,
take their rise
from atheism.

Scisme, Puritanisme, Brownisme, pa[pi]strie,   16
And such like hydra-headed errors, all
Proceed from thee, thou art the principall;

Thou w*h*ich wilt never graunt a Diety,

Vnlesse it be in poynt of pollicie,   20   The atheist thinks religion was devised to frighten children,

W*h*ich by religion dost not set a strawe,

Devisde, thou thinkst, but to keep fooles in awe ;

W*h*ich makest a moncking-stock of hell and devill,

Not in contempt of them, that they are evill,   24

But 'cause thou vainly dost thyselfe p*e*rswade,

Such toyes as these, such bugbears, were first made

On purpose to fright children.   Instantlie

The soule thou thinkst doth w*i*th the bodie dye. ·   28   and that the soul dies with the body.

Nature can*n*ot im*m*ortalize a man,

'Tis true indeed, but heavenly powers can.

 " That ther are no such things" (saist thou) "this age,

This vicious age, confirmes ; what need I wage   32

Other contentious arguments, when I

By this alone can proue noe Dietie ?

Were there a God, sinne would not flourish thus,   He says if there were a God sin would not flourish as it [leaf 3] does,

Neither would vertue (as it is) by vs   36

Be trodden vnder foote.   For ought I see

The lewdest p*e*rsons thriue best, and are free

From punnishment for sinne ; besides all this,

They that doe worship God doe often misse   40

The blessings of the world & suffer griefe ;   while the good suffer many things without help from Him.

Yet ther is none can giue to them relief.

They often fall in danger & mischance,

Yet never finde a full deliverance.   44

Were there a God, sure then he would defend

His children still, w*h*ich wholly doe depend

Vppon his mercy, & vpon them spread

His blessings in abundance : on the head   48

Of the vngodly, there alon should fall

His curses, crosses, punnishments ; but all

The righteous should escape."   Peace, impious elfe !

All thou hast saide is clean against thy selfe.   52   But these things tell against the atheist,

High Ioue p*e*rmits the sunne to cast his beames,

And the moyst cloudes to dropdowne plenteous streames,

Alike vpon the just & reprobate,
Yet are not both subjected by one fate ?   56

while in eternity they will be a cause of honour to the good.

The sunnes kinde heat, heavens fruitfull distillation,
Shall be a cause of greater condemnation
To the vngodlie ; but vnto *the* just,
(As gracious blessings w*hi*ch he doth entrust   60
Vnto his children) they well vsd' shall be
A cause of hono*u*r in eternity.

The wicked may flourish now, but they will go to hell in the end.

Well may the wicked flourish in this world,
But there will come a time they shall be hurld   ·64
From top of all their pleasures eminence,
And hell shalbe their place of residence.
Then shall the righteous shine like glorious starres

The righteous will shine as the stars and enjoy perpetual rest in heaven.

W*i*thin the sphear of heaven ; oppressions, warres, 68
Afflictions, p*er*secutions, iniuries,
Hatred, contempt, & all calamities
Shall be a crowne of hono*u*r to invest
Their then trivmphant browes ; eternall rest,   72
Perpetuall joy, subject to no mischance,
Shalbe their portion & inheritance.
    But against him that makes negation
Of principles in art, no disputation   76
Is to be held : deny God, & his Word
Can smale impression make ; it is the sword

[leaf 3, back]

Of iustice w*hi*ch must bring thee to confesse

God's Word must bring men to confess Him.

The powerfull Godhead ; yet I 'le somewhat presse 80
Thy irreligeous minde. Of thy creation
Take but a true consideration ;
For 'tis not Nature, as thou dost surmise,
That begets man in soule & qualities.   84
For thou must know, two parts must first conjoyne

Two parts conjoin to make a perfect man— soul and body.

Before we can a p*er*fect man define ;
The soule, an essence intellectuall,
The body, a substance corporeall ;   88
The first we imm*e*diatly receiue
From Ioue ; the other God to man doth leaue

(As a subordinat instrument)

To generat ; 'tis onlie incident   92

To man, to cause the bodies procreation ;

The soule's infusde by heavenly operation.

Looke on this with an intellectuall eye,

And it will teach thee ther 's a Diety.   96

View but the earth, which doth each year renew

Her drouping beauty, & clean change her hiew

Vpon the Springs approch ; doth it not shew

A supream Power, that governs things belowe ?   100

Looke on the heavens (which thou shalt ne're ascend,

Vnlesse it be with horrour to attend

Thie sentence of damnation ;) looke, I say,

Doth not their goodly opifice display   104

A power 'bove Nature ?   Dull conceited foole,

Ne'er trainèd vp but in dame Natures schoole,

Looke in thy selfe, when thou committst a sinne,

Doth not thy conscience prick thy soule within ?   108

If that ther be no God, what dost thou fear ?

Why doth remorse of conscience, or dispaire,

Afflict thee thus ?   This is enough to prove

(Were there no more) an Elohim, a Iove.   112

How canst thou then thus impiously deny

The sacred essence of the Diety ?

Recant this errour, least, to all mens wonder,

Revengefull Iove doe strike thee dead with thunder.

    Being once granted (this our true position)   117

Ther is a God ; let 's now make inquisition

What this God is ; which must be by relation

Vnto his workes, or else by meer negation   120

Of what he is not, we may make collection

Of what he is.   It is the times infection

[To b]¹e to curious in the mistery

Of searching his essentialitie,   124

Which simplie, as too glorious for the eye

¹ MS. worn off.

Marginal notes:

Look at the earth which, each year renewing its beauty, shows a supreme Power.

Look to the heavens, and they declare a Being who is above nature.

Look on yourself; if there is no God why does conscience make you fear ?

This is enough to prove there is a God.

Consider what God is.

It is the fashion now to be over curious in searching into [leaf 4] the Divine Being.

Of mortall vnderstanding to descrie,
We cannot comprehend ; let's therfore know him
In that sort onlie that the Scriptures shew him.   128

God is an Essence intellectuall,
A perfect Substance incorporeall ;
A Spirit whose being ne're begining knew,
Omnipotent, omniscient, ever true ;   132
Or rather, in the abstract :—Majestie,
Truth, mercy, wisdome, power, iustice, glorie ;
Which out of nothing this great world did frame,
And into nothing will rechange the same ;   136
Which made that glorious eye of heaven, the sunne
To rule the day, and for darke night the moone ;
Which joynes in friendly league each element,
And keeps the sea within his continent ;   140
Which of the dust mans body did create,
Into the which a soule he did translate,
Like his owne image pure ; vntill mans fall,
Left to his owne free-will, polluted all   144
That goodly microcosme ; for the which deed,
Had not the issue of the promisde seed,
The valiant Lion of stout Iudahs tribe,
The gentle Lambe vngentlie crucified,   148
Redeemd his life, borne his iniquity,
And conquerd Satan & his tyrannie,
He should haue been severely punnishèd
And everlastingly haue perishèd.   152

But now by him, all that make oblation
Of a true faith, assure their soules salvation ;
What the first Adam did by sinne destroy,
The Second hath restorde with duble ioye.   156
But leaving this moste heavenly meditation,
Let's shew for what effect was mans creation :
It was, it is, to serve this God alone,
With honour, loue, & true devotion.   160
The manner how were somewhat long to write,

Side notes:

God is an intellectual Essence, omnipotent, omniscient, and always true.

He made the earth, the sun, the moon, and elements, and sustains them.

He created man out of the dust and left him to his own free will.

Christ redeemed man from everlasting punishment, and restored what Adam lost.

Man was created to serve, honour, and love his Maker.

The Scripture all his precepts doth recite.
Which, cause we cannot in all parts fulfill,
In lieu of power he doth except our will.   164
But man, vngratefull man, this God withstandes,
And, like Briareus with his hundred handes,
Strives, as it were, to pull him from his throne
Which gave him being, & through whom alone   168
He his well-being has.   O, impious deed,
Which to recount my very heart doth bleed !
That wee (like to those giants, which made warre
Against the heavens) with such presumption dare   172
Lift vp our selues against our Maker by
So many kinde[1] of damnd impietie,
So many hellish sinnes, whose hideous cry
Percing the clowdes, mounting aboue the skie,   176
Affront Gods power, & doe deserve to finde
Another Deluge to destroy mankinde.
But God, this gracious God, with mercie strives
To bring vs to him & to saue our lives ;   180
And therfore hath chalkd out a ready way,
(That we no more might goe so farre astray)
His Gospell ; which path (if not trod amisse)
Will safelie bring vs to celestiall blisse.   184
This profferd grace some see not, some despise,
Although herein alone their safetie lies.
   Omitting Iewish superstition
With soule-profaning Turkish Alcheron,   188
And Infidels, which noe religion vse,
Whose ignorance cannot their sinne excuse :
We that doe boast of Christianity,
And knowledge in Gods holie misterie,   192
With sects & scismes our religion
Have made a chaos of confusion.
Our Anabaptists I will set aside,
With Families of Love, whose aimes are wide   196

[1] MS. tinde

Man strives against God and tries to pull Him from His throne. [leaf 4, back]

Like the fabled giants, we lift up ourselves against our Maker.

By our sins we affront Him and deserve a second deluge to destroy us.

He sent the Gospel to guide us to bliss, but while some see it not others despise it.

We who boast of our Christianity have made a chaos of our religion by our sects.

From the true faith.   There is a trinall kinde
Of seeming good religion, yet I finde
But one to be embrac'd, which must be drawne
From Papist, Protestant, or Puritane.   200

I will speak first of the Puritans who have become very numerous,   And first to speake of that pure seeming sect,
Which now of late beginneth to infect
The body of our land :—This kinde of men
Is strangelie (for I know not how nor when)   204
Become so populous, that with the number,

and cumber the Church, sticking as a disease within her bowels.   But more with new devises, it doth cumber
Our Catholique Church, & sticks as a disease
Within her bowels ; whilst it seems to please   208
With fainèd habite of true holinesse
Which is indeed the worst of wickednesse.

[leaf 5]   The thought of this hath set my Muse one fire,
And I must rage e're I can swage mine ire.   212
You hypocriticall precisians,
By vulgar phrase entitled Puritanes,

Of their apparent sanctity they make a cloak to hide their villany.   Which make of superficiall sanctitie
A cloke, to hide your inbred villanie ;   216
You soules-seducers vnto worst of evils,
You seeming saints & yet incarnat devils,
How dare ye slander our religion,
And make a scoffe at our devotion ?   220
How dare you with opprobrious wordes revile,

They revile the sacred orders of the Church ;   Or with vnhallowed actions thus defile
The sacred orders which our Church doth hold,
And sanctimonious customes, which of olde   224
Haue by grave counsels, to a godlie end,
Not superstition, as you doe pretend,
Been instituted ?   Cease your open wrongs !

even the bishops cannot escape their slanderous tongues.   Cannot our Bishops scape your slanderous tongues ?
No : you maligne their great authoritie,   229
Because they doe search out your villanie.
You must haue private meetings ! To what end ?
In bellie-cheer and lust your time to spend.   232

O rare devotion & strange holinesse,
Wh*i*ch endes in soule polluting beastlinesse!
Well may you blinde the eyes of com*m*on sence,

They pass for men of zeal amongst the simple, but God knows all, and He will punish their hypocrisy.

And passe for men of zeale & confidence   236
'Mongst simple worldlings, wh*i*ch by outward shew
Doth iudge the inward man; but God doth know
All yo*u*r intents, & w*i*th severity
Will castigate yo*u*r damnd hypocrisie.   240
In the mean time may you be forcd to dwell

Till then may they go to Amsterdam, or hell.

At Amsterdam, or else sent quicke to hell.
    For now my Muse doth hear another motion;—
"Ignorance is the mother of devotion!"   244

Ignorance is not the mother of devotion, as the papists say,

Erroneous papist, hast soe litle grace?
Thou knowst 'tis false, then how, or w*i*th what face
Canst thou maintaine against thy conscience
So manyfest an erro*u*r w*i*thout sence?   248
For how can he be good that knowes no cause
Whie he is good, but like a milhorse drawes,
Blindfolded, in a circle? Yet you teach

who teach religion in an unknown tongue, not daring to reveal their mysteries.

(For to the learnèd I addresse my speech)   252
Religion in an vnknowne tongue to those
Whom we call com*m*on people; I suppose,
Nay trulie may averre, you doe conceale
Yo*u*r misteries, not daring them reveale,   256
Lest that the people, knowing them for lies,

[leaf 5, back]

Should contemne you & hate yo*u*r heresies:
You that are worse then cannibals by oddes,

They are worse than cannibals, who only eat men, while the papists eat the gods.

For they devoure but men, you eat the gods!   260
Fro*m* whom doe you assume authoritie
To pardon capitall iniquity?
Why, not from God, the Pope's sufficient
To pardon sinne & divert punnishment.   264
Who taught you soe, you wilfully blinde fooles?
Sure Satan read this lecture in his schooles.
Wher did you learne? (was't in the Devils booke?

Where did they learn that it is lawful to murder princes?

For from Gods word I 'me sure you never tooke   268

Such damnable positions) that to murder
A prince, w*hi*ch doth not yo*u*r religion furder,
Is a moste lawfull act, yea commendable,
For w*hi*ch you will at any time enable   272

The man who attempts the murder of a prince

That man w*i*th your best benediction,
And all his sinnes free absolution,
And warrantize him heaven & happie day :
("A warrant seald w*i*th butter !" as we say).   276
All this, & more then this, you will pe*r*forme,
Be 't to the meanest abject, basest worme,
That dares attempt soe horrible a deed.
And though his enterprise doe not succeed,   280
(As God forbid it should) but he doe die
For his lewd treason, he shall instantlie

is canonized, as was Ravaillac for the murder of Henry IV. of France, May 14, 1610,

Be canonizd a Saint. Ravilliacke
Doth neither S*ai*nts nor Martires title lacke.   284
But you had reason : his vnhappy hand
Destroyde a kinge,[1] & almost brought a land
To vtter ruin ; for being thus defilde
With her owne princes blood, a tender childe   288
Was to succeed, & we know Scriptures say,
"Woe to those landes whose scepters children sway."

and Fawkes for his attempt on our King and Parliament in 1605.

But Faux & his confederats[2] are enrolde
For blessed S*ai*nts among you.—Who will holde   292
Yo*u*r piety authenticall, w*hi*ch makes
Such hell-houndes S*ai*nts? What godly heart not quakes
To hear such mischiefe, to record such evill,

The devil only could have put such a plot into a man's head.

As they would haue committed ? The grand Devill
Was their instructer sure, else could they not   297
Haue once devisde soe damnable a plott,
As by one blast o*u*r king to ruinat,
And our whole kingdome to depopulate,   300

---

[1] MS. kinde.

[2] Garnet and Oldcorn are set down as "martyrs" in an "Apologia " published at Cologne in 1610, written by A. E. Ioannes Cydonius, who justifies the killing of heretic kings. Others at that time did the same.

And spoile of her best treasure.   But high Ioue,
Against whose power in vaine their forces strove,
Crost their designes, & with a mighty arme   [leaf 6]
Delivered vs from the pernicious harme   304   But God delivered
                                                        us from the
Of that moste eminent danger ; to whose Name   danger,
All praise & all thanksgiving for the same   for which we give
                                                        Him thanks.
We doe ascribe ; beseching him to blesse
Our realme from you & your accomplices.   308
But to proceed : no man may kill his prince   No man may kill
                                                        his king, as might
Although a tyrant ; which I could evince   be proved from
By arguments drawne from the word of God,   the Bible.
But I too long one this haue made abode.   312

    Besides your errour I soe plaine repute,
As needs noe disputation to confute,
There are more errours of especiall note,   Besides this'
                                                        error, the Church
Which, if I list recite, I heer could cote ;   316   of Rome has
                                                        many others :—
But I doe leave them for the learned pen
Of great divines and more iudicious men.
Your holy water, purgatorie, bulles,   Holy water,
                                                        Purgatory, and
Wherwith you make the common people gulles,   320   bulls,
Are grosse abuses of phantastique braines
Subtillie devisd'e only for private gaines,   which are
                                                        devised for
Which you pull from the simple as you list,   private gain.
Keeping them blinded in black errours mist ;   324
And from the truth doe lead them clean astray,
Whilst of their substance you doe make your prey.
You false impostors of blinde ignorance,
Think you to 'scape eternall vengeance ?   328
'Tis not your Popes fond dispensation,   The Pope's dis-
                                                        pensation, works
Your workes of supererrogation,   of supererogation,
Your idle crossings, or your wearing haire   wearing of hair,
Next to your skin, or all your whipping-cheer,   332   whippings,
Your praiers & pilgrimage to Saints, your pixes,   pilgrimages,
                                                        pixes,
Your holy reliques, beads, & crucifixes,   relics, beads,
Your masses, Ave Maries, images,   masses, images,
Dirges, & such like idle fantasies   336   and such idle
                                                        fancies,

Of superstitiously polluted Rome,

Can saue your soules in that great day of doome.

Between these sects, as in a golden meane,

Stands the religion whervnto we leane ;   340

Vndoubted truth it is that we doe holde,

Yet is our zeale so frozen & so colde,

So chockt with thornes of covetous desire,

So hoggishlie polluted with the mire   344

Of carnall lusts, that our best sanctity

Is but a kinde of bastard piety.

And yet the times as now did ne're afford

Such plenty of dispencers of Gods word ;   348

For now the Gospell, like the midday sunne,

Displaies his beames over all Albion.

But we, as if by too much light strucke blinde,

Neglect this meanes of grace, which is assignd   352

For our soules health.   Some out of pride contemne it,

Others, bent vnto greedy gaine, condemne it,

Because it speakes against the slavish vice

Of soule-bewitching, sordid avarice.   356

Others, that follow Epicureus fashion,

Cannot abide to hear of reformation,

And therfore hate the Gospell, which doth cry

Against their brutish sensuality.   360

Many there are which live like libertines,

And the holy C[h]urch & good devines

Doe hold ridiculous ;—their homely homes

Will serve them well enough to pray, when 't comes

Into their fancies ; they cannot abide   365

Vnto Church orders strictlie to be tide.

Others, forsooth, will haue a congregation,

But that must be after another fashion   368

Then our Church doth allow,—no church at all,—

For that they say is too papisticall ;

Like[1] their profession, they themselves will sever

                    [1] MS. Likes.

From stone walles;—tut, their church shall last for ever;
Theire soules shalbe their tabernacles still,   373
That kinde of church doth only please their will.

Ioue separat me from these Separists,   *Jove, deliver me from such men!*
Which think they hold heavens kingdome in their fists,
And yet their life, if we into it prie,   .   377
Is full of sinne & damnd impiety.

  Some, more for fear of the lawes punnishment   *Some go to church because they fear the law.*
Then zeale vnto devotion, doe frequent   380
Gods holy temple, where they doe imploy
Themselves as ill as if they staide away;
On[e] part in sleeping, in discourse another;   *Some sleep, some talk;*
A third doth seeme to marke, but doth discover   384
Slilie some object that withdrawes his eye
From what he should attend; the yoonger frie   *others come to see and be seen.*
Come only to be seen & see : of all
Which doe repaire to church, the fruit is smale   388
That is collected by them.   I surmise
That wickednesse by this doth rather rise
To greater height, then anywise decaie;
For pride & lust it is the ready way   392
I 'me sure.   Of every new framd fashion,   *Every new fashion is displayed at church.*
This is the place to make moste ostentation,
To shew the bravery of our gay attire   ,
Hether to come on purpose; our desire   396
Is to be seen of all, whilst we observe   *[leaf 7]*
The like in others.   Though our soules doe sterve
For want of knowledge, we doe litle care;
From gazing vp and downe we cannot spare   400   *Not a moment can be spared from gazing about.*
A iot of time to hearken to Gods word,
When all 's to litle that we doe afforde
To our owne fancies; thus the time we spend,
Which devine service soone brings to an end;   404
And then againe we homeward doe advaunce,
Fuller of pride, as full of ignorance.
Is there a wench whose beauty is of note?   *If there's a pretty wench,*

Hether your gallants come, only to cote   408
Her rare perfections ; yea, this sacred place
Serves them to make (they have soe litle grace)
Compacts for lust.   Thus by these hellish evils
The howse of God is made a den of devils.   412

I speake not this to hinder the concourse
Of well affected mindes vnto that source,
That fountaine, blessed fountaine, which doth flow
With living waters, Gods word ; no, my bow   416

Aimes at another marke ; I onlie strive
To rectifie abuses which deprive
The Gospell of his propagation,
And plentifull encrease.   Our nation   420
Rather needs spurres to quicken his slow pace
Vnto religion & the house of grace.

For some there are which gape soe after gaine,
That on the Lords day they will not refraine,   424
So 't to their benefit tend, to exercise
Themselves in some laborious enterprise.
In towne & cuntrie this vngodlie sinne
To grow vnto a custome doth beginne ;   428

Your country swaines will moste familiarlie
Worke one this day & labour impiouslie.
But 'mongst our tradesmen specially, this vse,
Which I may iustlie call a damnd abuse,   432
Is most familiar.   Six dayes in the weeke
Are not sufficient, but the seventh must reeke
With sweat of their vngodly labour, when
They should repaire to church with other men,   436

To give vnto the Lord, the only Giver
Of blessings, & the gracious Forgiver
Of hell deserving sinnes, all praiers & praise.
What though the word of God expresly sayes,   440
" This is the day which thou must dedicate
Vnto my service, this day at no rate
Shalt thou performe thy worke, least thou doe draw

My heavy wrath vpon thee ?"   Though the law   444

Of man forbid the same, and doe inflict

A punnishment on those it doth convict

Of this offence; yet fearlesse of all danger,

From the man borne i' th' land vnto the stranger,   448

If they can cast a mist before the eye

Of sinne-correcting, strict authority,

Moste of our tradesmen will enact this crime ;

It stands not with their profit to loose time ;   452

They'l take their best advantage while they may ;

It is sufficient once a month to pray.

Vngracious villaines, how can you expect

A blessing to your labour, which neglect   456

The only meanes, Gods service, which alone

Can bring your workes vnto perfection ?

The manna gathered in the wildernesse

By the Iewes vnbeelieving wickednesse   460

Vpon their Sabboth, by the Lord forbidden,

Both putrifide & stuncke.   Nothing is hidden

Which shall not be reveald ; though you may blinde

The eyes of man, there is a God will finde   464

And punnish this lewd sinne.   I' th' meantime think

That all such labours in his nostrils stinke,

And therfore shall prove fruitlesse : men intend

But God it is that consummates the end.   468

   I cannot 'scape the blest Communion,

Which doth with God effect our vnion,

It is soe much abusd by sinfull man,—

To passe the papist & the Lutheran,   472

Their trans & consubstantiation,

Of both these errors to make no relation,—

We that doe holde the verity indeed,

That this same bred, wheron our soules doe feed,   476

This wine we drink, is reall bred and wine,

Although the mistery be moste devine ;

Even we, I say, though we doe represent

Side notes:

They despise the laws of God and [leaf 7, back] man which forbid this sin.

Most of our tradesmen are guilty of it, thinking once a month often enough to pray.

The manna collected on the Jewish sabbath putrified.

All Sunday labour is in vain.

The Holy Communion is much abused.

Passing by the Papist and the Lutheran, we

ourselves err in
our opinion of
this Sacrament.

The true opinion of the Sacrament,   480
Yet in the vse doe erre, nay rather sinne,
Which applide rightly is the meanes to winne
Eternall life. ' Some men, which are vnable

Some go to the
Holy Table to
please their
sense;

To iudge the worth, come to this Holy Table   484
Only to please their sence ; others there are
Which for so smale a pittaunce doe not care ;—
" What is a bitte of bread, a sip of wine ?"—
But that the law doth straightly them enioyne,   488
To be partakers of this holy meat

some think it is
not worth the
trouble, but go
because the law
compels them.

And sacred drink. By farre they'd rather eat
At their owne howses, wher their carnall sence
May be suffic'd ; their soules intelligence   492

[leaf 8]

May sterve for want of this spirituall food,
And they regard it not. That 's only good
In their grosse braines, whose visibility
And appetituall sensibility   496

Others esteem
themselves un-
worthy, and
refuse to go on
that account,

Lies open to their sence. Others ther be,
Which doe indeed esteem more reverendlie
Of the Lords Supper ; & because they knowe
The danger great, that to their soules may grow   500
By their vnworthy eating, quite refuse
To be partakers of it ; still they vse
Some let or other to detaine them back ;
Either they doe due preparation lacke,   504

or because they
are not in charity
with all men.

Or else they are not in true charity
With other men. Ther must noe malice be
In a communicant : 'tis true.—What then ?
Doe you surmise, O shallow-pated men,   508
That this excuse is all sufficient
To satisfie for such a foule intent ?

But remember,
the king made
his feast, and
that you were
bidden.

No, simple worldlings ; the king made his feast,
And you were bidden to it 'mongst the rest ;   512
But 'cause you would not come, you shall not tast
His sacred supper, but you shalbe cast
Into that pitt, with the ungodlie rout,

Where the worme dies not, the fire ne're goes out. 516
And soe shall likewise he that boldlie came
Without his wedding roabe ; I mean the same
Which comes vnto the Table of the Lord
As to some common, ordinarie bord,   520
And never seekes to make true preparation,
But even eats & drinkes his owne damnation.

You and he who came without his wedding garment will alike be cast into hell.

   It is a lamentable thing to see
The ignorance & strange stupidity   524
Of men now living in the clearest light
Of the resplendant Gospell, as if night
Of darkest errour still ecclips'd their eyes ;
They are so rude in the true misteries   528
Of their salvation, scarce one man 'mong ten
Can giue a true account of 's faith ; nor, when
He comes to due examination,
How he hath made his preparation   532 .
For the Lords Table, iustlie tell the number
Of Sacraments ; this only thing doth cumber
The wits of many & confounds their sence,
As I haue seen by plaine experience.   536
How far then are they from the perfect knowing
Of their true vse ! yet these men will be shewing
Themselues moste forward to receive ; but what
They know not, nor they care not much for that ; 540
But for the world, to purchase earthly gaine,
They follow that with dayly sweat and paine.

It is lamentable to see the ignorance and stupidity of men

in that which concerns their own salvation.

Some cannot even tell the number of the Sacraments,

or their true use.

[leaf 8, back]

   It is a custome, lewd enough I 'me sure,
(And I doe wonder that our lawes endure   544
Such profane vses) after the receate
Of that cœlestiall sacramentall meat,
For olde & young i' th' country frequently
Vpon that day to vse most luxurie.   548
Each on[e] must then vnto an alehouse run,
Drink drunk, act any sinne vnder the sunne.
Why ? this same day 's a day of iubile ;

After receiving the Holy Sacrament,

it is common for old and young to go to the alehouse.

It has been the custom; and they would rather lose their souls than their privileges.

It hath been an accustomd liberty   552
To spend this day in mirth, and th[e]y will choose
Rather their soules then priviledges loose.
And soe (I fear) not few among them will;
For they, which on this day doe drink & swill   556

Such men are like him who swept his house, after which seven evil spirits came to dwell with him.

In such lewd fashion, may be likened well
To him that swept the howse wher he did dwell,
And made it clean, & garnisht it full faire ;
After which act ther did to him repaire   560
Seven evill fiends worse then the former were ;
More ougly sinnes did enter & dwell there,
And by his falling to more wicked sinning,
He made his end far worse then his begining.   564

Satan stands ready to enter into them as he did into Judas.

So is 't with them that in this sort doe sinne,
Satan stands close ready to enter in,   ,
Even as he did in Iudas, which had eat
Vnworthily the sacramentall meat.   568
And yet fond man regardeth not one whit,
Till he have made himselfe the devils bit,
Who at two bits, for so his name imports,
Devours both soule & body, mans two parts.   572

So man, whose life is but a bubble, is blown from Christianity.

    Thus is man blowne, by every puffe of vanity,
From the true scope of Christianity,
His soules salvation.   Wretched, wicked man,
Returne, repent ! Thy life is but a spanne,   576
A breath, a buble ; think that thou must die
To live in joyes or endlesse miserie.
And if the comfort of celestiall blisse,

If the joys of heaven have not softened his heart,

Whose joy beyond imagination is,   580
Haue not sufficient power to mollifie
Thy heart, heart hardned in iniquity,

let the fear of hell do so.

Yet let the horrour of damnation,
Of whose strange paines no tongue can make relation,
Enforce repentance with a true contrition,   585
And that produce a forward disposition

To a new course of life ; refuse not grace
While it is offered ; while ther 's time & space
Dally not with repentance, least iust Ioue
Convert to furie his contemnèd love ;
And in that ire, iustly conceivèd ire,
Confine thy soule to hells tormenting fire.

588 While he has time
let him not dally
[leaf 9]
with repentance!

592

Satira 2.

[AGAINST SHAMS.]

ARGUMENTUM.

Fronti nulla fides, ludunt spectacula mentem ;
Non facies verum symptoma cordis habet.
Decipimur specie recti, sub imagine veri
Falsa latent; virtus dissimulata placet.

No poet has been
able to describe
the Mausoleum,

The brave erect Mausolian monument,

That famous vrne, the worlds seventh wonderment,

Whose sumptuous cost & curious workemanship

Noe poet, though in Helicon he dip   596

His pen, by verse is able to dilate,

Being made for wonder, not to imitate ;

which, for all its
outward beauty,
is full of
corruption.

For all his glorious outside, without staine,

Filth[1] & corruption doth within containe.   600

The sunne, whose spacious orbe in magnitude

Doth far exceed the earth, seemes to the rude,

Ignorant of the astronomicke art,

The sun looks no
bigger than a
cart-wheel.

Noe bigger then the wheel of Hobnols cart.   604

Counterfet gold, if we doe trust our eye,

Will passe for purest mettall currantlie.

The crocodile
sheds tears before
he devours his
prey.

The dredfull beast, ycleped crocodile,

Whose dwelling is about Ægiptian Nile,   608

Before he doth devoure his wished prey,

Pitty in outward semblance doth display ;

                    [1] MS. Fill.

For brinish teares from his false eyes distill,
When he is ready to destroy & kill.   612
Full dear seafaring passengers abie   *The Syrens by their melody entice sailors to their destruction.*
The Syrens sweet enchaunting melodie,
Which by their singing evermore presage
Death thretning danger by the furious rage   616
Of an ensuing storme.   Of Circes cup   *Circe's cup, though beautiful, changed him who drank from it into a brute.*
Who hath not heard, that who therof did sup
Was changd (strange metamorphosis in nature)
From humane forme into a brutish creature?   620
And yet the cup [w]as goodly to beholde,
Richly enchasde with pearle, composde of golde.

Glorious in view appeard Medusaes head,
Nathlesse it did strike the beholders dead.   624
Serpents & poysnous toads, as in their bowers,   *Serpents and toads lurk under sweet flowers.*
Doe closely lurke vnder the sweetest flowers.
But sencelesse things & sensuall beastes alone   *[leaf 9, back]*
Mislead not mans to rash opinion;   628
Even rationall creatures doe our iudgements cheat,
Man is to man a subject of deceite;   *Man is to man a subject of deceit;*
And that olde saying is vntrue, " the face
Is index of the heart."   False looking glasse   632
To view the thoughts of man, when there doe raine
Stormes of displeasure in mans vexèd braine;
When mists of sorrow reasons eyes doe blinde,
When revenge thunders in his ragefull minde,   636
His face can carry sunneshine of delight,   *his face is not the index to his heart,*
Allthough his soule be blacke as ougly night.
You erre, fond physiognomers, that hold
The inward minde followes the outward molde.   640
Philosophers, your axiome is vnsure,
The soule is as the bodies temperature;
Complexion noe certaine ground doth shew   *and his complexion does not always show his disposition.*
The disposition of a man to know;   644
Els why should Nisus, that same[1] pretty youth,

[1] MS. some.   Cf. Sat. 3. 1101; 4. 1397.

Be of soe lewd behaviour? when, in truth,

His bodies crasis is angelicall,

And his soules actions diabolicall. 648

If men were as they seem, detraction would not profess himself my friend.

Things are not as they seeme; for were they soe,

Detraction would professe himselfe my foe,

Shewing his rancors hate before my face,

And not behinde my backe worke my disgrace, 652

When in my presence he doth seem to be

As Damon to his Pithias, friend to me.

The tradesman seems civil and honest, but he'll cheat you.

Mechanico, reputed by moste men

An honest tradesman & grave citisen, 656

When thou dost come into his shop to buy,

Although it be the least commodity,

With kind salutes & good wordes will receave thee;

But trust him not, in 's deeds he will deceave thee. 660

Madam's face is painted and her hair only a periwig.

Madam Fucata seemeth wondrous faire,

And yet her face is painted, & her haire,

That seemes soe goodly, a false periwig.

Thus all her beauty is not worth a fig, 664

That doth appeare so glorious to the eye,

And strikes my gallant in loves lethurgie,

That soe doth boast of famous ancestry

And from great Iove derives his pedigree, 668

Her gallant shoots out oaths like artillery.

And speakes indeed, like Iove himselfe, in thunder;

For othes, as if they would rend heaven in sunder,

Shot out in vollies, like artillerie,

Flie from his mouth, that piece of blasphemie. 672

Like some great horse he paceth vp and downe,

He puts on a disdainful frown,
[leaf 10]

Gracing his lookes with a disdainefull frowne,

And takes vpon him in each company,

As if he held some petty monarchy. 676

If any man by chance discourse of warre,

He being present this discourse will marre

By intermixing his high martiall deeds,

and swears he has killed more

Swearing his manhood all mens else exceeds; 680

Vowing that his Herculean arme hath slaine

More men then populous London doth containe,

men than London contains.

Except the subvrbs.   He hath made to flie

He has put the Turk to flight.

The potent Turke, & got the victory   684

By his owne valour.   Charles the Fift of Spaine

Was nothing to him, nor great Tamburlaine ; ·

Stout Scanderbeg a childe ; he paralels

Strong sinnewed Sampson, or, indeed, excels.   688

Samson and Charles the Fifth were nothing to him.

What dares he not performe ?   Hee 'l vndertake

To make the Spanniards vtterly forsake

The Westerne Indies & their mines of gold,

With some few chosen men ; nay hee 'l vpholde   692

His force sufficient to reconquer Fraunce,

And with that kingdome once againe enhaunce

The faire revennewes of the English crowne,

Or lay their citties levell with the ground.   696

Hee 'l chase the Turke out of Hungaria,

He can drive the Turk out of Hungary and Greece,

And force him leave his seat in Grecia ;

Europe hee 'l free from his vexation,

And bring againe that scattered nation,   700

The Iewes, together to their Palestine,

and restore the Jews to Palestine.

Which he by force will conquer, & confine

To his obeisaunce.   These he dares be bolde,

And more then these, even acts that would make colde

The heartes of men only to hear recounted,   705

His martiall force, which Mars his force surmounted,

Shall vndertake.   Thou vainly bragging foole,

He's a vain, bragging fool.

[1] Ne're trainèd vp in brave Bellonaes schoole,   708

Doe not I know, for all thou lookest soe big,

Thou never yet durst see a sillie pig

Stucke to the heart ?   A frog would make thee run !

Thou kill a man ?   No, no ! thy mothers sonne,   712

His mother's only son was a coward.

Her only sonne, was a true coward bred.

I 'le vndertake a sword shall strike thee dead,

And never touch thee !   As for thy discent,

---

[1] *descript : of coragious brag :* in margin of MS. by a later hand.

He was born in
fertile Kent,
and his father
was a clown.

Though thou maist boast the place was firtill Kent 716
That gave thee birth, yet was thy syre a clowne,
And kept his wife in a course homespun gowne ;
Who, scraping vp a litle wealth, began
To fashion thee an ill shapd gentleman.   720

But, because he
has travelled
a little

And now, because thou hast, like Coriate,[1]
Traveld a litle ground, & canst relate

[leaf 10, back]

How many baudy houses thou hast seen
In the French country ; how the whores have been 724

and seen a little
of French life,

Kinder there to thee then *our* English punckes ;[2]
How many nunnes thou hast heard sing, & monckes
Say mattens ; thou thyselfe dost now repute
[3]The wort[h]iest wort[h]y of the race of Brute ;   728

he thinks he
excels all men in
bravery and
learning.

The rarest linguist England doth afford,
The bravest soldier that e're wore a sworde.
Vain vpstart braggadochio ! heartlesse cow !
Leave Mars his drum*m*e, goe holde thy fathers plow !

The Puritan's
wife lives in sin,

Fine M*istr*is Simula, the Puritane,   733
W*hi*ch as the plague shunnes all that are profane,
Ready to faint if she an oth but hear,
For all her outward holinesse doth blear   736

and is her coun-
try's shame.

The worldes dim*m*e eyes, plaies but the hypocrite,
Living in sinne & sensuall delight.
For, would you think it ? she was tane in bed
W*i*th a young, tender, smoothfacd Ganimed,   740
Her husbands prentice.   Out, lascivious whore !
Thy countries shame, thy husbands festered sore !
Are these the fruits thy frequentation

Do their meet-
ings lead to this,
while the world
thinks them so
good ?

Of learned sermons yeilds ?   Is this the fashion 744
Of *your* pure seeming sect ?   Your meetings tend
Surely vnto some such like holy ende.
And yet the world, blinde world, thinkes you to be
Men of most zeale & best integrity.   748
      Methinkes I see the rich chuffe, Sordido,

---

[1] Coryate's " Crudities " first appeared in 1611.
[2] See " Crudities," p. 26.   [3] /*I* in margin of MS.

How basely in apparrell he doth goe ;

Vpon his head a thrice turnd greasy felt,

His hose & dublet a tuffe ramskin pelt ;   752

His stockings of the coursest woole yspunne,

Full of broad patches, with thicke hobnaild shoone ;

His lockram bande sewde to his hempen shirt ;

A lethern thong doth serve his wast to girt,   756

At which a pouch full 20 winters olde

Hangs for his codpiece to keep out the colde.

How hunger-starvd he lookes ! With thin lank cheekes,

With beard vnkemd, with face fit soile for leekes,   760

I dare be sworne, who e'er should see the goat,

Would iudge him to be scarcely worth a groat.

And yet this boore, this miserable swine,

Hath landes & lordships, with good store of coine. 764

Slave to thy wealth, thus from thy selfe to rend

What thy next heir will soone as vainly spend !

   Scotus, thou hast deceiud the world enough,

Which takes thee, clothd in thy embrodered stuffe,

To be some lord at least.   Poore silly groome,   769

Which tother day wouldst faine have had the roome

Of some base trencher-scraper, so to put

Scraps twice runne over, in thy half starvd gutt.   77

And now, with often filling of the pot,

An office vnder my lords man hast got,

Being some bread-chipper or greasy cooke,

For much observance & respect dost looke.   776

Goe where thou wilt, thou gettest none of me,

I know too well thy genealogie.

Let ignorant asses bend their supple knees,

And cry, " God blesse your worship," for some fees 780

Of thy cast office ; I as much doe scorne,

As they desire the plenty of thy horne.

Proud meacocke,[1] make the world no more believe

The miser goes in a greasy hat, and coarse clothing, his linen collar stitched to his hempen shirt:

how hungry he looks ! His cheeks are thin, his beard uncombed, you would not judge him to be worth a groat.

The world takes Scotus for a lord at least, but the other day he was [leaf 11] half starved ;

and now, having a post under somebody, he looks for respect.

The ignorant may salute him,

but I scorn him,

----

¹ The *m* has been crossed out and *p* written over by another hand.

Gentility is pind vpon thy sleeve ;   784
For if thou doe, with my satirick verse,
Thy parentage & manners I 'le reherse,

and will make
the world laugh
at him and hiss
him.

And make the world, for thy monstrous othes,
To laugh & hisse thee out of thy fine clothes.   788
   He that sees Moros in his brave attire
Would deem him to be some discreet esquire,
He speakes soe seldome, soe demure doth looke.
But see how much a man may be mistooke ;—   792

Moros, who is
a very fool,
speaks so seldom
and looks so
demure, that
many think him
wise.

A verier foole dame Nature never bred,
That scarce knowes chalke from cheese, or blew from red ;
Yet amongst many which haue purblinde eyes
This foolish sot hath been thought wondrous wise. 796
I know a fellow (I 'le conceale his name)
Hath purchasd, & yet doth possess, the fame
Of a rare scholler, that hath noe one part
Of learning, not the smallest dramme of art.   800

I know a man
who gained a
repute for
learning

And will you know how he got his repute ?
I 'le tell you, soe you 'l promise to be mute
And make no wordes on 't.   'Tis his asses guise,
As soone as he from 's morning bed doth rise,   804

by attending
booksellers' shops
and asking to see
the writings of
famous authors—

After some turne or two in Paules, to drop
In the precinct of some knowne stationers shop,
And there, like a learnd Sir, with a grave voice
He doth demand to see some special choice   808
Of famous authors, whose true names by heart
The foole hath gotten, of what tongue or art

Montaigne, whose
Essays in French,
books 1 and 2, were
first published in
1580 ; books 1, 2,
and 3 in 1588.

It skills not much ; French, Latine, Hebrew, Greeke,
All 's one, he vnderstandeth all alike :   812
Montaignes Essaies in French,[1] the history
Of Philip Comineus,[2] poesie

[leaf 11, back]
Virgil, Horace,
Augustine,
Bernard,

Of Virgil, Horace, & such Latin writers,
St. Austine, Bernard, or some new enditers   816

---

[1] English translation published in 1603, 2nd ed. in 1613.
[2] Philip de Comines died in 1509.   He wrote memoirs of
his own time.

Of commentaries theologicall ;
And sometimes he 's for philosophicall,
And the best writers of astronomie,
With phisick, logicke, & geometrie.   820
Then Aristotle, Di[o]scorides,
Avicen, Galen, & Hypocrates ;
The Hebrew Rabbins, Ptolomeus, Plato
(Although the foole did never learne his Cato),   824
Are in his mouth familiar.   Some of these,
Which to demaund his fancy best doth please,
He for some hower or two will pore vpon,
Which time is worth your observation ;   828
For sometime smiling with a simpring grace,
In turning over those same leaves apace,
To shew his skill i' th' tongues, hee 'l nod his head,
As if the place which he doth seeme to read   832
Mov'd him to laughter ; then with thumb hee 'l cote,
As if that sentence were of speciall note,
And straight cry " pish !" as if he dislikd that
Which he as much knowes as his grandams cat.   836
Well, having (as he thinkes) sufficiently
Guld the opinion of the standers by
To his desire, the booke he downe doth lay,
Demaunds the price, dislikes it, goes his way.   840
Somtime perhaps, to blinde dull iudgements eye,
Some petty English pamphlet he will buie.
Thus hath this gull, among the common sort,
Which iudge by outward shewes, got the report   844
Of a great scholler, when, God knowes, the foole
Was never farther then the grammer schoole.
     Thus mans opinion doth him oft deceave,
And of true iudgement doth his minde bereave.   848
Iudging by outward shewes we iudge amisse,
For vice in vertues habite clothed is.
Hypocrisie seemes holinesse in looke,
Fixing his eyes on heaven or in his booke.   852

Margin notes:

Aristotle, Dioscorides, Galen,

Ptolemy, and Plato,

and poring over them for an hour or two.

Nodding his head, smiling,

and crying " Pish !" sometimes,

he demands the price, and sometimes will buy a petty English Pamphlet to gull the by-standers.

If we judge by outward appearances we judge amiss :

O, 'tis a most dissembling, harmfull devill,

That 's good in shew & yet in heart is evill.

hatred is often be-
neath salutation;

Backbiting slander, deep dissimulation,

Are inside hate, yet outside salutation.   856

valour is only
cowardice in
disguise;

Vanting in wordes true valour oft doth seeme,

Yet by his actions we him coward deem ;

flattery takes the
form of good
counsel;

Soothing vp ill, pernicious flattery,

In outward shew good counsel seemes to be.   860

[leaf 12]

Deformity, daubde with a face of paint,

With beauties title doth herselfe a[c]quaint ;

avarice is ac-
counted thrift;

Base avarice & sordid parsimony

Is thrift[1] accounted, & good husbandry ;   864

prodigality,

Excessive spending, sensuall prodigality,

liberality.

Is thought all one with liberality ;

Impudent boldnesse, rash temerity,

Is held for vertuous audacity ;   868

Ignorance passes
for learning,
while learning
is held in no
repute.

Ignorance in his scarlet robe yclad,

Accounted learning, in respect is had,

When vertuous[2] art, clothed in poor aray,

Is held in no repute, till time bewray   872

The seeming good that ignorance hath not,

And the not seeming good that art hath got.

Put no trust in
seeming.

Thus ther 's no trust to be reposde in seeming,

Since virtue 's knowne by act, not by esteeming.   876

---

[1] MS. thirift.

[2] Originally written *vertcous*, but altered apparently by another hand into *vertuous*.

Sat[ira] 3.

[AGAINST PRIDE, ETC.]

ARGUMENTUM.

Dum tendit superos ambire superbia cœlos,
    Decidit ad Stigium fulmine quassa lacum.
Æterno verum sic indignata perisse,
    Cœcos mortales ad sua regna trahit.

After the fabricke of heaven, earth, & seas

Were gloriously composde, it then did please

High Ioue (e're he began mans operation)

To give vnto the Angels their creation.   880

No earthy substance was in them at all,

Their formes were heavenly & spirituall.

Yet some of these, vpon the very day

They were by God created (if I say   884

Vntruth, I can alleadge mine author for it),

Swelling with pride (oh, I to write abhor it)

Because they were such glorious creatures, strove

To take possession of the throne of Ioue.   888

But he, displeasde with such ambition,

Struck them with lightning downe to Acheron,

And them confined perpetually to dwell

In the darke horrour of infernall hell.   892

Thus were faire angels ougly devils made,

And one dayes sinne an everlasting trade.

[side notes]
After the creation of the heavens and the earth, angels were called into being.

On the very day of their creation they attempted to dethrone the Almighty,

who drove them into hell.

After the fall of these, man was created and woman made to be his associate

After the fall of these was man compacted,
And from him sleeping woman was extracted   896
And made to be a kinde associat
Vnto him.   Now the devill shewes his hate

[leaf 12, back]

And swelling envie 'gainst God in his creature
Formd to his image, man ; to make defeature   900
Of his estate in blisse, he doth intend
And fittest opportunity attend.

To work their fall Lucifer seeks an opportunity,

To worke this feat proud Lucifer's enioynd,
And goe[s] about it swifter then the winde.   904
" Shall I," quoth he, " fall from celestiall blisse
Into the horrour of hells blacke abysse,
And man escape ?   Shall I in torment live,
And man in pleasure ?   Shall I only grieve,   908

thinking to ease his own pain by making man co-partner in his grief

And man goe scotfree ?   No, 'twill ease my paine
If in my griefe I him copartner gaine ;
And I will doe it : if my plots hit right,
I 'le bring his soule vnto perpetuall night."   912
This saide, the serpents shape he takes & hies
Vnto the tree in midst of Paradise.
There findes the woman, after naméd Eve,
The weakest vessell, easiest to deceave ;   916

Eve's mind he inspires with pride,

Whose minde with hellish pride he straight inspirde
That she [the] trees forbidden fruit desirde ;
The tree of which alone she might not eat,
The tree forbidden by the Lord for meat.   920

causing her to eat of the tree of knowledge.

The tree of knowledge, knowledge of much evill,
She gathers straight, seducéd by the devill,
Which greedilie, without advice, she tasted,
And then to give her husband of it hasted.   924
Whom when she had allurde vnto her will,
And both had tasted, then they knew their ill ;

Grown wise, Adam and Eve

But all too late (first Phrigians[1]) they grew wise,

[1] This may refer to the Phrygian oracle which promised empire to him who untied the Gordian knot, cut by Alexander the Great.   Or it may be an allusion to the low estimate in which Phrygian character was held by the ancients.

Being both thrust forth Edens Paradise ;   928 lost Paradise,
Which happy place man ever had possessed,   which man would ever have possessed.
If they had never in this sorte transgressed.
Vnhappy three, first causers of our evill,
Fond man, proude woman, & accursèd devill !   932
Since this hath pride increasd with Adams seed,   Since this, pride has gone on increasing in Adam's seed.
And Lucifer companions shall not need ;
Man with soe many kindes of pride doth swell
As if he strove headlong to run to hell.   936

　　Some shew their pride in raysing stately bowers,   Some show their pride in stately buildings,
Which seem to threatne heaven like Babell towers ;
Building so strong, erecting them so high,
As if they ment to live eternally,   940
In spite of Ioue.   Others bestow more cost   and some in houses built for pleasure.
In houses built for pleasure, which they boast
Are but for shew, then would maintaine & cherish   [leaf 13]
Thousands of poore soules which are like to perish : 944
Confusion sure will light on their pretence
Which wast their treasure in soe vaine expence.
Others there be which, clad in gay attire,   Others, in fine clothing and lofty looks, aspire above their rank.
In stately gate & loftie lookes, aspire   948
Above their ranke ; holding inferiors base,
Scarsely permitting equalles come in place
Of fellowship, vnlesse their peacock sutes
Gaine them admittance in their proud reputes.   952
O, these are men of admiration,
Which follow each fantastique fashion,   These follow each vain fashion, but their gay apparel covers little wit.
To be observde with reverence & respect ;
When, if we could the inward man detect,   956
God knowes that I am not deceavd a whit,
Their gay apparrell covers litle witt.

　　Most of our women are extreamly proud   Most of our women are proud—they paint their faces.
Of their faire lookes, & therfore doe enshroud   960
Their beauties in a maske ; with greater care
Their faces then their soules, to keepen faire.
Some of this kinde when beauty gins decay,

By art restore what nature takes away,   964
Painting their visage.   Cursed Iesabell
That taught them this, will bring them all to hell.
This vice in woeman only doth not bide,

The men curl
their pates and
wear love-locks;
others paint their
faces.

Men alsoe are infected with this pride.   968
Some curle their pates to make their lookes more fair,[1]
Others delight to wear a locke of haire,
A lovelocke, which being of the longest size
Doth the lewd wearer quite effeminize.   972
Nay some with fucus will besmear their face,
It ads to their complexion better grace.

I know one who
is ever looking in
his glass, setting
his perfumed
beard or combing
his hair.

I knowe a snowt-faire, selfe-conceited asse,
Which is still prying in a looking glasse   976
To see his fooles face, washt with ly o 'th' chamber,
And set his beard, perfumde with greece of amber,
Or kembe his civet lockes, soe far in love
With his owne beauty, that I fear hee'l proove   980
Sicke with conceat ; for the which maladie
I can prescribe no better remedy
Then wish the glasse, wherin he views his face,

The fate of
Narcissus might
cure him.

A river, him to take Narcissus place,   984
So the next time he came on 's face to looke
He should be drenchèd in the liquid brooke.
But leaving him a courting in the glasse
His owne vaine shadowe, I this coxcome passe.   988

[leaf 13, back] Others there be which, selfe-conceited wise,
Take a great pride in their owne vaine surmise,

Some delight in
heaiing them-
selves speak, and
tire all men with
their chatter.

That all men think them soe ; these take delight
To hear themselves speak ; if they can recite   992
A thing scarce worth the hearing, they will prate
Till they tire all men with their idle chatt.

Some, like
Phaeton, aspire
at honours far
above what they
deserve,

Others, ambitious like fond Phaeton,
Aspire to guide the chariot of the sunne,   996
Aiming at honours far above their place,
Till by their pride they worke their owne disgrace.

        [1] Margin worn away: may have been *faire*.

Presumptuous pride in others doth remaine,

And these high Ioves almighty power disdaine,   1000

And (like those giants) fight against the gods,

Till, Pharoah like, they scourgèd are with rods

Of dire affliction, & their hardned hearts

Vnto their guilty soule dispaire impartes.   1004

But I too much insist in generall :—

Pride in particular must be dealt withall.

He that desires to breake a bunch of wandes,

Must not take all at once into his handes,   1008

But singlie, one by one ; and if he trie,

He may then break them with facility.

Reader, doe thou the application make,

For I to other matters me betake.   1012

Proud Romish prelat, triple crownèd Pope,

Which vauntst of Peters heavenly keis, that ope

The dore that leads vnto celestiall blisse ;

Which makst great princes stoope thy foote to kisse,

Emperours vpon thy stirrop to attend,   1017

When as thou wilt thy stately horse ascend ;

Damd Antichrist, proud Lucifers first sonne,

Ambitious beast, great whore of Babilon !   1020

Thou false vsurper of Gods regal throne,

How darst assume his honour, which, alone

Monarch of heaven & earth, disdaine[s] to see

Corrivals in his sacred Emperie ?   1024

How darst thou take vpon thee such authority

Which doth belong to Gods high majesty,

To forgive sinnes, to award heaven & hell

At thine owne pleasure ?   Wher didst learne to swell

With such ambition ?   Thinkst thou Peeters chaire

Can sheild thee from Gods wrath ?   Can once impaire

And lessen thy deservèd punnishment ?

Can free thee from eternall detriment ?   1032

Thinkst thou that he presumption can abide,

Which did not spare his angels for their pride ?

Marginal notes:

and are punished for their presumption.

I have dealt long enough with generalities, I come now to particulars.

The Pope makes princes kiss his feet, and emperors hold his stirrup, as Frederick Barbarossa did that of Alexander III. [*Coryate's Crudities*, p. 201, ed. 1611.]

He is a false usurper of God's honour.

Peter's chair can not shield him from God's anger.

No. Thou shalt finde that he will vengeance take,

Sending thee headlong to the Stygian lake.   1036

Maddam Poppæa is soe stately growne

That she can neither sit nor walke alone ;

Store of attendants still must wait vpon her,

And doe obsequious homage to her honour.   1040

The ground she thinkes vnworthy is to bear

Her precious body ; when she doth vprear

Her selfe vpon her feet, there must be spread

Rich clothes of Arras wher she goes to tread.   1044

If she doe ride, the horse that must vpholde

So rare a burden must be shod with golde.

When she intends to wash her selfe she hath

Of goats pure milck a sweet preparèd bath.   1048

Musick beyond the musick of the spheares

Must still attend vpon her itching[1] eares.

Her food must be Ambrosian delicates,

Dissolvèd pearle her drink.   Impartiall fates !   1052

How can ye suffer this lascivious quean

Thus swell in pride, thus swim in pleasures streame,

And holde your thunder fast ?   Proud, stately dame,

Which more respectst thy body then thy fame,   1056

Or thy soules health, know that all working Power

Which did confound (by wormes that did devour

His cursed body) Herods lofty pride,

Will, when thou thinkst thou art most diefied,   1060

Severarly punnish with confusion,

To thy soules horrour, this presumption.

Lucius spends his substance & his store,

To keep in gallant fashion his proud whore,   1064

Yet al 's to litle to maintaine her pride ;

She must be coatcht, forsooth, & bravely ride.

Lackies before her charriot must run,

And she in spangled gold, clothd like the sunne,   1068

Dazels the eyes of men, or she complaines

[1] MS. 'itching.

He loves her not, & such a man maintaines
His love in better fashion! Then his land
Must flie, for soe his mistris doth command,   1072
To bolster vp her pride.   O foolish sot,
Thus to procure thy reputations blot,
Thy states vndooing, & thy soules perdition
For on[e] soe base & of soe vile condition !   1076

 Drusus, that fashion-imitating ape,
Delights to follow each fantastique shape ;
Every new habit of hell-hac[t]hed sinne,
Though it vndooe him, hee'l be clothèd in ;   1080
And prodigally vpon every toy
Lash out his substance ; 'tis his only ioy
To see himselfe not differing in a hair
From the true stamp of a brave Cavaleer.   1084

 Vain Epainnutus, selfe-admiring gull,
Doth speake orations, write whole volumes full
Of his owne praises.   Silly, simple sotte,
Hast thou that auncient, true saide sawe forgot,   1088
That " a mans praise in his owne mouth doth stinke " ?
Or dost (foole if thou dost) absurdly think
This age such shallow pated men affords,
That will give credit to thy boasting wordes ?   1092
Because in gay apparell thou art drest
Some puppet-like thou dost advaunce thy crest,
And swell in big lookes like some turkie cocke,
Ready to burst with pride, & even to choake   1096
With selfe-conceit of thy perfection,
Which is iust nowe, though the infection
Of thy high leveld thoughts lets thee not see
The ougly face of thy deformity.   1100
Thou which thinkst Adon, that same lovely boy,
Dame Natures dareling, Cithereas joy,
A taunie Negro, or Barbarian Moore,
Comparèd to thy selfe, & dost adore   1104
Even thine owne beauty like some demigod,

His lands go to minister to her pride.

Drusus imitates the fashions like an ape, and will dress like cavalier.

[leaf 14, back] Another writes volumes of his own praises,

and because he is well-dressed is bursting with pride.

He thinks Adonis a Negro compared to himself,

Which (for on purpose thou dost goe abroad

and fancies his good looks ravish the eyes of all who see him,

To shew thy selfe), thou vainely dost surmise

Doth even ravish the beholders eyes. 1108

Noe wench that sees thee, but straight fals in love

With thy rare feature, & doth wish to prove

and that one kiss from him would be endless bliss.

The tast of thy Ambrosian lip ; one kisse

From thy mirre-breathing mouth were endless blisse ;

But gavst thou other joyes (which in thee lies) 1113

They would be thought 'bove ioyes of paradise.

But he is only like a bladder puft up with vanity.

Thou bladder full puft vp with vanity,

Whom with my pen I prick, that ther migh[t] flie 1116

Out into open aire all windy pride,

All self-conceit ; then being repurifide,

Before the purchase of all earthly pelfe

Learn Solons saying, " Mortall, know thy selfe." 1120

Neotimus, why art thou growne so proud,

Instead of Iuno to embrace a cloud

Another is proud of empty honours,

I' nothing worth ? These honours heapd vpon thee

Are but as shadowes, & will soone flie from thee. 1124

Ther is an everlasting dignity

Of greater worth and more insignity,

To be sought out, which thou shalt ne're attaine,

If pride in thy aspiring thoughts doe reigne. 1128

[leaf 15] and forgets that he might have been as low as those whom he despises.

Contemne not them because thy selfe art high,

Who, if the heavens had pleasd, might equally

Have rankd with thee, yet now are low in state ;

All men are not predestind to on[e] fate. 1132

Become more humble, & cast downe thy looke,

Least prides bait snare thee on the devils hooke,

And having caught thee, hale thee downe to hell,

With fiends in everlasting paines to dwell. 1136

For why shouldst thou be proud 'cause thou art high

In titles of renownèd dignity ?

Honour is a flower, a vapour, and is soon blown away.

Honour 's a flower that will soon decay ;

Honour 's a vapour, quickly blowne away ; 1140

And 'tis a saying held for true of all,

" A sudden rising hath a sudden fall."

Philarchus (w*hi*ch in his ambitious minde

Devoures whole kingdomes) doth smale comfort finde

In his olde vnckles new-framde married[1] life,　　1145

But lesse in the male issue of his wife.

The bastard brat (for soe he calles his cozen)

Defrauds his expectation of a dozen　　1148

Of goodly lordships, w*hi*ch (his hopes were faire)

Should come to him, as the next lawfull heire.

But now this boy, w*hi*ch stands as a crosse-barre

Twixt him & home, doth all his fortunes marre.　1152

But long he shall not soe, if figs of Spaine,

Or pils of Italy[2] their force retaine ;

If ther be meanes that his pretence will furder,

If ther be hands that dare enact a murder,　　1156

Hee'l send his soule (wher himselfe ne're shall come)

To Abrahams bosome (mans long lookd for home).

Nor shall his aged vnckle 'scape this net,

Least if he live he doe more sonnes beget ;　　1160

Least he more issue by this marriage have,

He shalbe wedded shortly to his grave.

But then his vnckles wife surviues, purchance

Left quick w*i*th childe ; & then he may goe dance　1164

For a new living ; no, he likes not that,

She shall be soone pact after too, that 's flat ;

Besides, her ioynture, in his heart engravde

With duble greatnesse, by her death is savde.　　1168

Ambitious slave ! wilt make a crimsen flood

Of thy neare dearest kinsmens vitall blood,

To wash thy murdrous handes ?　Think not at all

Vpon a deed so much vnnaturall !　　1172

Shall hope of some vain titles move thy minde,

To doe an act p*er*petually combinde

W*i*th horrour of a guilty conscience

Marginal notes:

Philarchus is annoyed because his old uncle is married and has a son,

who, if he lives, will defraud him of the property he expected.

The child and his father must be got rid of, and so must the wife.

He will bathe his hands in his kinsmen's blood

[leaf 15, back]

---

[1] This word seems to have been originally written *marriag.*

[2] Referring to the practice of secret poisoning.

(A most deservèd & due recompence)   1176

to gain a little
land.
Wilt thou for purchase of a litle land,

With innocent blood distaine thy guilty hand?

Desist ; for murder 's an iniquity

Their blood will
cry to heaven for
vengeance.
That for iust vengeance vnto heaven doth crie.   1180

And darst thou then insist in thy invention?

Is there noe hope to alter thine intention?

No !   Thou art flesht in sinne, & dost despise

My Christian counsell; Satan blinde[s] thine eyes. 1184

Goe forward then in this lewd preparation,

But know thou headlong runst vnto damnation.

Thus Lucifer
strives to increase
the inhabitants of
hell.
Thus Lucifer, which through ambition fell,

Strives dayly to bring company to hell   1188

Of each degree & sex, from every nation.

Mortals, become more wise ; make preparation

Of armes defensiue to resist this devill

Which would procure your everlasting evill.   1192

But you, whose vnrelenting heartes persist

In fearfull pride, will then cry, " had I wist,"

When it is too
late men will see
their error.
Yet all too late, when each his sinne shall rue ;

You having your iust meed, & hell his due.   1196

Thoug[h] God awhile his punnishment delay,

A thing deferd 's not taken quite away.

But now enough of Luciferian pride,

Ther 's other vices in the world beside.   1200

Sat[ira] 4.

[AGAINST AVARICE, BRIBERY, APOSTASY.]

ARGUMENTUM.

Effodiuntur opes ex imo viscere terræ,
    Quæ fiunt miseri causa, cibus*que* mali.
Omnia sunt auro nostræ væmalia Romæ,
    Ius, pudor, & probitas, favor & ipse deus.

Insatiate Avarice then first began

To raigne in the depravèd minde of man

After his fall ; & then his mother Earth,

That gave first being to his bodies birth,   1204

Vngracious childe, he did begin to wound,

And rend the bowels of the harmelesse ground ;

For precious metals & rare minerals[1] ies

Her veines, her sinnewes, & her arteries.   1208

Among these, Golde, Dame Tellus glittering sunne,

Was with his sister Sylver, earth[s] bright moone,

Digd from the center of rich Aurimont,

Sol & his sister Phebe to confront.   1212

But for that silver golde in price doth follow,

Because from him, as Cynthia from Apollo,

She takes her light, & other mettals all

Are but his vassaile starres ; they well may fall   1216

Side notes:
Avarice soon took possession of man's min l,

and induced him to search the earth for treasures,

for gold and silver and rare minerals.

[leaf 16]

---

[1] The final *s* is 'smudged,' and the Author's comma is after *ies*—thus : *minerals ies*, . The sense is not very clear, but it seems to mean, Avarice, for precious metals and minerals, eyes (i. e. searches) her veins, &c.

Vnder his title, therfore I 'le expresse
Others in him, the great includes the lesse.

He who first
sought gold was
the cause of
'wronging right.'

He that first searched the teeming earth for golde,
Now as a demigod perhaps enrolde   1220
In Fames eternal booke, was the chief cause
Of wronging right & abrogating lawes.
For since these mines bewi[t]chd the mindes of men,
What mischiefs haue ensude my worthlesse pen   1224
Cannot delineat, but we all can tell
The number infinitly doth excell;
Omitting former ages & strange climes,

The mischiefs
which have
ensued are
numberless.

The vices of our nation in these times,   1228
So far excede in quality & number,
That to recite them would whole volumes cumber.
        Iustice, opprest by golden bribery,
Hath left the earth-stage of mortality   1232
And fled to heaven for succour & defence,
Wher she doth keep eternall residence;

Justice, oppressed
by Bribery, has
left the earth.

And now our lawes for Mammons cursed golde
Like as at open mart are bought & solde.   1236
Our lawyers, like Demosthenes, are mute,
And will not speak, though in a rightfull sute,
Vnlesse a golden kei vnlocke their tongue;
Then how thei 'l sweat, be it for right or wrong, 1240
And get their cause too, or it shall goe hard,

Lawyers plead no
man's cause
unpaid.

When the poore client, of his right debard,
Cursing the law, first for mans good ordainde,
Grieves at his losse, which ne're can be regainde. 1244
Let some damnd villaine of all grace bereft

Murder, sacrilege,
theft, lust, are all
purged by money.

Commit a murder, sacriledge, or theft,
And if he can procure but store of pence
Our iustice then will with the law dispence,   1248
And grant the hell-hound life, when, for lesse cause,
Poore men abide the rigor of the lawes.
Let lustfull Ioue, that virgins would defloure,
In Danaes lap rain but a golden shower,   1252

Her chastety will soone be washt away,
And she be ready for his amarous play.
Let some rich cuffe, Thersites-like in shape,
Of far worse qualeties then an olde ape,   1256   An old wretch
    who can't speak
Which hath nought in him that may speake him man,   without slavering
But a good purse ; although he scarcely can
Speake without slavering, goe without a crutch,
Be rivall to a man that is not such   1260
In wealth, though far above him in desertes,
As good discent, rare features, vertuous partes ;
Yet for all this, I ten to one will lay,   [leaf 16, back]
    will gain a wife
The richer man carries the wench away.   1264   where a poor man
    of good parts
    Honours & offices, which in times of olde   will fail.
Were given for deserts, are bought for golde.
Sir Iohn Lacklattin, one that ne're did passe
In any place, but for an ignorant asse,   1268
If he can grease his patron in the fist,
Shall for his gold be richly beneficde ;
When he that better doth deserve the place,   Honours and
    offices are
If poore, shall be repulsèd with disgrace.   1272   bestowed upon
    the ignorant
Lode but a silly asse with store of golde   because they can
And he will enter in the strongest holde.   pay.
Let a foole passe by in a golden coate,
He shalbe reckond for a man of note   1276
By those that know him not, when on[e] that 's wise,
Poore in arraie, seemes abiect in their eyes.
    Tradesmen make no account for golden gaine   Tradesmen cheat,
    and cozen and
To sell their soules vnto eternall paine ;   1280   forswear
Daily each one, in vttering of his wares,   themselves.
Cosens his chapmen & himselfe forsweares.
The vserer hords golde vp in his chest,   The usurer hoards
    up gold
Making an idole of it.   To be blest   1284
Is to get store of golde, the wre[t]ch doth thinke ;
When the fruition scarcely lets him winke,
For sleep he cannot, till i' th' end his pelfe
Shipwracks his soule vpon hels rocky shelfe.   1288   and shipwrecks
    his soul.

Many for golde have turnd (like Iulian)
Apostates to true religion,

Some, Judas like, sell Jesus for gold.

And have, with wicked Iudas, Iesus solde
For the vaine purchase of a litle golde.   1292
          Thus doth the devill, full of slie deceits,
Fish for the soules of men with golden baites ;
And to increase his kingdome, doth assay
By this temptation to pervert our way.   1296

The Lacedæmonians banished gold from their commonwealth.

Well did the Lacedæmons banish golde
Out of their common wealth ; well did they holde
Community of all things necessary ;
For by this meanes they were not accessary   1300
Vnto the many kindes of wickednes,
Which the vnsatiable greedinesse
Of golde in this our iron age begets ;

He who gains most is best off, for the world may be led in a golden string.

Which to entrap, so many kinde of nets,   1304
So many damnèd plots are dayly laide ;
He that gets moste thinks himselfe best apaide,
And well he may, for in a golden string
A man may lead the world to any thing.   1308

[leaf 17]

What in these days may not a man command,
That seekes to purchase with a golden hand ?
          Fortunate Fatuo was late dubd a knight,
Not for his wit, or for his martiall fight ;   1312
For wit ne're blest him, valour never knewe him ;
What may the cause be then that only drew him

One is dubbed a knight because by stealth he can buy the honour.

To this preferment?   Faith, his store of wealth,
For honours now ar[e] purchasèd by stealth   1316
Of vndermining bribes.   Canst thou disburse
Good store of coine from a well lined purse ?
Thou shalt not want authority to grace thee,
And in an office of repute to place thee,   1320
Be thy life ne're so vilde.   O evill times,

Men now esteem great means more than greatness, and goods more than goodness.

And ill conditioned men, that act such crimes,
Which great meanes then good meaning better deeme,
And more of goods then goodnesse doe esteeme ! 1324

But bootelesse I exclaime on this same age,

This vnrelenting age, whose furious rage

Will not be mollified as it hath been,

But is now hardned in vngodly sinne.　　1328

Yet, though the world nothing the better grow,

I 'le rip vp all the villanies I know.

　Flavia, because her meanes are somewhat scant,

Doth sell her body to relieve her want,　　1332

Yet scornes to be reputed as a quean,

Though with moste nations she have been vnclean.

English, Scots, Dutch, French, Spannish, yea, black
　　Moor[es],[1]

If they bring store of gold, her open dores　　1336

Conveigh to private lust; bee 't day or night,

Golde vshers them to sensuall delight.

Thus often fighting vnder Cupids banner

Perhaps she 's sometimes taken in the manner,　1340

And being brought before authority,

Which should correct her hell-bread villany,

If golde speake for her in the present tense,

The officer deputed for th' offence　　1344

Will winck at smale faultes & remit correction.

This foolish, knavish pittie 's an infection

Spread through our land, & hurtes our common wealth—

Iustice restore her to her former health!　　1348

For true 's the saying (magistrates, beware!)

"He harmes the good that doth the evill spare."

　Midas is patron to a goodly living,

And Stolido, that dunce, hath now been driving　1352

A price for it.　What, benefices solde?

This was not wont to be in times of olde,

But Simonie is now soe common growne,

That 'tis account noe sinne, if kept vnknowne.　1356

Or[2] otherwise, lawes danger to prevent,

The patron with the parson will indent

Side notes:

Though the world may be none the better, I'll expose all its villanies.

Flavia, scorning to be called a quean, sells her body to all comers,

no matter of what nation they may be.

If she's brought before the magistrate the prosecutor can be bribed.

Benefices are bought and sold:

[leaf 17, back] Simony is so common that men don't care to hide it.

---

[1] MS. worn away.　　　[2] MS. O^r.

That he shall have the living in this wise,

Suffering him yearly to reserve his tithes;   1360

When the whole parish knowes the better part

Of all the living, those his tithes imparte.

It is very wrong to deceive the Church and dissemble with God.

Thou wicked imp, thus to abuse the C[h]urch,

And with such sacrilegious handes to lurch   1364

Gods sacred duties, which he doth afford

To the dispensers of his holy word!

How dar'st thou with all-seeing Iove dissemble?

Me thinkes thou shouldst with great amazment tremble

At that most fearfull yet just punnishment   1369

Powrd downe one Ananias, whose intent,

Men who do so should remember the fate of Ananias

Like thine, was in most damnd hypocrisie

To mocke God with a shew of charity.   1372

But for this sinne he & his cursèd wife

Suddenly fell downe dead & lost his life.

Take heed the like plague fall not on thy head,

If thou persist, high Iove can strike thee dead;   1376

Though he awhile forbear to shew his ire,

His mercy keeps back what thy sinnes require.

The man who is ignorant of the law is made a Justice of the Peace,

Signior Necessity, that hath no law,

Scarce ever read his Litleton,¹ a daw   1380

To a solliciter, is now become

Iustice of peace & coram; takes his roome

'Mongst grave & learned Iudges; is still cald

Right worshipfull, his wit & pate both bald.   1384

And yet the foole expects th' ensuing year

To be elect high sherif of all the sheire.

I, & he hath great hopes, for the whole tribe

and expects to be sheriff and M. P. He'll bribe the lot to gain his end.

Of voices that elect the sherif hee 'l bribe;   1388

And after that he hopes to get consent

By this meanes to be knight o' th' parliament.

Base minded peasants, which for some few pence

Give to [a] foole such place of eminence!   1392

Ignoble Crassus did in litle time

¹ Littleton died in 1481.

Vnto the top of honours mountaine clime ;
If you aske how he rose, let this suffice,
His wealth was great, & therfore needs must rise. 1396

Ruffino, that same roring boy of fame,
By braules & wenches is diseasde & lame ;
Yet hath some store of crownes left in his purse,
Which he with all his heart would fain disburse, 1400
And those that healpt him benefactours call,
To get a place in the new hospitall.
Fear not Ruffino, for it is decreed
Those that have meanes to give shall only speed. 1404

Loth am I to rip vp my nurces shame,
Or to accuse for this those schooles of fame,
The Academies : yet for reformation
Of this abuse, I must reprove the fashion 1408
Of divers seniors, which for private gaine
Permit some ignorant asse, some dunce, attaine
A schollers or a fellowes place among 'em.
Some think perhaps of malice I doe wrong 'em, 1412
But the poore students know it to be true,
Which wanting meanes, as often want their due.
Art was not thus rejected heertofore,
But plenty now hath made a scholler poore. 1416
Learning was wont to be the highest staire,
Vpon whose top was fixd preferments chaire ;
In which the best deserver was install,
The worthiest man to highest honour cald. 1420
But now the world 's altred, changèd is the molde,
And learnings step is turnd to massie golde.
To get preferment who doth now intend,
He by a golden ladder must ascend. 1424
Thus cursed golde doth bear soe great a sway
That nurseries of learning doe decay ;
For not the meanes of taking our degrees
Are quite exempt from bribes ; for duble fees 1428
A dunce may turne a Doctour, & in state

Men whose wealth is great must rise.

Even admission to the hospital is to be gained by money.
[leaf 18]

The Universities are not free from blame.

A dunce may buy a fellowship.

Learning used to be the ladder to preferment,

but now the ladder is made of gold.

For double fees a dunce may be a doctor and walk in scarlet.

Walke in his scarlet !   O, vnhappy fate !

When paltry pelfe doth worthlesse ignorance

Vnto the top of learnings mount advaunce.   1432

Cocus, that faine would thrive, hath a[n] intent,

To curry favour, to dresse meat in Lent—

How is 't to be obtainde ? hast store of golde ?

And canst thou spare a litle ? then be bolde,   1436

Persue thy project, & I 'le vndertake

The overseers will a licence make,

By which is granted leav to dresse for th' sicke,—

Vnder the colour of which pretty tricke   1440

Thou mayst make sale of it to whom thou list.

Sayth master mony-taker, greasd i' th' fist,

"And if tho[u] comst in danger, for a noble

I 'le stand thy friend, & healp thee out of trouble." 1444

But these are petty crimes which now I cote,

This vicious age acts sinnes of greater note,

And them by greater persons, in which sence

Th' offenders greatnesse aggravates th' offence.   1448

Taurus, that ruffen, in his drunken fit

An execrable murder did committe,

For the which fact he straight was apprehended,

And should, had right tooke place, have been condemnèd.   1452

But marke th' event ; his mony stood his friend,

And sav'd the caitife from a shamefull end.

For having the chief iudge sollicited

With bribes, from iustice him he quite misled ;   1456

Who when he should pronounce[1] his condemnation,

Instead therof gave him his approbation,

Vowing there was good reason him to clear,

'Cause 40 angels did to him appear,   1460

Which spake him guiltlesse.   O,[2] rare vision,

And admirable golden apparition,

---

[1] MS. *of pronounce*, with *h*, and a partially-formed *a* crossed out, between the two words.   [2] MS. ô.

That had the power to make good such evill,
And turne a demigod into a devill !   1464

Turnus his enemy would faine supplant,
Yet how to doe it iustly, cause doth want.
His Machiavillian[1] pate doth then devise
To overthrow him by meer forgeries ;   1468
Then saith he is a traiter to his[2] prince,
And that he can of treason him convince.
Divers seditious wordes are then invented,
For w*hi*ch he is before the iudge convented ;   1472
But there wants witnesse to confirme this lie,—
Tut, they are easily found ; his neighbou*r*s by
Are knights o' th' post,[3] and for a litle coine
Will swear what ever he doth them enjo[i]ne.   1476
Thus armde, he brings to passe his damnèd will,
And like a villian guiltlesse blood doth spill.
But he & 's knights o' th' post will post to hell,
That thus their soules vnto damnation sell.   1480

Codrus to his poore cottage had some land,
W*i*th w*hi*ch, & w*i*th *the* labou*r* of his hand,
Six litle children & his sickly wife
He did maintaine in such estate of life   1484
As his best meanes could yeild, sufficient
Because they therw*i*thall did live content.
But now Antilegon, his neighbou*r* by,
Because the ground did lye com*m*odiously   1488
For his owne vse to make a garden plot,
Hath encroacht all & sure possession got,
W*hi*ch he maintaines by force.   Poor Codrus is
Constraind to sue *sub formâ pauperis*,   1492
(As wanting friends & mony) to regaine
What is his owne.   T' other doth entertaine
The best of counsell, & his golde 'gainst lawes
O're throwes the poor man in his rightfull cause ; 1496

Side notes:

If a man wants to supplant his enemy

he accuses him of treason and bribes his

neighbours to give witness against him.

The poor man with six children and a sickly wife owns a cottage and a bit of land;

but his rich neighbour wants it for a garden.

With the best of counsel and gold he gains his end,

---

[1] Machiavelli died 1527.   [2] *to his* repeated in MS.
[3] Professional perjurers, &c.

and the poor man is undone.

Who with his family are quite vndone,
Through this vnjust & damnd oppression.

[leaf 19]

  Thus Iustice eyes closde vp in golden sleep,
The ravenous woolfe eats vp the harmlesse sheep. 1500
Thou wicked Ahab, which hast got possession
By such iniurious transgression,

If God punishes those who have no compassion upon the poor,

Think that if God inflict damnation
On them that doe not take compassion   1504
Of their poore bretheren, & their wants relieve,
What will he doe to thee, which seekst to grieve
With an oppressours hand the innocent !
Being not only not to give content,   1508
But even to take away by cursed wrong
All that in right doth to the poore belong ?

He will most severely punish those who oppress them,

Vnlesse thou doe due restitution make,
And to a better life thy selfe betake ;   1512
Vnlesse repentance purchase grace from Ioue
And his iust iudgements from thee quite remooue,

especially unjust judges.

Surely the Lord (which doth such sinne detest)
With horrid tormentes will thy soule invest.   1516
And you, which should true equity dispense,
Yet bear a gold-corrupted conscience,
Looke for some plague vpon your heades to light,
That suffer rich wrong to oppresse poore right.   1520

All lawyers are not guilty of this sin,

All lawyers I cannot heerof accuse,
For some there are that doe a conscience vse
In their profession.   This our land containes
Some in whose heart devine Astræa raignes.   1524
To these, whose vertue keeps our land in peace,

and I wish all prosperity to the impartial.

I wish all good, all happines encrease.
Go forward then, and with impartiall handes
Hold Iustice ballance in faire Albians landes.   1528

  Olde greedy minded Pandarus hath a paire
Of daughters whom the world reputeth faire,
And faire indeed they are to outward eyes,
Which not discerne inward deformities ;   1532

These, for the purchase of a litle golde,

By the olde miser vnto lust are solde.

This slave will even vsher his disgrace,

Bringing his daughters vnto any place   1536

Which is appointed to commerce with sinne,

And himselfe keep the dore, whilst that within

The shamlesse strumpetes are with lust defilde,

Having the gallants of their golde beguilde.   1540

Impious villaine ! to defame the fruit

Of thine owne loynes, & basely prostitute

Thy childrens body to such luxurie,

Whom with paternall care & industrie   1544

Thou shouldst traine vp in vertuous education,

For want whereof theire horrid imprecation

Will light vpon thy soule, &, which is worse,

Gods fearfull plaugues[1] second thy childrens curse. 1548

   Me thinkes the hellish & mad lunacy[2]

Of them that doe commit apostacie

For gold, might well a Christian heart affright

Only to hear another but recite   1552

So damnd a sinne ; yet every day their fall

In these relapses diabolicall

Many, too many,—Christians shall I name them ?

Ah, noe ! their actions otherwise defame them.   1556

Some have tur[n]d Turkes for gaine, yet live despisde

After they once have been but circumcisde.

Base slaves, which Dagon 'bove the Arcke doe set,

And for true Christ adore false Mahomet.   1560

But Mahomet, as Dagon did, shall fall,

And all those wicked priests that worship Baal.

Others, that would to high preferment come,

Leave vs, & flie vnto the Sea of Rome.   1564

But how dost prosper with them being there?

Pandarus sells his two daughters for gold,

and keeps the door while their gallants are within.

[leaf 19, back] In the end his children will curse him.

Those who apostatize for gold are many.

Shall I call them Christians?

Some join the Church of Rome,

---

[1] This word twice written : *plages;* the letter over the ∧ is uncertain. This is crossed through and *plaugues* written, but here the first *u* is blurred.   [2] MS. lunary. See Glossary.

Contemptibly they live, & full of feare.

and are employed to murder princes. Is ther some damned enterprise in hand,

To murder princes, ruinate a land?   1568

These be the men that must be actours in it,

Who ever were the author to beginne it.

If they refuse, 'tis death; if they proceed

Death & damnation waites vpon their deed.   1572

Thus chaind in wre[t]ched servitude, doth live

A runagate, & English fugitive;

Like fools they submit their necks to the yoke of the Pope. And yet like fooles, they doe submit their necke

Vnto the slavish yoke & proudest checke   1576

Of Romes insulting tyrant, vpon hope

That their demerits will win larger scope;

Many which theither dayly flocke apace

To worke their owne confusion & disgrace   1580

Witnesse their fearfull endes & wre[t]ched lives :

"Needs must when the devil drives." "But goe they must because the devill drives."

Carrier of late would have made his career

If Carrier, who died (? at Liege) before midsummer, 1614, (Thinking perhaps to be esteemèd dear   1584

Of th' antichristian prelate) to the citty

Of seven hilld Rome, "O, &," say some, "'twas pitty

That his (how e're they grant it lewd) intent

Met not a look't for prosperous event.   1588

For he, because his learning[1] was not small,

had succeeded in reaching Rome, he might have become a Cardinal. Might in short time have been a Cardinall."

What the successe had prov'd I dare not say,

For he was cut of from his wishèd prey;   1592

High Iove incensd that thus he should backslide

Stroke him, & in a neighbour land he died.

Some think he was not Apostolicall,

But alwaies in his heart papisticall;   1596

[leaf 20] Certaine it is, how e're they can excuse him,

The devill in this act did but abuse him.

He was either an apostate or a hypocrite. And were he not apostate in his flight,

In his stay heer he was an hypocrite.   1600

[1] MS. *learming*.

Pistor was falln into great poverty,

How come he to grow rich thus sodenly ?

For[1] he of late hath matchd his daughter well

Vnto a gentleman, as I hear tell,   1604

Of faire demeanes, & great extent of ground,

And made her portion worth five thousand pound.

Why, once within these five year (as was thought)

Ten poundes would all the wealth he had have bought,

And now he 's in his thousandes ! This quick change,

This sodaine metamorphosis is strange.

Belike he hath found out some mine of golde,

Or else the Fairies bring him heapes vntolde   1612

Because he sweeps his house cleane, sets a light,

Faire water in a basen, every night,

And other pretty toyes, to doe them pleasure ;

Or else some spirit shewes him hidden treasure.   1616

O now you hitt it, 'twas indeed a spirit,

To whom, for certaine tearme of yeares t' inherit

His ease and pleasure with aboundant wealth,

He hath made sale of his soules dearest health.   1620

And in a deed engrost, signd with his blood,

Sould soule & body with all hope of good

In heavenly ioyes to come, vnto the devill.

O horrid act ! O execrable evill !   1624

Another Faustus, haplesse, hopelesse man,

What wilt thou doe, when as that litle sand

Of thy soone emptied houreglasse, is spent ?

When horrour of thy conscience keeps repent   1628

From thy black spotted soule ?   O (but in vaine)

Thou wilt then wish (& think it ease, not paine)

" That I had that estate of grace I solde

[For the] fruition of a litle golde.   1632

Thoug[h] I liv'de ne're soe miserablie poore,

And like an abject begd at every doore

Millions of yeares, I could be well content

                    [1] Originally *Why : For* written over.

Marginal notes:

Pistor, who was poor, matches his daughter with a rich man.

Perhaps the Fairies bring him gold, perhaps a spirit.

He has signed a contract with the devil.

What will he do in the end?

He will be willing to be a beggar if he can

thereby escape
hell.
To 'scape the everlasting punnishment   1636
Of hells infernall lake, & purchase heaven,
Of *which* for ever I am now bereaven."
Then wilt thou curse thy selfe, thy wretched fate,
The wombe that bare thee, him that thee begat ; 1640
Wish thou hadst been a beast, a sencelesse stone,
To 'scape that horrour of confusion.

He will curse all
men, but in vain.
But wishes, vowes, & horrid execration
Cannot preserve thee from damnation.   1644

So every honour
is bought and
sold : let buyers
and sellers
beware.
   Thus each thing of esteem is bought and solde
For mindes-corrupting, soules-confounding golde.
Sellers take heed, & byers have a care,
This is no com*m*on ordinary ware !   1648

[leaf 20, back]
Looke to 't betimes, lest you to late repent
The poore mans curse, earths plague, hells punnishment !

Sat[ira] 5.

[AGAINST GLUTTONY, DRUNKENNESS, AND TOBACCO.]

———

ARGUMENTUM.

Nobiscum in terris Epicuri vivitur instar
  Delitijs : ventri mille placere modi.
Turpior ebrietas animam cum corpore fœdat,
  Et demum ad Stygias ducit vtrumque domos.

From thirst of wealth & golden villany
I now am come to brutish gluttonie,
Of which my Muse doth almost loath to treat,
It is soe base a crime, yet growne soe great   1654
In customary action, that 'tis deemd
If sinne, a smale one, not to be esteemd.
This vice doth not alone it selfe extend
T' excesse in meat, but eke doth comprehend   1658
That base vnmanly sinne of drunkennesse,
Whose worse then worst of brutish beastlinesse
Defiles both soule & body, & doth bring
Both of them to eternall ruining.   1662
This age of men to *that* excesse is growne
That was I think in Sodome never knowne,
Although it were *that* capitall offence,
Which iustly did all-seeing Ioue incense   1666
Them & their citty vtterly to quell
With fire which from heavens architecture fell.

Side notes:

I now come to brutish gluttony, which is very common,

and drunkenness, which defiles body and soul.

The present age is worse than Sodom ever was.

How can we wretches in this sinfull time
Expect lesse vengeance for as damnd a crime?   1670
For to speake first of our excesse in meat,
Though man should eat to live, not live to eate,

Many care only
for what they
shall eat.
Many there are which only vse their care
In dainty banquetes and delitious fare.   1674

What beast doth breed in our Britannicke soile
That doth delight the tast, but we doe toile

Every beast, bird,
and fish is
captured for
their tables,
To take & kill?   What bird doth cut the aire
With her swift wing, but that we doe repaire   1678
Therwith our tables?   We doe fish all seas
To catch the rarest dish, therby to please
Our dainty palates : & yet fish, bests, birdes,
Which in aboundance this our land affordes,   1682

and yet they
must have
delicacies from
other nations.
Are not sufficient ; we must have more cates
From other nations at excessive rates
To furnish out our table, which (like swine
That eat the fruit, but ne're cast vp their eyen   1686
To the faire tree) we dayly doe devour
Without thankesgiving to that heavenly power,
Whose gracious goodnesse doth such blessinges give,
And suffers vs so peaceably to live   1690
In such a land of plenty that doth flow
With milck & hony, which we doe bestow

[leaf 21]
We pamper
ourselves, and
live like epicures,
To pamper our selves & please our sence
Like Epicures ; as if alone from thence   1694
We had our being, & vnto that end,
The cause of our creation, did intend.
Thus are the guiftes,[1] wherwith God man doth blesse,
Abusd'e by vaine & riotus excesse.   1698
Like the rich gluttons in the Gospell are
The feastes we make, from which we doe debarre

without regarding
the poor who
crave charity at
our doors.
The poorer sort of men.   Well may they lie
Before our dores, & crave our charity ;   1702
But with poore Lazarus they shall obtaine

               [1] MS. guistes.

Cold comfort, & small reliefe to sustaine
Their hunger-starvèd bodies, while within
The richer sort doe stand vp to the chin
In delicates, & euen with excesse,
Are like to surfet ; while the wantonnesse
Of their insatiat appetite, that feeds
On such plurality of viands, breeds
Offensive humors.   This I thinke the cause
Which our rich men to such diseases drawes,
Wherwith we dayly see they are tormented,
When if with moderate fare they were contented
They might both keep their bodies in good health,
And save the residue of all their wealth
To feed the hungry soule, the naked cherrish,
Which wanting succour still one heaps doe perish.

   But now let me discourse of drunkennes,
Which is a part of gluttony, whose excesse
Is likewise of the belly, & is made
Even a common ordinary trade.
We count the nation of the German Dutch
The greatest drunkard, but our land as much,
Or rather more, is with this vice infected,
Which doth deserue sharply to be corrected,
And yet 'tis slackly punnishd ; but 'twere good
That Dracoes [laws] for ours in vertue stood.
This vice, I say, with vs as frequent is
As with the Dutchmen, who, if I not misse
Mine aime, were the first founders of this sinne
Within our country; but we now beginne
T' appropriate to our selves their noted vice,
So apt we are to follow each devise
That tendes to wickednesse & villany;
After forbidden things we swiftly flie,
When after that from which much good may growe,
Although by force compeld, we slowly goe.
But man must follow the times fashion,

1706

1710

1714

1718

1722

1726

1730

1734

1738

The rich over-
feed themselves,

and draw on
themselves many
of the diseases
from which they
suffer.

Drunkenness
is common.

We are worse
than the
Germans.

The Dutch first
began this vice,

but we quickly
imitated and now
often excel them.

And shew himselfe an ape in imitation
Of every new found & hell-hatched sinne
Or else he is not counted worth a pinne. 1742

He that cannot sit quaffing all the day,
Carousing healths till wit & wealth decay;
Which will not vpon every lewd request
Drink drunk in kindenesse, why, he 's made a jest 1746
To those companions, whose licentious veine

And drunken humours still doe entertaine
The basest speeches, & in their mad fit
Doe speake at randome without fear or wit. 1750
How far vnlike Lacedemonians,
Though they were hethen & we Christians,
Are men in this our age ? To them this crime
Soe loathsome was, that they would finde a time 1754

To make the Helottes drunk, which wer their slaves,
A sort of loutish, abject-minded knaves ;
And being in the basest sort disguisde,
Shew them their children, mock them as despisde 1758
And debaush creatures, by their beastlynesse,
To teach their young to loath all drunkennesse.
But if others will not doe it for vs
Will[1] even fox ourselves till all abhorre vs. 1762
  Well may it fit this our vntemperate age,
To shew a drunkard in his equipage.

I 'le passe Apitius, which spent all the year,
In brave carrousing, & fine belly-cheer ; 1766
He that to please his sence had at one feast
His thousand severall dishes at the least,
Although he had noe other company
But his sole single selfe to satisfie ; 1770

For all the flesh that Noahs Arke contained,
The whole seas fish, if he had entertained
His friends, could not sufficient store afforde,
To furnish out th' insatiate gluttons borde. 1774

[1] ? We'll.

Thus he run one, till on[e] yeares gluttony

Brought him from millions vnto poverty :

I will omit the brave Ægiptian Dame,

Which by her death hath got eternall fame,   1778

Proud Cleopatra, Anthonies loose minion,

Who, to obtaine her lovers good opinion,

Did in a cup of wine, drunk to his health,

Carouse dissolvèd pearles of infinite wealth ;   1782

Her great excesse & sensuall gluttony

Procurde her owne & his sad tragedie.

I 'le leave th' Assirian Sardanapalus,

With that lewd Roman, Heliogabolus ;   1786

Only their riot was the fatall knife

That cut them of from empire & from life.

Examples from soe farre I need not fetch,

We have more moderne ones within our reach ;   1790

In this our native Isle, each day, each hower

Millions of such like subiects doe ever shower

Before our eyes, which live in vaine excesse

Of soule-polluting, beastly drunkennesse.   1794

On[e] pot companion & his fashion

I will describe, & make relation

Of what my selfe have seene, that they that hear it

May hate the like, & hating may forbear it.   1798

   Cervisius is a most accomplisht man,

Whether he deale at halfe pot or whole can,

No flincher, but as true a drunkard bred

As ever lifted cup vnto his head.   1802

A right good fellow, a true ioviall boy,

And on[e] that of his purse is nothing coy ;

Hee 'l spend his dozen of beer with any friend,

And fox him if he can, before hee 'l end ;   1806

I, or hee 'l fox himselfe, but that 's no wonder

The fox & he are seldome time a sunder.

But if the man, to sobernesse inclinde,

Refuse to follow his inordinate minde,   1810

brought himself
to poverty.

Cleopatra, to gain
her lover's good
opinion, drank
dissolved pearls.

Sardanapalus
lost his life not
through such
means

as millions in our
own country now
[leaf 22]
practise.

Cervisius is a
true drunkard

and a right good
fellow,

but if a man
declines to drink
with him he is

ready to compel him.

Because his nature cannot brooke to doe it,
His stab is ready to compell him to it.
This alehouse-haunter think*es* himselfe a safe

He drinks with his companions and makes them drink with him,

If he w*i*th his companions, George & Rafe,   1814
Doe meet together to drink vpsefreese
Till they have made themselves as wise as geese.
O ther this man (like lord w*i*thin a hutch)
Will pay for all & ne're his mony grutch ;   1818
Th[e]y must not part till they have drunk a barrell,

or else he will quarrel with them.

Or straight this royster will begin to quarrell.
Wher e're they meet, to th' alehouse they must goe,
He sweares they shall, & they must not say noe. 1822
As soone as e're the alehouse them receives.
The tapster, duble diligent, straight leaves
His other guest*es*, in course to take his cup,
And make the full messe of these drunkards vp ; 1826

As it is sweetest drinking at the spring, they go into the cellar

He knowes what best belongs vnto his gaine,
These are the men he seekes to entertaine.
Then straight into the seller hee 'l them bring,—
'Tis sweetest drinking at the verry spring,—   1830
Wher as a barrell, for the nonce set out,
Must straight be pearc'd, then each must haue his bout
And drink vp all ; to leave a litle snuffe
Is petty treason ; & such pretious stuffe   1834

and drink till their hands shake and their heads are addled.

Must not be throwne away.   Thus they drink round,
Vntill their adle heads doe make the ground
Seeme blew vnto them ; till their hands doe shake,
Their tongues speak duble, & their braines do ake. 1838
But they proceed till one drop[s] downe dead drunke,
Wher he doth lie long time, a sencelesse trunk ;
And all the rest in a sweet pickle brought
(Such op*er*ation hath the barrell wrought),   1842

[leaf 22, back] One falls dead drunk, a second goes to sleep, the third is sick,

Lie downe beside him.   One straight fall*es* a sleep
Ready to drowne himselfe, in that doth keep
The broken beer from spoiling ; then another
Fall*es* into spuing, & is like to smother   1846

Himselfe in his owne vomit. He that least

Seemes to be drunk, yet shew*es* himselfe a beast,

And that 's the tapster, w*h*ich hath got a tricke,

Because he would prevent his being sick,   1850

To force himselfe to cast, then on the barrell

To take a nap. Thus ends this drinking quarrell.

After some 3 howers sleep*es* strong ope*r*ation

Hath brought their braines into a better fashion,   1854

They gin to wake, & finding themselves ill

Of their late surfet, w*h*ich hath force to kill

The strongest body, to 't afresh they goe,

To drink away their paine ; such heartsick woe   1858

By an im*m*oderate drunkennesse procurde,

Must by " a haire of the same dog " be curde.

Then once againe the pot must keep his round,

Vntill the barrell, w*i*th his hollow sound,   1862

Fortell his emptinesse. Trivmphantly

They doe then eccho forth this victory,

As 'twere a conquest, that deserv'd w*i*th golde

In Fames eternall booke to be enrolde.   1866

But still Cervicius paies for all, his purse

Defraies all recknings ; there must none disburse

A penny but himselfe. " Tut, I have land*es*

W*h*ich now of late are come into my hand*es*,   1870

And whilst they last, I will not want good drink,

Nor boon companions. Wherfore was my chinck

Made but to spend ? And can 't be better spent

Then 'mongst good ladd*es* in ioviall meriment ?   1874

Faith, no. Flie, brasse ! More precious I do holde

Malt*es* pure quintessence then king Harries golde.

Good liquor breeds good blood, good blood best health,

And that 's a iewell to be prisde 'bove wealth.   1878

Drink round, sweet George, to me, my turne is next,

And I'le charge honest Rafe ; let 's ply our text

W*i*thout digression. Tapster, take yo*u*r bout,

Leave not a drop, you'r best, but drink all out.   1882

while the tapster vomits and goes to sleep on the barrel.

Three hours later they all wake and go to it again till the barrel is empty,

because " a hair of the same dog " must cure them.

Cervisius pays for all;

so long as he has money he will not want good drink,

which breeds good blood, and good blood best health.

Why soe, brave boyes, this gear doth cotten well,

He thinks the four would beat any four in Europe.

I think we foure might win the silver bell
Of any 4 in Europe, for our drink.
Let 's make a challenge, Rafe ; I doe not think 1886
But we shall put downe all that dare contest
With vs in this, if we but doe our best.
And yet ther were 4 roring boyes, they say,
That drunk a hogshead dry in one poor day. 1890

This conceit makes him dry, and he drinks hoping to meet again next day.

Tapster, some beer ; the conceit makes me dry !
Heer honest rogue, night partes good cumpany ;
But my good lades, let 's meet againe to morrow,
And at this fountaine we will drinke downe sorrowe."

[leaf 23]

Thus he runs on his course, til 's drunken vaine
Ruines his substance, makes him entertaine
For his companion penurious want.—
All other friends doe then wax wondrous scant ; 1898

In the end comes poverty, and it alone sticks to him.

But this alone, when men fall in decay,
Will never leave them till their dying day.
His substance poore, his soule more poore in grace,
Getes him contempt on earth, in hell a place 1902
Of everlasting paine, vnlesse the smart
Of misery reforme his wicked heart.
For sometimes want & hard calamity
Even Athiestes turnes to Christianity. 1906

Another scorns to get drunk on beer or bottled-ale.

But Bacchanall is of a higher straine,
He scornes soe base a thought to entertaine,
As to drink drunk with beer or botle-ale ;
Noe, he contemnes the vse, that fashion 's stale. 1910
Marry, your true elixar, all rare wine,
That doth enspire, & make the thoughtes divine !
Whie, he esteemes the nectar of the goddes,

Nepenthe to him falls far short of delicious wine,

Homers Nepenthe, to come short by oddes 1914
Of [this] delicious iuice. Rich Malago,
Canarie, Sherry, with brave Charnico ;
Phalerno, with your richest Orleance wine,
Pure Rhenish, Hippocras, white Muskadine, 1918

With the true bloud of Bacchus, Allegant,   and claret is but
That addes new vigour which the backe doth want   "so-so."
Are precious wines. Marrie, your white or Charret
Is but so so ; he cares not greatly for it ;   1922
But for the rest, whose vertuous operation   Wines cheer the
Doth cheer the heart opprest with passion,   heart and elevate
the senses.
Doth rapsodize the soules intelligence
Above the levell of inferiour sence,   1926
Why, had he to his wish the cranes long necke   If Bacchanal had
To tast with more delight, he would not wrecke   but the neck of a
crane, to taste
Of all celestiall ioyes ; this were a treasure   with more
delight!
To be preferd above that heavenly pleasure.   1930
From thine owne mouth, thou beastly Epicure,
Dost thou condemne thy selfe, thou shalt be sure
Never indeed to tast celestiall bliss !
But know withall (though thou those joyes doe misse)
That thou (when as thy soule will be agast)   1935
Shalt of the cup of Godes iust vengeance tast !

    Fower kindes of drunkardes this our age hath quoted,   There are four
kinds of
Which, since by observation I have noted,   1938   drunkards:
It shall not be amisse heer to insert,
That we may know how much each doth pervert
The soule of man. The first is merry drunk,   1. The merry
And this, although his braines be somewhat shrunk   drunk : his sport
is called
I' th' wetting, hath, they say, but litle hart   1943   harmless ;
In his demeanour ; to make harmles sport
Is all his practise. In what fashion ?
Is baudie talke, & damnèd prophanation   1946
Of Godes most holy name, a harmlesse thing ?   [leaf 23, back]
Are apish tricks & toies, which vse to bring   but bawdy talk
Men in dirision, sportes to breed delight ?   and apish tricks
are not harmless.
Is that which makes the soule as black as night,   1950
Which takes away the perfect vse of sence,
Which is the high way to incontinence,
A thing of nothing ? Whie, if this be soe,
I graunt you then a drunken sot may goe   1954

For one that is innocuous ; otherwise
He is a beast & worse, let that suffice.
And if this be the hurtlesse sport you meant,
Iove keepe me from such harmlesse merriment.   1958

2. The maudlin drunk, whose drink seems to fall from his eyes.

The second kinde we maudline drunkard*es* call.
I thinke the humid stuffe they drink doth fall
Out of their eyes againe, for they distill

Women can cry when they will,

Teares in great plenty. Woemen when they will 1962
Can weep, we say, but these doe never cry
Except they first be drunk ; but then they dry
The fountaine of their teares quite vp before

but he only when he's drunk.

They cease from weeping, or doe once give o're   1966
Their dolefull lamentation.   I suppose
The name of " Maudline drunk " from hence arose.
This kinde of drunkard is the kindest creature
That ever did converse with mortall nature ;   1970
When he is in his fit, you may commaund
All that he has, his purse, his heart, his hand,
To do you service ; why hee 'l ever kill

If you'll sit and swill with him he's happy.

Your heart with kindenesse, soe you 'l sit & swill 1974
In his loathd presence ; keep him company
And he is pleasde, ther 's his felicity.
      And now I call to minde an accident
That did befall to one of his lewd bent,   1978
One of these maudline drunkards (I will passe
Over it briefly).   In this sort it was :

Once a wealthy young gentleman

A certain wealthy-left young gentleman,
One that had more skill how to quaffe a can   1982
Then manage his revenewes, for his ease

let out his land to a crafty old fox,

Put out the best part of his land to lease,
And had to tennant an olde crafty fox,

who knew on which side his bread was buttered.

Who, though his landlord made him a right oxe, 1986
Knewe for all that on which side of his bread
The sweetnesse of the butter was yspread ;
Knew how to turn all to his best of gaine,
And therfore did with patience entertaine   1990

His supposde wrong.   What cannot thirst of golde
Performe when men to wickednesse are solde ?
This old sinckanter, when he came to pay
His landlord*es* rent at the appointed day,   1994
Was for the most part sure to finde him fast
Within a taverne ; whilst his coine did last
Ther was his randevous.   The mony tolde,
Wh*i*ch was as welcome vnto him as golde,   1998
They needs must drink together ere they part.
Then is wine cal'd for, & quart after quart
Comes marching in, till my young gallant fals
Into his maudline fit, & then he calles   2002
Afresh for wine, & w*i*th right weeping eyes
Hugging his ten*n*ant, "You are welcome !" cryes,
"In faith you are, be God you are ! Beleeve it,
What is it thou willt have & I will give it.   2006
Sha 't have a new lease for a hundred yeares,
Of all the land thou holdst !—I speake in teares
Of my affection,—& shalt yearly pay
A peppercorne, a nutt, a bunch of may,   2010
Or some such trifle.   Tut, man ! I desire
To have thee thrive,—I only doe aspire
To purchase credit ; thou the gaine shalt reap ;—
Hang him that will not let his land*es* good cheap !"
   Well, for this time they part.   Next quarter comes,
And after that a third ; he payes the sum*m*es,
And findes his landlord in this humo*u*r still.
Then doth the crafty fox begin to fill   2018
His braines w*i*th cun*n*ing ; if his plot*es* doe hit
To his desire, his landlord*es* want of wit
Shall make him rich for ever.   Vpon this
He makes a feast to w*h*ich he doth not misse   2022
To invite his landlord ; but before, compacted
With an atturney by whose healp directed,
A paire of large indentures, fairely drawne,
Are formally composde.   These as a pawne   2026

TIME'S W.   5

When he came
to pay his rent he

always found his
landlord at the
tavern,

[leaf 24]

where he was
welcomed and
treated,

and offered his
land at a pepper-
corn rent

by his maudlin
drunk landlord.

This time they
part, but before
they meet again
he prepares
indentures.

Of his deer hopes he keeps, & when the fit

Hath quite deprivde my gallant of his wit,

Hee 'l make his landlord set both hand & seale

Men act for their own advantage.   To this new lease.   Men of experience deale   2030

To their best proffit ; & it were as good

That he should be a gainer as the brood

Of cut-throat vintners. Well, to make short worke,

My gentleman, his braines as light as corke   2634

With brave carrousing, fals to his odd vaine

The landlord complains that his offer is not accepted.   Of weeping kindenesse ; nay, seemes to complaine

That his kinde offer findes noe acceptation !

Olde Gray-beard knowes his cue, & by gradation   2038

Still drawes him one, till the kinde foole protestes

Were the indentures drawne, so firme he restes

In his opinion, ther should be a match,

And his hand soone should all the rest despatch.   2042

Then the Indenture is produced and signed, and he is robbed.   Straight vpon this are the indentures brought ;

Witnesse there needs not, for the house[1] is fraught

With store [of] guestes ; then the kinde harted gull

Seales and subscribes to all : his wits are dull   2046

And sencelesse of this wrong. Thus is he[2] shorne

Of eight score poundes a year for one poore corne

Of pepper, & the lease, that hath noe flawe,

For a whole hundred yeares is good in lawe.   2050

[leaf 24, back]   But now to passe this & to make reporte

3. "Lion-drunk-ards" come next.   Of lyon-drunkardes, which is the third sorte.

Your lyon-drunkard is a kinde of man

That in his fitt will rage, sweare, curse, & banne,   2054

Break glasses, & throw pottes against the wall,

Quarrell with any man, & fight with all

They are far worse than Hercules.   That yield not to his rage. Mad Hercules,

In the extreamest rage of his disease,   2058

Clad in the shirt which Deianira sent,

Dipt in the blood of Nessus, to prevent

---

[1] A letter like *O* is written before the word *house*.

[2] MS. this is the

His love to Iöle, when the poyson boylde
In every veine, & with the torment spoilde   2062   This drunkard
is worse than
a madman.
And quite bereaft him of true reasons vse,
Making him teare vp trees, & break all truce
With man & beast, was not yet halfe soe madde
As this outragious drunkard, nor soe bad   2066
T' encounter with ; for this man is indeed
Worse then a mad man.   Let that man take heed
Which comes within his reach ; vnlesse he have
More lives then one, this wretch will dig his grave.
These are the men that make soe many fraies,   2071   These are they
who commit so
many murders.
That stab & kill soe many now adayes,
On whom just vengeance oftentimes attendes,
Bringing their lives vnto most shamefull endes.   2074
     The fowerth & last kinde of this drunken crewe
Is beastly drunk, & these men vse to spue,   4. The beastly
drunk, who lie in
gutters like
swine.
Lying in gutters, & in filthy mire,
More like to swine then men.   Promethean fire   2078
Is quite extinct in them ; yea, vse of sence
Hath within them noe place of residence.
Some of this kinde, as if a deadly potion
Had wrought th' effect, doe seeme to have no motion
Of vitall faculties ; a man would deeme   2083
That they were dead indeed, for soe they seeme,   They are dead
drunk.
When only superfluity of drink
Deceives the eye, & makes the heart misthink.   2086
On[e] of these men (I am about to tell
Noe fable, reader, therfore marke it well)
Vpon mine owne moste true intelligence,
Being dead drunk i' th' time of pestilence,   2090   One of these was
missed during
the pestilence
which raged in
1603. [See *Defoe's*
History of the
Plague of 1665, p.
68, ed. Bohn.]
Was thought t' have dide o' th' plague, & seeming dead,
Was amongst others alive burièd.
But being by some of his companions mist,
And diligent enquirie made, they wist   2094
At length what was become of him, & went
Vnto his place of buriall, with intent

If it were possible to save his life.

He had been
buried alive.

The grave digd vp, they saw with how great strife 2098

The drunken man, to wonted sence restorde,

Had vsde himselfe, being all with blood begorde

[leaf 25]

With violence to help himselfe was wrought,

But all in vaine ; for not the aide they brought, 2102

Which came too late, nor his owne power, could shend

This wretched man from a moste fearfull end.

This serves as an
example of God's
hatred of this
sin.

Surely this iust example doth expresse,

How much God hates this beastly wickednesse. 2106

Yet sinfull man, whose very heart should bleed

With recordation of soe straunge a deed,

Is not reformd a iot from this lewd sinne,

But every day more deeply plungèd in. 2110

Nay, drunkennesse hath got an arch-defender,

Yea, more then that, a principall commander,

But a certain
physician says
it is necessary
to drink.

A great phisitian, which prescribes some dayes

Wherin 'tis necessary, as he saies, 2114

To drink drunk for the bodies better health,

And being done in private & by stealth,

It is a thing of nothing ! What phisitian,

Whose vertuous minde, religious condition, 2118

Speak him a Christian, would once entertaine

Soe vilde a thought, or such a lye maintaine ?

He must be an
atheist or an
Epicure.

It is some at[h]eist sure, vpon my life,

Some Epicure, for 'mongst such men ar[e] rife 2122

These damnd opinions ; on[e] that knowes noe God,

Was neuer scourgèd with afflictions rod,

And therfore luld a sleep in pleasures lap,

Securely sinnes, & feares no after-clap. 2126

This man, which only setteth vp his rest

In that which man communicates with beast,

He denies the
immortality of
the soul.

The soule of sence, denies th' eternity

Of th' intellectual part, & doth apply 2130

All his endevours to delight the sence ;

Noe marle though he with drunkennesse dispence,

Which, though it may the bodies health secure,
The soules continuall death it doth procure.   2134

   Old Monsier Gray-beard with your poynts vntrust,   Old Gray-beard
Dublet vnbuttond, ready for your lust;   who hangs his
                                                          chamber with
You, which the chamber wher you lay your head   baudy pictures,
With baudie pictures round about doe spread;   2138
Which make your maide daunce naked to your eyes,
Only to see her veines & arteries;
Which hast given out this foolish prophesie,
That, vnlesse throngd to death, thou ne're shalt die;   thinks he will
                                                          only die by being
And therfore neither vnto church nor faire,   2143 thronged.
Nor any publicke meeting darst repaire,
But idlie livest at home in ease, secure,
A very atheist, & meer Epicure,   2146
This is your axiome, "drunkennesse is good   He too thinks
                                                      drunkenness good
To clear the stomach, & to purge the blood."   sometimes.
Well maist thou be a good phisitian
But I am[1] certaine a bad Christian.   2150
After the killing of some hundred men,   [leaf 25, back]
And yet I scarcely recken one for ten,
To trie the working of thy minerals,
Thy hearbes, thy drugges & such materials,   2154 In his experi-
                                                          ments to test his
Perhaps some litle knowledge thou hast gaind   drugs he has
To ease the head or stomach, being painde;   killed many.
To help an ague-shaken bodie, cure
A fever, dropsie, gout, or cicature;   2158
All this, & more then this, as farre as nature
Permites thy skill to healp a mortall creature,
Suppose thou canst performe; graunt thou couldst give
To a dead body force againe to live,   2162
As poetes faine that Æsculapious   Though he has
                                                      learned some-
Did to vnjustly slaine Hypolitus;   thing, yet,
                                                      ignorant of his
Yet all thy skill wherof thou makst thy vaunt   soul, his learning
Is nothing worth, because thou standst in want   2166 is useless.
Of the true knowledge of thy soules salvation,

          [1] Not unlike *ar* in MS.

The sweetnesse of whose only contemplation,
The vertue of thy art doe passe, as farre
As bright Apollo doth the meanest starre.   2170

We may not do evil that good may come.

Which if thou knewst, it would thee quickly teach
Another lesson, far above thy reach
Of principles in phisick :¹—that noe evill
(Which had it's first begin[in]g from the devill)   2174
Though good ensue therby, must be committed,
Yea though the ill with more good be requitted.
How much more then soe horrible a crime

Drunkenness darkens the splendour of our country,

As drunkennesse, whose putrefactious slime   2178
Darkens the splendour of our common wealth,
Must not be acted to secure the health
Of the base body (I doe call it base
In reference to the soule), so to deface   2182
The purer part of man ; yea, by such action,
The loathsomnesse of whose infection

and makes man worse than a beast.

Makes man, indued with reason, worse then beast ;
Both soule & body doe become vnblest,   2186
Vnsanctifièd members, & vnlesse
Godes grace in time this wickednesse represse,
Th' all² both together perish, & remaine
In hels eternally tormenting paine.   2190

Besides ale and wine, we now have Tobacco,

Besides ale, beer, & sundry sortes of wine
From forren nationes, whose more fruitfull vine
Yeilds plenty of god Bacchus, we have got
Another kinde of drinke, which well I wot   2194
Is of smale goodnesse, though our vaine delight
Follow it with excessive appetite ;

a rare Indian weed of great virtues,

And that 's Tobacco, a rare Indian weed,
Which, because far fetcht only, doth exceed   2198
In vertue all our native hearbes,—for what ?
For many pretious vses, vertues that

---

¹ The sense seems to require "the reach of principles in phisick," or, "thy reach in principles of phisicke."
² MS. Th'all for they 'll.

May be applide to phisicke ?   Graunt it soe,

Although I see great reason to say noe ;   2202

How can that iustifie our common taking

In such excesse, our even for that forsaking

All other nutrime[n]tes ?   Doe we applie

Phisick in this sorte ?   If I should say I,   2206

I should belie my knowledge ; phisicks vse

Serv's only to reforme the knowne abuse

Of the distempered body, & must be

But seldome, & with mediocrity,   2210

Applide on speciall causes when they fall ;

To take Tobacco thus were phisicall,

And might perhaps doe good ; but this excesse

And ordinarie practise, questionlesse,   2214

Annoyes th' internall partes & makes them foule,

But I am sure commaculates the soule.

Yet in these dayes hee 's deemd a very gull

That cannot take Tobacco ; every skull   2218

And skip-iacke now will have his pipe of smoke,

And whiff it bravely till hee 's like to choke.

You shall have a poore snake, whose best of meanes

Is but to live on that he dayly gleanes   2222

By drudgery from others, which will spend

His pot of nappy ale vpon his friend,

And his Tobacco with as ioviall grace,

As if he were a lord of some faire place   2226

And great revenewes !   "Tut, why should he not ?

I hope a man may spend what he hath got,

Without offence to any.   What he spendes

Is his owne monie, & among his friendes   2230

He will bestowe it."   I, & doe soe still,

Follow the swinge of thy vngoverned will,

See what 'twill bring thee too ; for I fore see

Thy end wilbe both shame & beggerie.   2234

    Whom have we yonder with a pipe at 's head ?

He lookes as if he were true Indian bred.

[leaf 26]
which, even if good in itself, cannot justify the excessive use of it.

Physic is used seldom and with moderation,

and if tobacco were so used it might do good.

But now every skip-jack must have his pipe

and pot of ale.

And why should a man not spend what is his own ?

Fumoso is the best of smokers;

O, 'tis Fumoso with the tallow face,
He that of late hath got a speciall grace,   2238
And that 's to be the best Tobacconist
That ever held a pipe within his fist.

but he has ruined himself by the practice;

It cost him dear enough ; for the fame goes
H'as smokd out all his living at his nose   2242
To purchase this rare skill. But hee 'l repaire
This losse with greater wealth vnto a haire,—
He has the rediest meanes this gap to stop.

he means to regain his wealth by selling tobacco and bottled ale.

"What 's that ?" Why he intends to keep a shop   2246
For smoke & botle-ale, which soone will drawe
Good store of gallantes (even as iet doth strawe)
Vnto his custome, &, for greater gaine,
A bonny lasse or two hee 'l entertaine.   2250

[leaf 26, back]

As take me e're a shop subvrbian
That selles such ware, without a curtezane,
And we will have the deed cronologizde,
Nay it may well be now immortalizde.   2254
Doth a tobacco pipe hang before the dore,

A woman is always kept at these shops.

'Tis a sure signe within ther is a whore.
"A whore," sayes he ; "O, fie ! you speake to broad ;
A punck, or else one of the dealing trade ;   2258
And such a one I mean to keep, & she
Will help, I hope, to keep & maintaine me.
O, 'tis the only thriving meanes of all

He will purchase riches in abundance,

To rayse mans fortunes vp by womans fall."   2262
An excellent project, follow thy designe,
And thou shalt purchase a rich golden mine,
And hell with all to boote ;—soe thou hast golde
It makes noe matter. But perhaps being olde,   2266
One foote already within Charons bote,
Thou thinkst it time enough to change thy cote
To a more Christian habit, if th' intend,
How vile so e're thy life have been, thine end   2270

but must lose his soul in the end.

Shalbe repentant, though thou doe deferre
To the last minute, yet thou darst aver

'Twill be sufficient.   From the theefe o' th' crosse
Thou dost example take ; God seekes the losse   2274
Of no mans soule ; his Sonne he therfore gave
The soules of sinners, soe we are all, to save.

Thou silly sott, how well thou canst invent   *Faith only can gain a man admission to heaven.*
Against thy selfe to make an argument !   2278
Foole, Foole !   Not every dying man shall enter,
That saith " Lord, Lord," into the heavenly center
Of everlasting blisse ; true faith must be
The only meanes to this eternity.   2282
And how doth that but by good workes appear,
Good woorkes are true faiths handmaides, & are dear
In the Almighties eyes, though (I confesse)
Not of sufficient power to release   2286   *and faith shows itself in good works.*
The soule from everlasting punnishment
(As papistes doe persuade by argument)
And purchase heaven.   Godes mercy, not deserte
Of mortall man, can heavenly ioyes impart.   2290

But to returne to thee which thinkst to die
In the true faith, yet livst in villanie ;
That makst account to purchase heavenly grace   *They who hope to purchase heaven at the last hour are deceived.*
At thy last hower, yet dayly sinst apace ;   2294
Presumpteous slave, thy error doth deceive thee,
And of those heavenly ioes will quite bereave thee !
For if the truth thou doe exactly scanne,
As is the life, so is the end of man.   2298
Wheras the theefs example thou dost bring,
Who being ready, his last requiem sing
Vpon the crosse, was in that instant hower   *The example of the thief on the Cross was only to*
From shamefull death to the celestiall bower   2302
Of Paradise transported ; learne to know   *[leaf 27]*
That this example was indeed to shew
Gods mercy infinite, his power to save,
Though man belike to drop into his grave.   2306
The vse of this we rightly may applie
To comfort them whose huge iniquity   *comfort such as*

Their conscience doth oppresse, & make them faint,

Lest black dispaire their guilty soules attaint.   2310

But as this one, so but this only one,

To keep man from such damnd presumption

As thou dost fall into, Godes word containes,

How darst thou then presume? Wher are thy braines?

How is thy iudgement from truth alienated?   2315

How is thy soule, which should be consecrated

Vnto Godes service, dedicat to sinne,

To such presumpteous sinne? If thou shouldst winne

All thy lives precious time to clear this blot,   2319

To purge thy conscience of soe foule a spot,

To wash thy sinne in true repentant teares,

Yet all thy sorrowes, all thy Christian cares   2322

Are not sufficient to appease Godes wrath.[1]

Vnlesse his mercy helpe to expiate[1]

The foulnesse of thie crime; without his grace,

Hell shalbe thy perpetuall dwelling place.   2326

And you rich gluttons, drunkardes, Epicures,

Whom carnall sence & appetite immures

From God & goodnesse, think not (though you live

Like beastes) that you noe strict account shall give 2330

How you have spent your time, consumd'e your treasure,

Livd' brutishlie in ease, delight, & pleasure.

Yes, for each act, for every word & thought,

Before Godes high tribunal being brought,   2334

You must all answeare, yet you wilbe mute,

For your owne conscience will your cause confute.

Then to your terrour shall that sentence be,

"Depart ye cursed to helles miserie!"   2338

But I too long vpon this vice have staide,

Ther's something else of others to be saide.   2340

---

[1] *So* in MS.

Sat[ira] 6.

[AGAINST LASCIVIOUSNESS.]

ARGUMENTUM.

Vndique squalenti scelerata libidine terra
Affluit, & templis spargitur vsque Venus ;
Luxurians ætas læna, meretrice, cinædo
Polluitur, mœchos angulus omnis alit.

Having discoursd of sensuall gluttonie,   Excess of
It followes now I speake of venerie ;   delicates is the
                                                                 heart of lust.
For these companions as inseperable
Are linckt together with sinnes ougly cable ;   2344
The heart of lust 's excesse in delicates,
And in this vice the soule precipitates.
Lot was first drunk, & in this drunken fit   Lot was drunk
He that incestuous sinne did straight committ.   2348   when he sinned.
But I leave recordes of antiquity   [leaf 27, back]
And take me to this times iniquity.
Lust, as a poyson that infects the blood,
Boyles in the veines of man ; the raging floud   2352
Of Neptunes kingdome, when th' impetuous might
Of the fierce windes doth make it seem to fight   Now lust as a
With monstrous billowes 'gainst the loftie cloud,   poison infects the
                                                                 blood,
Is calmer then the sea of lust, though loud   2356
Vnto the eare of sence, & is more safe ;
For this can only drowne the worser hafe

Of man, the bodie ; but lust*es* ocean
O'rewhelms both soule & body ; yet fond man   2360
Runnes in this gulfe of sinne w*i*thout all stay,
And wilfully doth cast himselfe away.

and if ever a
nation were
defiled it is
our own.

  If ever age or nation w*i*th this crime
Were beastiallie defilde, now is the time,   2364
And ours that nation, whose libidinous heat,
Whose fire of brutish lust, is growne soe great
That it doth threaten w*i*th proud Phaeton
To give the world a new combustion.   2368

Both sexes and
all ages are given
to this sin.

Both sexes, each degree, both young & olde,
Themselves vnto this filthy sinne have solde ;
Yea, even the tribe of Levie (w*hi*ch should be
The mirro*u*rs of vnspotted chastety)   2372
Are slaves to lust !   I speake not this alone

Popish priests
are guilty not-
withstanding
their vows.

Of Popish priest*es*, w*hi*ch make profession
Of an im*m*aculate virginity,
Yet live in whoredome & adultery ;   2376
But alsoe to o*u*r clergie, which to blame,
Preach continence, but follow not the same.
And their example 's able to seduce
Well given mind*es* vnto this knowne abuse ;   2380
For euery man doth vse in imitation
To follow his instruct*ou*rs fashion.

One country
parson keeps
his whore,

The country parson may, as in a string,
Lead the whole parish vnto any thing.   2384
  Eulalius hath had good education,
Pens sermons well, hath good pronuntiation,
Stiflie inveighs 'gainst sinne, as gluttonie,
Pride, envie, wrath, sloth, brutish lecherie,   2388
Covetousnes, & such like, no man more,—
Yet every man can tell he keeps a whore.

while another
defiles his
neighbour's wife,

Philogonous doth love his lust as well,
But he would clear from all suspition dwell ;   2392
'Tis safest gutting at a loafe begunne,
And therfore he his neighbo*u*r[s] wife hath wonne

To be his paramour; they may suspect,
But hee's soe wary, no man can detect   2396
His close encounters.   O, but heers the spite,   *but is not satisfied with one or two.*
On[e] wench cannot suffice his appetite !
His first must then•be baude vnto another,
She to a third, the daughter to the mother,   2400
Til like the parish bull he serves them still,   *[leaf 28]*
And dabbes their husbandes clean against their will.
But he that knew him not, & heard him preach,   *If a man heard*
Would think it were impossible to teach   2404 *him preach he would think he*
Vertue with such a fervent seeming zeale,   *could not sin thus.*
And yet thus looslie in his actions deale.
You lustfull swine ! that know the will of God,
Yet follow your owne waies, think that his rod   2408
(For soe he saith himselfe) shall scourge your sinne
With many stripes ;—with you he will beginne.
The greater man, the higher is the evill
He doth committ, & he the viler devill.   2412
Turne convertites, & make true recantation,   *Let him repent, or God will judge*
And leave at last to act your owne damnation,   *and condemn him.*
Lest your reward be Godes just vengeance,
And hell your portion & inheritance.   2416
    Sempronia's married to a gentleman
That in the joyes of Venus litle can ;
'Tis very likely, & you may believe her,
And you, her honest neighbours, should relieve her.
Saith lustfull Spurio, " Would she me accept,   2421 *Women, for various reasons,*
I'de pawne my head to please her e're I slept,
And save the paines of suing a divorce."
Yet Messalina doth, without remorse   2424
Of conscience for the act, take to her bed
A second husband ere the first be dead,   *are guilty of adultery.*
With whom she lives but an adulteresse
In brutish sinne & sensuall beastlinesse.   2428
Pray Iove he please her well, or, though 't be strange,
This second for a third I fear shee'l change.

Borgia 's in quiet, & is let alone,

Although his sister & his whore be one ;   2432

The father likewise doth (a hellish fact !)

With his owne daughter cursed incest act.

Who dares to let him ?   Hee 's a great commander,

Romes triple crownèd Pope, Sixt Alexander !   2436

Incestuous slaves ! think you to scape the rod

Of the Almighty sinne-revenging God ?

No, though the world doe wink at your offence

God never will with wickednesse dispence.   2440

Sulpitia, leave at last to wrong thy spouse,

Lest thou the furious sleeping lion rouse ;

Desist to act thy aged husbandes scorne,

He hath olde plenty, give him not the horne,   2444

And I 'le not tell the world thy hatefull sinne,

How full of luxury thy life hath been,

How many severall lovers thou hast had,

How often thou hast faind to see thy dad,   2448

That by such meanes thou mightst have free accesse

and robs him to
put money into
the hands of her
lover.
[leaf 28, back]
To meet thy paramour.   Nor will I presse

Thy conscience with recitall of that ill

When thou, thy letchers purse with golde to fill,   2452

Emtiedst thy husbandes bagges ; the diamond ringes,

The sutes of sattin, & such pretty thinges,

Which thou, as pledges of thy lewd desire,

Gavst to thy sweetheart for his lustfull hire,   2456

I 'le not once name ; no, I will hold my peace,

Soe thou wilt from thy filthy lust surcease.

Let the man who
has escaped the
penalty for rape
be careful.
Drugo, although thou lately didst escape

The daunger of the lawe, which for a rape   2460

Awardeth death, be wise & sinne noe more,

Least that thou run soe much vpon the score

Of wickednesse, that thou canst never pay it ;

And soe for want of meanes how to defraie it,   2464

By death arrested, in helles prison cast,

Thou pine in torment which shall ever last.

Sodomeo scorneth women ; all his joy

Sodomy is not unknown in the land.

Is in a rarely featurde lively boy,   2468

With whom (I shame to speake it) in his bed

He plaies like Ioue with Phrigian Ganimede.

Monster of men, worse then the sensuall beast !

Which by instinct doth follow the behest   2472

Of nature in his kinde, but thou dost fall

Into a sinne that 's moste vnnaturall.

Degenerate bastard ! by some devill got,

Such men must be the children of the devil.

For man could never, sure, beget a spot   2476

Of such vncleannesse ; how dost dare enact

Soe damnd a crime, soe lewde a loathsome fact ?

Dost thou not fear that iust Ioue, in his ire,

Will raine downe brimstone & consuming fire ;   2480

As in his wrath, though many ages since,

He did one Sodome, whose concupiscence,

Like thine, deservde black helles damnation ?

Or that some fearfull invndation   2484

In his swift streame, should hurry thee to hell,

He who punished Sodom will punish them.

With damnèd fiendes & torturde ghoastes to dwell ?

Methinks such thoughts as these should purge thy
    soule,

And keep thy bodie from an act so foule.   2488

But 'tis noe marvell though thou be not free

From the contagion of this villanie,

When the whole land 's thus plagued[1] with this sore,

Whose beastlinesse then now was never more :   2492

In Academie, country, citty, Courte,[2]

The Universities, the City,

Infinite are defiled with this spurt.

O, grant, my dearest nourse, from whose full brest

I have suckt all (if ought I have) that 's best,   2496

Suffer me to condole the misery

and the Court, are alike guilty.

Which thou gronst vnder by this villanie !

---

[1] Spelling uncertain : it appears to have been *plaguied*,
but the *i* is undotted and the *e* is blurred.

[2] MS. Corrte.

I grieve at the vices which prevail at the Universities.
[leaf 29]

How many towardly young[1] gentlemen
(Instead of ink, with teares I fill my pen   2500
To write it) sent vnto thee by theyr friendes
For art & education, the true endes
Their parentes aime at, are with this infection
Poysned by them whose best protection   2504
Should keep them from all sinne ! Alacke the while !

Each pedant Tutour should his pupill spoile.

Each pedant Tutor spoils his pupils.

O, how I grieve at this vnhappy fate,
Because this vice is soe inveterate,   2508
Growne to so strong a custome that (I fear)
The world shall end ere they this sinne forbear !

I pray for a speedy reformation.

But I leave thee with my best exoration
For thy moste speedy & true reformation.   2512

Nothus, without crossing the sea, has been into France.

Nothus which came into the world by chaunce
At a bye window, hath been late in France,
Yet never crost the seas, it cannot bee ;
'Tis newes that passes our capacity !   2516
'Tis soe, & by th' event I wilbe tride,
For I am sure hee 's hugely Frenchifide,
Gallicus morbus is his owne, I swear,
He has it paide. him home vnto a haire.   2520

Let those pity him who choose; he gets none from me.

Pitty him they that list, soe will not I,
Hee 's iustly plagud for his damnd luxurie,
He might have keapt his whore-house-haunting feet
Out of Picthatch, the Spitle, Turnboll street ;[2]   2524
He might, forewarnd, have left his pockie drabbes,
They must have veriuice that will squeese such crabbes.
But he had cause to love a puncke the more,
Because his mother was an arrant whore.   2528

I cannot chuse but grieve at the mishap

Claudia has caught a clap.

Of Cloudia, which of late hath caught a clap.
Alack, poore wench ! the trust of promisde marriage

---

[1] MS. goung. It may have been originally *goune*, as the final letter seems to have been altered. Cf. Taylor, " Gown-men," Works, fo. p. 178.
[2] All notorious haunts of prostitutes.

Hath loded thee with an vnvsuall carriadge.   2532   A promise of marriage has been her ruin.
Take comfort lasse, & I a time will spie
To shew thy lover his discourtesie,
And though he have thee in this sort beguilde,
He shall give somewhat to bring vp the childe;   2536
A litle mony from the law will quite thee,
Fee but the Sumner, & he shall not cite thee;   Fee the summoner and the law will hold you innocent.
Or if he doe, only for fashion sake,
The lawe of thee shall no advantage take.   2540
And though due pennance thou deservst to doe
For tredding thus awry thy slippery shoe,
Be not dismaide at all; if thou dost flow
In thy frank guiftes, & thy golde freely stow,   2544
The principall will make thy pennance ebbe.
The Comissaries court 's a spiders webbe,   The Comissary's court is like a cobweb which only holds small flies.
That doth entangle all the lesser flies,
But the great ones break through; it never ties   2548
Them in his circling net.   Wher golde makes way
Ther is no interruption, noe delay
Can hinder his proceeding; therfore, wench,   [leaf 29, back]
Thou maist with a bolde face confront the bench.   2552
If thy forerunners bribes have made thy peace,   Bribery will cover your shame,
Thy shame shall vanish, but thy sinne encrease,
And when thou once hast scapèd this annoy,
Goe to it roundly for another boy;   2556
Lose not an inch of pleasure, though thou gaine,   but increase your sin.
For momentarie ioyes, eternall paine.
But yet be sure, if thou still goe about
To play the drab, my pen shall paint thee out,   2560
And thy lewde actes vpon thy forehead score,
That all the world may note thee for a whore.

O Linceus,[1] that I had thy searching eye!   If I had the eyes of Lynceus I could expose the vices of this age.
Then would I in each secret corner prie,   2564
To finde the hidden knaveries of this age,

---

[1] Lynceus, one of the Argonauts, could see through the earth, and distinguish objects at a great distance.

And lay them open to this paper stage.

Then Glabria should not, with her wanton eye,

Allure faire Quintus to her villanie,   2568

But I would straight detect her for the crime,

And hinder their appoynted meeting time.

Then Lusco, 'cause his wife's in years decaide,

Should not entise to ill her waiting maide,   2572

But I would spie them out, & note[1] them downe,

To her discredit & his smale renowne.

Then Scilla, 'cause she might without suspect

Play the lewd harlot, & none might detect   2576

Her lustfull conversation, should not hide

Her loosnesse in a masculine outside,

[2]But with my pen I soone would her vncase,

And lay her open to noe mean disgrace.   2580

Then Galla, that insatiate citty dame,

(Which loves a player, 'cause he hath the fame

Of a rare Actour, & doth in his part

Conquer huge giantes, & captive the hart   2584

Of amarous ladies) should not him intice,

Prone (as all players are) vnto this vice,

With goodlie presentes. I their match would lett,

Or catch them sleeping in a Vulcanes nett,   2588

And having caught them to the world display

How lusty Mars with lustfull Venus lay.

Then lustfull Ioue, what shape soe e're he tooke

Should not deceive mine eye, nor scape my booke. 2592

Thy lust Pasiphae I'de sett to th' full,

Whose bestiall appetite desirde a bull.

Mirrha, thou shouldst not scape, that didst desire,

To make thy father to thy childe a sire.   2596

But since I cannot, as I would, be fitted,

Let me detect what I have knowne committed.

It was my fortune, with some others moe,

On[e] summers day a progresse for to goe   2600

---

[1] Final e by a later hand.   [2] /I† in margin.

Into the countrie, as the time of year   [leaf 30]
Required, to make merrie with good cheer.
Imagine Islington to be the place,   to go to Islington
The jorney to eat cream.   Vnder the face   2604 to eat cream.
Of these lewd meetings, on set purpose fitted,
Much villanie is howerly committed.
But to proceed; some thought there would not be
Good mirth without faire wenches companie,   2608 To make good
And therfore had provided, a forehand,   company,
Of wiues & maides a iust proportiond band
In number to the men of vs; each on[e]
Might have his wench vnto himselfe alone.   2612 a wench was
I that, till afterwardes, not comprehended   provided for each.
Whereto this meeting chieflie was intended,
But thought indeed the only true intent
To spend the time in honest merriment,—   2616
Went 'mongst the thickest, & had intercourse
In many a mad & sensuall discourse.
   Among the women kinde a wife ther was,   Among them
Her name I could not learne, I therfore passe   2620 was a married
It over; but a fainèd one to frame,   woman,
Call her Veneria, that's the fittest name.
This wife, which with the maides did holde her walke,
I chanc'd to overhear in her lewde talke,   2624 whom I will call
How she did them by argumentes perswade   Veneria,
To vse the pleasure of the common trade,
I will repeat, that you may iudge with me,
Women moste prone to filthy luxurie.   ·   2628
" My friendes," quoth she, "first, all of you must knowe,
Good things more common doe the better grow;
For 'tis an axiome in morality,   who persuaded
Which you must all believe for verity.   2632 the maidens to
If, then, community doe goodnesse adde   lust.
To actions that are good, who'd be so mad
To lose the vertue of this common good
When 't may be purchasde without losse of blood? 2636

For that 'tis good, I think you 'l not deny,
Or if you doe, then thus I doe replie :—

To doe our friend a pleasur 's a good deed,
If it be done for love, & not for meed ;   2640
To doe an act *that* addes to our delight
Is it not good? what foole will once deny 't?

Besides, the name import*es* it to be good,
For we a good turne call it. With my blood,   2644
If all this be to weake, I will maintaine
Ther 's none of all our sexe that would refraine
To vse *the* pleasure of this knowne delight,
If fear did not restraine their appetite.   2648

And this I holde, *that* secret letcherie
Is a lesse sinne then close hypocrisie.
A preacher tolde me that the action wrought
(Because more seldome then the wandring thought)

Is not soe great a fault, soe we chuse time   2653
And place convenient to conceile our crime ;
And that we will not want, nor lusty boyes
Able to give a wench her fill of ioyes.   2656

Then to it, lasses, when you have desire,
'Tis dangerous to suppresse a flaming fire ! "
To hear this lewdnesse both mine eares did glow,

But I bit in my tongue, lest there should grow   2660
Some discontentment 'mongst them by my speach,
W*h*ich happily might have procur'de a breach
Among vs ; & indeed soe much the rather,

Because by circumstances I did gather   2664
Wherfore this meeting was, & did intend
to observe all vnto the very end.

    By this time we th' appointed place attainde,
Where straight with welcomes we were entertaind. 2668

Musicke was sent for, & good chear preparde,
With w*h*ich more like to Epicures we farde
Then Christian*es* ; plenty of wine & creame
Did even vpon our table seeme to streame,   2672

With other dainties.   Not a fidlers boy
But with the relicks of our feast did cloy
His hungry stomach.   After this repast
(Which feast with many a baudy song was gracd) 2676
Some fell to dauncing (& dauncing is a cause
That many vnto fornication drawes),
In which lascivious kinde of merriment,
Till the darke evening did approch, we spent   2680
The lightsome day.   But now the time drew nigh
That was comprisd'e to act their villany ;
And therfore after candles were brought in
(For then the night grew on) we did beginne   2684
The fidlers to discharge, who being gone,
There straight was held a consultation,
In which, when each man had his wench assignde,
The filthinesse of this lewde act to blinde   2688
With darkenesse, all the candles were put out,
Which favouring my intent, I left the rout,
And closely stole away, having defraide
A great part of the reckning ; which I paide   2692
Whilst they were all full busie in the darke,
Because they should not think I came to sharke
Only for vittailes.   How the rest agreed,
Iudge you which doe this true narration read.   2696
But leaving this mad crew, I have to say
Somewhat of bawdes, cheife actours in this play.

  Gabrina, in her youth a pretty ducke,
Hath been, they say, as good as ever strucke.   2700
It was her fortune (long she could not tarry
'Cause she was faire) with a rich foole to marrie.
I call him foole, because he let her have
Her minde soe much, that he became her slave   2704
To his vndooing.   She must keep her coach,
Consort with ladies ; each new set abroach
Fantastique fashion which she did affect,
His gold must flie for ; yet she did respect   2708

Side notes:

After the feast some fell to dancing, which lasted till dark.

When the candles were brought in the fiddlers were discharged.

As soon as the lights were put out I escaped.

Gabrina married a rich fool.

[leaf 31]

She kept her coach and con- sorted with ladies.

Others above him, vpon whom she spent
His wealth ; her lust his care could not prevent.

Her pride and
sensuality
brought him to
beggaiy, and
broke his heart.

Thus soone her pride & sensuality
Brought him vnto disgrace & beggery,   2712
Till griefe for her lewd life, his ruind state
Broke his weak heart, & made him yeild to fate.
Then was she glad her whores flag to advaunce,
And get her living by a Scottish daunce.   2716
Thus with her sister, such another piece,
Many a gallant of his golde they fleece.

In their age she
and her sister
hiie out a crew
of whores.

Now ceazd with age, & both of them turnd bawdes,
Olde hackny women, they hire out their jades,   2720
A crew of whores far worse then crocodiles,
Killing with fainèd teares & forgèd smiles.
Confusion with their fortunes ever dwell,
That keep the dores that ope to sinne & hell !   2724

These bawds up-
hold their state

These bawdes which doe inhabite Troynovant,[1]
And iet it vp & downe i' th' streetes, aflaunt
In the best fashion, thus vpholde their state,
As I haue heard a friend of mine relate,   2728
Who once in privat manner with another
Went purposly their fashions to discover.

by keeping wives
as well as com-
mon whores.

They doe retaine besides these common queanes,
Even mens wives which are of greatest meanes,   2732
That yearly pay them tribute for their lust,
Vpon whose secrecie they doe entrust
Their blotted reputation, for which pleasure
They lewdly doe consume their husbandes treasure. 2736
The custome of these bawdes is thus : if any
Repaire vnto them (as God knowes too many
Run to this sinck of sinne), at the first view

When a man
comes in, they
show the cheapest
wares first.

To shew their cheapest ware ; if they will glue   2740
Their slimy bodies to those common whores,
The bawdes proceed no farther, keep the dores,
The price paide, which repentaunce findes to dear,

---

[1] London. See Taylor, Works, fol. 491.

And the act done, doe straight the men cashier. 2744

But if some gallant, whose out side doth holde

But if he looks
rich he is shown
into a private
room

Great expectation that good store of golde

Will from his bounty shower into their lapp*es*,

Come to demaund (for soe it often hap̃p*es*) 2748

To see their choysest beauties, him they bring

(After request [not]¹ to say any thing)

Into a privat roome, w*hi*ch round about

Is hung w*i*th pictures ; all w*hi*ch goodly rout 2752

hung round with
portraits of City
dames.

Is fram'de of Venus fashion, femals all,

Whom if I name whores, I noe whit miscall,

For soe they are, whom these doe represent.

[leaf 31, back]

All citty dames, w*hi*ch vsually frequent 2756

This cursed place, who, though they goe full brave,

Are in their lust insatiat as the grave.

That picture w*hi*ch doth best affect the eye

The picture
which takes his
fancy is soon
replaced by its
"lively sub-
stance."

Of this luxurious gallant, instantly 2760

Is by some traine brought thether in true shape

Of lively substance.   Then good Bacchus grape

Flowes in abundance ; Ceres must be by,

For w*i*thout them ther is noe venerie. 2764

Provocatives to stir vp appetite

Wines and
nutritious food
are provided in
abundance.

To brutish lust & sensùall delight,

Must not be wanting ; lobsters buttered thighs,

Hartichoke, marrowbone,² potato pies, 2768

Anchoves, lambes artificiallie drest stones,

Fine gellies of decocted sparrowes bones.

Or if these faile, th' apothecaries trade

Lobsters, pies,
jellies, mar-
malade,

Must furnish them w*i*th rarest marmalade, 2772

Candid eringoes, & rich marchpaine stuffe ;

Vpon w*hi*ch cates ther is consumde enough

To give sufficient to a hundred men,

Spent but on ordinarie fare.   But then 2776

These dainties must be washd downe well w*i*th wine,

¹ Blank in MS.; something erased.
² Very much like Moorrowbone in MS.

sack, eggs,
Muscadine,
Alicant,
With sacke & sugar, egges & muskadine,

With Allegant, the blood of Venerie,

That strengthens much the backes infirmity.   2780

and dainties
enough to crack
a man's purse-
strings.
Abundance of these dainties they 'l not lacke,

Although it make my gallantes purstrings cracke.

And yet sometimes these cittie dames will spend

As if their husbandes wealth could ne're have end.   2784

Then after this libidinous collation

They doe proceed to act their owne damnation.

Thus is our great
city made a
brothel.
Thus is the worthiest citty of our land

Made a base brothel-house, by a lewde band   2788

Of shamelesse strumpets, whose vncurbèd swing

Many poore soules vnto confusion bring.

The Magistrates
should rid it of
this cursed crew.
You magistrates, which holde Astræas sword,

For countries cause joyne all with one accord   2792

To clear the citty of this cursed crew,

Least the whole land the noysomenesse doe rewe

Of their contagion.   For the better health

Of the whole body of the commonwealth,   2796

Cut of these rotten members, & beginne

First at the head of this notorious sinne.

Remove the
cause, and the
effect will perish.
For this is written one the Lidian stone,

"The effect doth perish when the cause is gone." 2800

These bawdes & panders which doe give receat

(Being indeed the meanes wherby they eat)

[leaf 32]
To whores & ruffians, whose damnd villanie

Doth purchase gold & sell iniquity ;   2804

Were they expeld the cittie, ther would grow

More continence, for[1] them these heades doe flow ;

The springs of lust, these fountaines, being drawne dry

The lesser streames would stint immediatly.   2808

Lop off these
ulcered members
with the hand
of justice.
Lop of these vlcerd members of our land,

These putrifièd members ; with the hand

Of iustice chase hence this vngodly rout,—

Subtract the fewell & the fire goes out,—   2812

---

[1] ? from.

And let our land this damnèd devillish crew,
As excrementes, out of her bosome spewe ;
And then you manifestly shall perceave
The greater part their brutish lust will leave.   2816
For every man this olde saide saw beleeves,
"Were no receivers there would be no theeves."   "No receivers,
                                                         no thieves."
    Thus City scapes not, nor the Court is free
From obsceane actes of hatefull luxurie.   2820
Those men or women that doe make resorte,
In hope of gaine or honour, to the Court,   The Court is not
                                                   free from these
Doe live soe idely, & in such excesse,   sins.
That it must needs produce this wickednesse.   2824
    Vitellius hath gotten a good place,
And might live well i' th' Court, had he the grace
To keep it to good endes, & vse it soe,
"But lightly come," we say, "doth lightly goe."   2828   "Lightly come,
                                                                 lightly go."
It cost him nothing but a supple knee,
[1] And oyly mouth & much observancie,
But he doth vpon worse then nothing spend it,
Yet 'tis well spent, he saies, & hee 'l defend it.   2832
He keeps a whore i' th' city, what needs that ?   City and Court
                                                          are alike.
Ther 's whores enough i' th' Court, which (as a cat
Waites to supprise a mouse) watch to espie
[2] Whom they can draw vnto their villanie,   2836
Some for meer lust, others for greedinesse
Of gaine ; as, 'mongst all your court landresses
If but one honest woman can be found,   Scarce one honest
                                               woman to be
I 'le give her leave to give me twenty pound.[3]   2840   found.
But these are stale ; Vitellius must have one
That 's a rare piece of the best fashion,
Although she make these three thinges fare the worse,
His soule, his body, & his strouting purse.   2844   They ruin soul,
                                                            body, and purse.
His purse, her gay apparel & fine fare
Have made allready very thin & bare ;

---

[1] /Ion in margin of MS.
[2] /I in margin of MS.   [3] MS. 20¹.

Bodily disease.

His bodie, her vnwholsome luxurie
Hath brought to *the* disease of venery ;   2848
And I much fear this their lewde fashion
Will bring his soule vnto damnation.

[leaf 32, back]
I need not talk
of Silvius and
City dames,

    Silvius doth shew *the* citty dames brave sights,
And they for *that* doe pleasure him a night*es*.   2852
Citty & country are beholding to him,
And glad w*i*th purse & body both to woe him.

when higher
personages are
guilty.

But what talke I of these, when brighter starres
Darken their splendant beauty w*i*th *the* scarres   2856
Of this insatiate sinne ?   If hono*u*r fall
Gentry must need*es* submit himselfe a thrall.
But whether climst thou, my aspiring Muse ?
It wilbe thought presumption & abuse   2860

Forbear, m*y*
Muse, to tax
nobility !

To taxe nobility !   Forbear, forbear !
Thou art an orbe above thy native spheare,
Something thou canst not in oblivion drowne ;—
Why come one then, & briefly set it downe.   2864

One boasts that
he has made
fifty-one cuckolds
in the year:

    I heard Brusano by his hono*u*r sweare
He on[e] & fifty cuckold*es* made last yeare.
Pitty it was he did noe farther goe,
Each weeke would have done well to struck a doe, 2868
And given *the* keeper his due fee to seeke
When as he came to th' two & fiftith weeke.

but he who made
so many,

Whom shall we finde to make vp *the* iust number ?
To bring 't about it my conceit doth cumber.   2872
Why, what a foole am I to seek thus farre !
You did soe many cuckold*es* make or marre ?

is himself the
fifty-second.

Well then, i' faith you may, for all yo*u*r pelfe,
Make vp the two & fiftieth yo*u*r selfe !   2876
    Madame Emilia hath a proper squire
To vsher her vnto *the* filthy mire

Madam's page
knows all her
arrangements,

Of soule-polluting lust, who knowes his cues
Wher he must leave her, where attendance vse ; 2880
And can while 's lady act*es* the horrid crime,
W*i*th picking rushes trifle out *the* time ;

And for a need, when she wantes fresh supplie,

Her sensuall desires satisfie.   2884

Base slave! which standest centinell to lust,

Suffering thy soule, polluted with the rust

Of canckered sinne, by thy neglect to perish,

Which above all thinges thou shouldst love & cherish!

Thou instrument of sinne & Sathans[1] rage!   2889

Incarnate devill! pandarizing page!

Be sure (vnlesse repentance pardon gaine)

There doth a place in hell for thee remaine.   2892

   And for those lechers which will never linne

(Accounting lust but as a veniall sinne)

To committ incest, whoredome, sodomie,

Defile the land with damnd adulterie,   2896

Which strive not to suppresse their lewde desires,

But fewell ad to their lust-burning fires,

By seeking wicked opportunities

To act their damnable iniquities,   2900

Till they have ruind all their hope of blisse,

Devilles will hale them to helles darke abisse.

Side notes:
- and can at times supply her wants himself.
- But he may rest assured that there's a place reserved in hell for him,
- as well as for all who are guilty of incest, whoredom, sodomy, and adultery.
- [leaf 33]

[1] MS. Sathange.

Sat[ira] 7.

[AGAINST THE PASSIONS OF THE MIND.]

ARGUMENTUM.

Reginam mentis rationem, serva rebellis
Passio devincit, calce tyranna premit,
Dum gerit immodicos (victa ratione) trivmphos,
Incautos homines, ad mala damna rapit.

God gave to man a reasonable soul that he might govern all things.	God gave to man a reasonable soule, That he might govern vnder his controle All other creatures in the world beside, Yet man wantes reason how himselfe to guide. 2906
Reason is the queen of the soul,	Reason, *the* soules queen, whose imperious sway Should rule the microcosme of man, & stay By her wise governing authority Each insolent affections tyranny, 2910
but she is become the slave of her subject,	Is through much, too much, sufferaunce become Slave to her subiect, who vsurps her roome. Ambitiously aspiring passion, Ever delighting in rebellion, 2914 Collects her forces, meets her prince i' th' field,
who boldly rebels against her.	Subdues her power in conflict, make[s] her yeild. And now *the* tyrannesse beares all *the* stroke, Clogging her suffering neck with servile yoke, 2918 And proud insulting in her victorie, Trivmphs o're mans base imbecillity.

Thus his owne servant, every base affection,

Keeps him in slavish t[h]raldome & subjection. 2922

By love or hatred, by ioy, griefe, or feare,

Desire, boldenesse, anger, hope, dispaire,

Man is enthrald, & doth submitt his will

Their tyrannies & pleasures to fulfill.   2926

The Amoretto, pearc'd with Cupides stroke,

Must straight submitt his neck vnto the yoke

Of peevish love.   Either his mistrisse haire,

Or else her forehead is beyond compare ;   2930

Her eyes are starres, & her cheekes roses be,

Her lips pure rubies, her teeth ivorie,

Her breath perfume, her voice sweet harmonie

Passing Threician Orpheus melody ;   2934

The path between her brestes a whiter way

Then that celestiall via lactea ;

Her veines pure azure, or what colour 's best,

Her skin sleck sattin or the cygnettes brest ;   2938

A Venus in whom all good partes doe hitt,

More then a second Pallas in her witt ;

In stately pace and dazeling maiestie,

Another Iuno ; in pure chastety   2942

Spotlesse Diana.   Thus is all her feature

Beyond the fashion of a humane creature.

Then what "ay mees !" what crossing of his armes,

What sighs, what teares, what love-compelling charmes

He vseth, would enforce a sicke man smile !   2947

Yet all the paines he takes is to beguile

His sillie soule ; for having once enioyed

The thing, for which he erst was soe anoyde,   2950

The tide is turnd, the saint doth seem a devill,

And he repentes that soule-bewitching evill

[1] Which once his fancy as a good adorde ;—

His mistresse love, I mean, is now abhorde.   2954

Anothers minde by hate distempered is,

[1] /I in margin of MS.

Marginal notes:

Every base affection keeps man in thraldom.

If man falls in love he must submit to the yoke of peevish fancy,

and compare his mistress to

[leaf 33, back]

Venus, Pallas, Juno, and Diana,

Then to hear his "*Ah me's !*" till he gets dis-enchanted !

Then his "saint" seems a devil.

The mind of another is over-come by hate,

Malicing whom in shew he seemes to kisse.

This base affection causeth dismall strife,

Despoileth honour, & destroyeth life.   2958

which he hides by dissimulation. Yet in these dayes 'tis counted pollicie

To vse dissimulation ; villanie

Masqu'd[1] vnder friendships title (worst of hate)

Makes a man liue secure & fortunate.   2962

These Machiavillians are *th*e men alone

.That thrive i' th' world, & gett promotion.

Such as he are worse than Timon of Athens. Athenian Timon, in his hatefull moode,

Was ne're soe bad as some of this damnde broode, 2966

This brood of Cain*es*, these dissembling knaves,

These mankinde-haters, bloody minded slaves,

W*h*i*c*h all *th*e world w*i*th horrid murders fill,

Laughing one those whom they intend to kill.   2970

A third sort have their minds overwhelmed with joy. A third ther is, w*h*i*c*h gaining some vaine toy,

Is overwhelmèd through excessive ioy.

The husbandman, if that his crops proove well,

Hath his heart fild w*i*th joy 'cause his barnes swell ;

The marchant, if his gaines doe safe come in,   2975

Is w*i*th ioy ready to leape out on 's skinne ;

The vehemency of this passion 's such,

Many have[2] died by joying overmuch.   2978

Another, shuning comfort & reliefe,

Some are over-come with grief, Suffers himselfe to be surchargde w*i*th griefe,

And soe this passion doth his reason blinde

That it begett*es* a frenzie in his minde.   2982

Another, if that fear doe him assaile,

Doth suffer that affection to prevaile,

[leaf 34] And doth bring him [in]to such franticke fitt*es*,

As you would judge him to be out on 's witt*es*.   2986

and some with fear. Each bush doth fright him, & each flying bird,

Yea his owne shadowe maketh him afeard.

---

[1] *Masque* originally written ; altered into *Masqu'd.*

[2] This *have* seems to have been *o'ave*, but a line is drawn
. through the *o*.

Desire in others sheweth forth his mighte,
Making them follow brutish appetite. 2990
Desire of honour fires th' ambitious minde ;
Desire of wealth the covetous doth blinde ;
The lecher cannot lustfull thoughtes withstand :
Reason 's controlde by passions that commaund. 2994
Another, rash & indiscreetly bolde,
Hazardes himselfe in dangers manifolde,
Yet thinks himselfe (mislead by his temerity)
To vse true valour & dexterity ; 2998
When folly his companion is assignde,
For " who soe bolde as bayard that is blynde ?
With rashnesse is conioynèd impudence,
With which my Muse in noe case can dispence. 3002
His talke is bawdry, he doth rather choose
His soule then a prophane conceite to loose.

Mischiefe-procurer anger rules another,
That knowes not friend from foe ; stranger or brother,
All 's one to him ; for in his bedlem fitt, 3007
Which quite deprives him of his litle witt,
He cares not whom he strikes, or what vile wordes
That cutt like razors, or sharp edgèd swordes, 3010
Flie from his hasty tongue.   This passion swaies
And rules over too many now adayes,
For each vaine toy stirreth vp man to furie,
When he in patience greatest wrongs should burie. 3014

Hope & affection is that doth least harme
Vnto the soule of man ; for it doth arme
With constancy in trouble to endure
The worst of evill that sad fates procure. 3018
It makes the prisoner, bound in gives of steele,
In expectation of release, to feele
Noe torment in bis bondage ; cures the sicke
Of his diseases ; makes the halfe dead quicke. 3022
Yet is this good conioynèd with some evill ;
To hope on God is good, but from the devill

Honour fires
the ambitious.

Rashness by some
is mistaken for
valour.

Impudence is
often conjoined
with rashness.

Anger rules some,
and deprives
them of their
wits.

They care not
whom they
wound.

Hope and affec-
tion do the least
harm.

They console
the prisoner and
cure the sick.

Don't expect aid
from the devil.

To expect healp, as they doe which attend

With expectation of a happy end   3026

To some ill act, is diabolicall,

And not by Christians to be vsde at all.

But when I come to think vpon dispaire

(Which to withstand the rediest meanes is praier) 3030

Despair drives
men to suicide.

I muse to think it should soe much bewitch

The minde of man, making the soule (like pitch)

Commit such deeds of darkenesse, such damnd ill,

As with our owne handes our owne lives to spill. 3034

[leaf 34, back]

Farre be it from me all passion to exclude

Out of mans soule, my meaning's not so rude ;

A man void of
passion is void
of good.

For 'tis an axiome not to be withstood,

" He that is void of passion's voide of good." [1]   3038

Love of that love deserving Diety,

Which doth produce effectes of charity,

Love to God
kindles devotion.

And kindles in mans heart [2] devotion,

Once to extenuate were a sinfull motion   3042

Of a pestiferous braine ; noe, I desire

To ad more fewell to that holy fire.

Godly hate is
commendable.

Nor can I but commend of godlie hate,

Detesting sinne, that doth commaculate   3046

The soule of man ; this passion's worth commending,

That hates the offence, yet loves the man offending.

Neither will I restraine the heart from joy

Joy in modera-
tion is good,

Soe that with moderation we imploy   3050

This passion to good vses ; hartes rejoyce,

But let the cause be singuler & choice.

Grief likewise must abounde in every man

That will indeed be a true Christian,   3054

so are godly
sorrow and
filial fear.

Sorrow the badge of true repentance weares,

Sinne must be purgde by a whole flood of teares.

[3] To filial feare I likewise doe assent,

---

[1] *blood* was first written, then a line drawn through it, and
good written after.
[2] MS. heard.   [3] */I and* written in margin of MS.

That 's awd from sinne by love, not punishment. 3058
Salvations hope, celestiall ioyes desire,
Vertuous boldenesse, with religious ire,   Virtuous boldness
                                                            and religious ire,
Are heavenly passions not to be denide,
But as occasion serves, to be applide   3062
To their true endes.   Affectiones of such kinde
Mie Muse disclaimes not ; but all such as blinde   my Muse dis-
                                                            claims not ;
The eyes of reason, & doe quite pervert   but all such
                                                            affections as lead
The soule, mans better intellectuall part,   3066   man to sin.
That keep him from the path of his salvation,
And lead the way which brings vnto damnation,
These, these they be, on which I doe engage
My vexèd Muse to wreck her spleenfull rage.   3070
     Philautus with his very soule doth love   Philautus loves
A wench as faire as Venus milck white dove ;   many things,
He loves his hunting-horse, his hauke, his hound,
His meat & drink, his morning sleeps profound ; 3074
He loves to follow each new-fangled fashion,
He loves to hear men speake his commendation,
He loves his landes, that bring him store of pelfe,
But above all thinges he doth love himselfe.   3078   but himself
                                                            most of all.
In all this love noe love of God I finde,
Noe love of goodnesse, but a love confinde
To sensuall delights, to sinne & ease,
A love to others soe himselfe to please.   3082
Thou impious worldling, leave this vaine affection,   [leaf 35]
Which only on thy selfe hath a reflection ;
This sinne relinquish, lest incensèd Ioue   This is love
Doe iustly plague thy misapplyèd love.   3086   misapplied.
     I saw (a sight that made me much affraide)
Amorphus kisse his mothers kitchin-maide.
Me thought as both their heades together came,   Amorphous is in
                                                            love with his
I saw the devill kissing of his dam :[1]   3090   mother's kitchen-
                                                            maid.
And yet this foole 's in love with her 'bove measure,
Calls her the mistresse of his[2] ioy & pleasure ;

        [1] Final *e* crossed out.   [2] MS. *her*.
    TIME'S W.   7

Sweares *that* faire roses grow vpon her cheekes,
When I 'le be sworne 'tis fitter place for leekes ; 3094
Saies her sweet breath his amarous fires increase,
When she smell*es* filthy strong of durt & grease.

It is a case of
like to like;
the collier and
the devil.
" But like to like, *th*e collier & *th*e devill,"
He & his wench ; she stam*m*ers, he doth drivell ; 3098
He squints, & she doth gogle wondrous faire ;
His botle-nose is red, soe is her haire ;
She hath a crooked backe, he a polte foote ;
His face is blacke, & hers begrimd'e w*i*th soote ; 3102
A loving lovely couple most divine,
Pitty it were *that* they should not combine.

Pamphila is in
love with every
man she sees.
Pamphila is in love w*i*th every man
That comes w*i*thin her sight, & if she can   3106
Will prostitute her body to his will,
And never leave till she her lust fullfill.

Stepmother Phœdra woos her husband*es* sonne,
Hypolitus, but he w*i*th care doth shunne   3110
Phœdra's love to
her stepson is
turned to hate.
Her odious lust, loathing a sinne soe vile
As his sires bed w*i*th incest to defile ;
But still she sues, & still he doth denie,
Till vrgde to farre, he doth her presence flie.   3114
Lust thus by verteous chastetie w*i*thstood
Is turnd to hate, & hate thirsts after blood ;
And his hart*es* blood it is this thirst must ease ;
Only his death can her fell hate appease.   3118

True Machiavillian Cæcilius
Honorius is per-
secuted because
of his virtues.
W*i*th hate doth prosecute Honorius,
Because his vertues did deserve more love,
And he i' th' Court respected was above   3122
His high aspiring selfe.   Yet till *th*e end
In outward shew he seemd to be his friend.
But when *that* Fortune had once turnd her wheele
He was *th*e first *that* did his furie feele ;   3126
For then his rage burst forth, & it is thought
This one mans hate his sad destruction wrought.

Misotochus (which his hand will sooner lend
To bring his neighbour to vntimely end   3130
Then save his life) hath horded vp his corne,
Ready to burst his garners with the horne
Of his aboundance, & doth hope his seed
Kept from the market will a famine breed ;   3134
And therfore will not sell a graine this year,
Nor to sustaine his householde thresh an eare ;
But lives one rootes like a Diogenes,
With poor thin drink, & course bread mad[e] of pease.
What though the poore doe want, begge, starve, & dye,
They get from him noe healp in miserie.
Their hunger feeds him fat, he ioyes to see
Their death-procuring sad calamity.   3142
Thou hateful cynick-dog, belov'd of none,
Because none loving, not thy selfe alone !
Inhuman devill ! think some fatall hower
Will bring huge troupes of vermine, to devoure   3146
Thy graine & thee ; or that from heaven will fall
Consuming fyer & destroy it all.
Looke for some fearfull vengeance to be sent,
Some plague vnheard of, some straunge punnishment ;
For such damnd hatred, iust revenging God   3151
Will scourge thy sinne with some vnusuall rodde.

Nænius hath with much officious labour
Recoverèd his mistrisses lost favour,   3154
For the which act the foole's soe overioyde
That through excesse therof he is annoide.
When she vouchsafte that he might kiss her hand,
The asse had much adoe on 's feet to stand,   3158
He was soe inly ravisht with delight
Of that rare pleasure : such another fight
Twixt reason & his passion would have sent
A foolish soule to Plutoes regiment.   3162
When Carthaginian Hanniball, that stout
And politicke captaine, which soe often fought

Marginal notes:

A man who would rather help to kill than save life,
[leaf 35, back] keeps his corn till there's a famine.

Though the poor die of want they get no help from him.

But troops of vermin devour him and his corn.

One fool was so overjoyed at his mistress's favours,

that another fit like it would have killed him.

With Roman Consuls in their native soile,
And their best forces many times did foile,   3166
It is recorded by cronologers,
And excellent histriographers,

A Roman matron heard that her two sons were killed in the battle of Cannæ.

In *tha*t vnluckie Cannas overthrowe,
When few or none escapte deaths fatall blowe,   3170
A certaine woman dwelling then at Rome
Heard her two sonnes had their eternall doome;
For w*hi*ch (as nature would) she did lament,
Her eyes (bare witnesse) all w*i*th teares besprent. 3174

But they escaped, and she was so overcome when she saw them, that she died.

But *th*e young men scaping by flight their foe
Recover.Rome & to their mother goe ;
She hearing both alive returnèd were
And bid her former sorrow to forbeare,   3178
Will not beleeve reporte, but trust her eyes,
When sodainly opprest w*i*th ioy she dies.

[leaf 36]

One dies in the act of sin.

Mopsa, they say, o'recome w*i*th joy lies dead,
But how ? i' th' act of her lost mayden head !   3182
A fearfull end, to die in act of sinne,
And in this death a second death beginne,
A dayly living death, yet dying paine
W*hi*ch shall in p*er*petuity remaine.   3186

Another mourns her puppy's death.

Luctantia, cease thy lamentation !
Thou mone'st thy puppies death w*i*th greater passion
Then *th*e offences *tha*t thou dost committe
'Gainst thy Creat*our* ; w*hi*ch iust ne're a whit   3190
Grieve thy seard conscience ; noe remorse for sinne
On[e] tear enforceth, but for every pinne,
For every trifle else, that doth distast
Thy foolish liking, thou dost even wast   3194
Thy selfe in sorrow.   Wash thy blubbered eyes,

She should weep for iniquity.

And cry no more for shame ! If thou be wise
See that hence forth thou keep thy fludgates dry,
And weep for nothing but iniquity.   3198
    Mutius, why art thou thus opprest w*i*th griefe ?
Take comfort man, & thou shalt finde reliefe ;

Be not dejected, bear a constant minde :
What though the tempest of an [a]dverse winde   3202
Hath blowne thy fortunes downe, ruind thy state ?
Wilt thou for this accuse *the* god of fate,
And yeild to sorrow ?   Doe not soe ; beware,
'Twas mercy in him then thy life to spare.   3206
When he destroide thy goods, had 't been his pleasure
He might have ruinde thee & them together.
But now thy substaunce & thy wealth is lost,
Thou art vndone, & all thy hopes are crost ;   3210
Ther is noe meanes to rise : who once doth fall
Is still kept downe, & cannot climbe at all.
Fear not, Antæus more couragious grew,
And by his fall did still his strength renew.   3214
Be thou like him ; may be this misery
Was pre-ordainde for thy felicity.
Grieve not at all, ther 's blessing still in store,
And he *that* tooke thy good*es* can give thee more.   3218
     Ther 's three ill feares (to one good filiall)
A worldly, servile, & a naturall :
A worldly feare is when some worldly gaine
Makes vs doe evill, or from good abstaine ;   3222
When for *our* proffit, pleasure, & *our* ease,
We doe not good, but men fear to displease.
There is a worldly fear, a fear to lacke
Things necessary for *th*e maw or backe,   3226
W*hi*ch hath in nature greater confidence,
Then in Gods all-foreseeing providence.
Naturall fear is a distraction
Of mind & senses, by th' iniection   3230
Of some moste eminent danger ; & this passion
Is great where faith doth want his op*er*ation.
A servile fear 's a fear of punnishment
Vnto *the* reprobate coincident,   3234
Whom oftentimes vnto good act*es* doth drawe,
Not fear of God, but fear of humane lawe.

Side notes:

If adversity come do not be cast down,

Antæus became more courageous by his fall.

There are three ill fears :

A worldly fear, or fear for want of things necessary.

[leaf 36, back]

A servile fear, or a fear of punnishment for ill deeds.

Letia doth fear to play *the* whore with any,
And yet she loves the sport as well as many   3238
That act the sinne ; what hinders her intent ?[1]
O she 's afraide of shame & punnishment.

A man would steal, but he fears punishment. Irus is poore, yet feares to play *the* theefe,
And yet his fingers itch to get reliefe,   3242
" But the burnt childe (we say) doth dread *the* fire ;"—
Hee 's burnt i' th' hand, the next is halters hire.

Romanus keeps his monthly residence
The Church dignitary would neglect his duty, only he fears the consequences. At church, although against his conscience ;   3246
He would refraine (because he doth abhor it)
But *that* he feares to be presented for it.

Bellina, tost in a tempestuous sea,
Fears drowning much, & fear doth make her pray. 3250
And yet her prayers, w*hi*ch doe seeme profounde,
Are but lip-labo*ur* & a hollow sound ;
For set a shore, vnlesse apparent evill
Affright her much, she fears nor God nor devill.   3254

Phorbus has been frightened, but it was only a cat, Phorbus, what makes thee looke soe like a ghoast ?
Thy face is pale, thy sences are quite lost,
Thy haire vpon thy head doth stand vpright
As if thou hadst been haunted w*i*th a spright.   3258
Why soe thou hast, thou thinkst ; what, hast thou soe ?
How scapdst thou from him ? would he let thee goe ?

which he thought was the devil. Sure 'twas a very honest devill, friend,
Wer he hobgoblin, fairie, elve, or fiend.   3262
Thou fearfull idiot ! looke, it was a catt,
That frights thee thus, I sawe her wher she satt ;
But thou w*i*th conscience guilty of much evill
Dost deeme *the* cat to be a very devill.   3266

Caligula creeps under the bed, but it is a poor shelter. Caligula, creepst vnderneath thy bed ?
That 's a poore shelter to defend thy head
'Gainst Ioves feard thunderbolte ; huge Atlas hill
Cannot preserve thee, when he meanes to kill.   3270

One wishes for an estate Votarius wisheth for a great estate,

_____
[1] MS. intentent.

And saith *the* poore should then participate
Of all his blessings ; yet doth nothing give
Although he be exceeding well to live,   3274
And might healp others, till his substaunce grew ;
But *the* olde proverbe is exceeding true,
" That these great wishers, & these com*m*on woulders,
Are never (for *the* moste part) good householders." 3278

[leaf 37]
that he might
assist others.

Timophila her part of heaven would sell
To be a ladie, she so much doth swell
W*i*th this ambitious longing, to be cald
Madam at every word ; to be enstalde   3282
In such a chaire of state, were heaven it selfe.
Ambitious woman, high aspiring elfe !
All thy desires are wicked, thou vnblest,
Vnlesse God*es* Spirit, working in thy brest,   3286
Change thy desire from vaine & earthly toies
To covet truely after heavenly ioyes.

Another would
sell heaven to be
a lady and be
called Madam.

Chremes is troubled with *the* greedy minde
Of golde-desiring Midas ; he doth finde   3290
Noe comfort but in gaping after gaine.
Would to his wish awarded were *the* paine
That Midas felt ; who, thirsting after golde,
Wishd *tha*t what e're he touchd might change *the*
        mould   3294
Into *tha*t purer mettall.   Phœbus graunt
Confirmd *the* misers wish, but soone did daunt
The wretches minde ; for all *the* foode he tooke
To comfort nature, cleane his forme forsooke 3298
And turnd to golde.   The asse had surely starvde
Had not Apolloes power his life preservde
By taking of his wish.   May the intent
Of Chremes meet with *the* like punnishment ; 3302
Or, since *tha*t Midas greedy minde he beares,
May he w*i*th Midas wear *the* asses eares.

Chremes is
greedy, and his
only comfort is
in gain.

Midas wished all
things turned
into gold,

and had starved
had not Apollo
taken off his
wish.

Dame Polupragma, gossip Title-tatle,
Suffers her tongue, let loose at randome, pratle 3306

Dame Tittle-
tattle

Of all occurrent*es* ; comes to publike feastes

W*i*thout invitement, 'mongst *th*e worthiest guest*es*

Takes vp her roome at table, where, more bolde

Then truely welcome, she discourse will holde   3310

Of state affaires, talke of divinity

As moves *th*e hearers to deride her folly,

But grieves me to *th*e heart, that thing*es* soe holy,

Things wh*i*ch in greatest estimation stand,   3314

Should by her foolish lips be soe propha*n*de.

But Betterice let me thee this lesson teach,

To leave those thing*es* *tha*t are above thy reach.

Temerus, wh*i*ch i' th' warre had borne a launce, 3318

Vpon some great exploite would need*es* advaunce

Hi*s* high attempting minde, & doe some act,

To make *th*e world applaud his worthy fact.

Then (ne're regarding what might him befall)   3322

He takes in hand to kill *th*e generall

Of the foes armie ; but his vaine intent

Met w*i*th as ill successe ; care did prevent

His desperate boldenesse, ere he could come nigh 3326

His wish*è*d end ; for, taken for a spie,

And brought to th' racke, torture did him compell

The truth of his straunge stratagem to tell ;

For wh*i*ch *th*e wretch in horrid torment lies,   3330

Being iustly plagu'de for his rash enterprise.

          Anaidus, art soe clean devoide of grace ?

Hast thou soe impudent a brasen face,

Not only to act sinne w*i*th greedinesse,   3334

But to make boast of thy damnde wickednesse ?

Was 't not enough w*i*th word*es* to have beguild

Thy mothers maide & gotten her w*i*th childe,

But *tha*t thou must most shamefully beginne   3338

To make a iest of this thy hellish sinne

'Mongst thy companions ?   Thou p*er*haps dost think,

Because thy law-p*er*verting curs*è*d chink

Hath freed thee from *th*e standing in a sheet   3342

(A punnishment for thy offence moste meet)
That there remaines noe more ? Yes, ymp of hell,
There is a Iudge w*h*ich in the heavens doth dwell, *but an uncor-*
rupted Judge
An vncorrupted Iudge, *that* will award   3346 *dwells in heaven.*
Damnation for thy sinne, vnlesse regard
Of *that* vnhappy state wherin thou art,
Softning (I fear) thy vnrelenting heart,
Shew thee thy soules deformity, & in   3350
Repentaunce fountaine make thee purge thy sinne.

  Looke vpon Adrus in his furious ire ! *The limbs of*
Adrus shake
He seemes to burne like some red cole of fire ; *with anger.*
How his eyes flame ! how his limbs shake w*i*th rage !
How his voice thunders, as he ment to wage   3355
Warre against heaven ! Surely the cause is great
That makes him in this sort himselfe forget ;
It can*n*ot but be matter of much consequence,   3358 *What moves him*
so ?
That moves *the* man to this impatience ?
Faith no, you are deceivde ; *the* cause was smale,
A better man then he would put vp all,
Were *the* disgrace more hainous, w*h*ich is none   3362
But *that* his cholericke humo*u*r makes it one.
This asse (w*h*ich for *the* wagging of a straw *He'll draw his*
dagger upon
His dagger vpon any man will drawe) *any man :—*
Walking i' th' street, was iustled fro*m* *the* wall   3366 *why ? Somebody*
pushed him into
Downe almost to *the* channell ; this is all *the gutter !*
That putt*es* him in this fume ! Would you surmise, *[leaf 38]*
A man that hath the vse of reasons eyes
To guide himselfe, should for a cause soe light,   3370
Soe smale a matter, be in such a plight ?
Ready to frett himselfe to death, to sweare,
To curse, & banne, as if [he] meant to teare *And all this fury*
because he
The earth in su*n*der, only for this end,   3374 *knows not on*
whom to bend
Because he knowes not vpon whom to bend *his fury !*
The furie of his rage ! Thou irefull foole !
Vse henceforth to frequent *the* learned schoole
Of sacred vertue, w*h*ich will thee inspire   3378

With patience to moderat thine ire.

Good Mistriss Orgia, holde your hasty hand*es* !

Because your maides have not pind in your band*es*

You who lay the
stick about your
servants'
shoulders,

According to your minde, must th*e* stick flie   3382

About their shoulders straight ?   Should they replie

In your owne language to you, you were servde

According as your rage had well deservde.

But this is nothing with this furious dame,   3386

Ther's other matters th*at* deserve more blame.

and break your
husband's head,

She will not stick to breake her husband*es* head,

Revile[1] him to his face & wish him dead

In most reproachfull manner ; he, good man,   3390

Dares not replie a worde, but gett*es* him gone

Till her fit's past, & doth with patience

Endure his wives outragious insolence.

learn to rule
your passions.

Thou furious vixen, learne to rule thy passion,   3394

And vse thy husband in a better fashion,

Or I will have thy name to be enrolde

For a moste shamelesse & notorious scolde !

Manlius lives in
hope of inherit-
ing his uncle's
lands.

Manlius hath a very mean estate,   3398

Yet lives in longing hope of better fate ;

He hath an vnkle above measure rich,

And cares not much if he lay dead i' th' ditch ;

Hopes he cannot last long because hee's olde ;   3402

And then he hopes to seaze vpon his golde.

Foole, how dost know th*at* thou shalt him outlive ?

'Twere better for thee, did he something give

A bird in the
hand is worth
two in the bush ;
and he who
waits for dead
men's shoes may
go barefoot.

Now while thy wantt*es* desire reliefe ; "one thrush 3406

I' th' hand is worth more then are two i' th' bush ; "

And " he th*at* hopes to put one dead mens shoos,

It often comes to passe he barefoote goes."

Elpinas, which with seas doth traffique holde,   3410

Hath made a ship out for West Indian golde,

And all his hopes doe in this venture lie :

---

[1] *Reveale* originally.   The stroke over the second *e* is con-
tinued till it looks more like *j—Revjle.*

Should she miscarry sure *th*e man would die ;
But hope, w*hi*ch holds him like a violent fever,   3414
Flatters him still he shalbe made for ever
At her returne ; & since she first began
To cut *th*e billowes of *th*e ocean
With her swift keel, his minde, more swift then she,
Followes her in *th*e voyage, & doth see   3419
With eyes of selfe-delighting fantasie
(W*hi*ch sometime wrap him in an extasie)
Her prospe*r*ous traffique.   If *th*e day be faire   3422
He hopes *th*at homeward she doth then repaire ;
If stormes obscure *th*e brightnesse of *th*e skie,
He hopes she doth in safest harbo*u*r lie.
The time w*hi*ch slowlie seemes to passe away   3426
Vnto his longing hopes, he day by day
Tell*es* o're i*n* minutes ; not a puffe of winde
Blowes, but *th*at straight his advantageous minde
Carries it to his ship.   Sometime his thought   3430
Runnes on *th*e gold wherw*i*th his ship is fraught,
Imagining in his still working braine,
How to imploy it to his best of gaine.
Thou greedy minded slave ! whose hopes are fixd 3434
Only on wealth, w*i*th pleasure inte[r]mixt,
And ne're hop'st after heaven, how canst thou thinke
But *th*at iust Iove should in *th*e ocean sinke
All thy fond hopes, & drive thee to dispaire,   3438
Wh*i*ch ne're implorst his ayde by hearty praier ?
Returne at last, and fix thy hopes one him,
Whose only power can make thee sink or swimme.

   Alston, whose life hath been accounted evill,   3442
And therfore cal'de by many the blew devill,
S[t]ruck w*i*th remorse of his ill gotten pelfe,
Would in dispaire have made away himselfe,
One while by drowning, when *th*at would not be, 3446
He drew his knife to worke his tragedie,
Intending w*i*th *th*at fatall instrument

[leaf 38, back]
The merchant is
all anxiety about
his ship.

He daily tells
over the time for
her return in
minutes.

Sometimes he
decides what to
do with the gold
she will bring
home.

But his hopes
may all be
confounded !

Alston, in a fit of
" blue devils,"
would have com-
mitted suicide,

To cut his owne throte.   Fearfull punnishment
Of a dispairing minde ! O, who can tell   3450
The pangs *that* in a guilty conscience dwell?

but God's mercy
restrained him,

Had not *th*e gracious mercy of *th*e Lord
Restraind him from a sinne soe much abhord,   3453
W*i*th his owne hand*es* he would have stopt his breath
And w*i*th his bodie sent his soule to death.

Thrice happie mortall, w*hi*ch this grace didst finde,
Soe *that* henceforth thou bear a better minde,
And let thy actions to his glorie tende   3458

and saved him
from such an
end.

That savde thy life from such a fearfull end.
Returne thanksgiving, & desire in praier
His grace to sheild thee fro*m* forlorne dispaire.

[leaf 39]
Latro added
murder to
robbery,

Latro did act a damnèd villanie,   3462
Adding blacke murder to his robbery,
Yet 'cause 'twas closely done he might conceale it,
For, save himselfe, none living could reveale it.
But see *th*e iust revenge for this offence ;—   3466

but conscience

After *th*e deed, his guilty conscience
Torturing his soule, enforc'd him still to think
The act disclosde, & he in dangers brinke.   3469
He thought *th*e birds still in their language said it ;
He thought *th*e whistling of *th*e winde bewraide it ;
He cald to minde *that* murder was forbidden,
And though a while, it could not long be hidden.
Destract in minde, & fearfull in his place,   3474

and the devil

Having noe power to call to God for grace,
The devill doth suborne him to dispaire,
Tells him 'tis pitty he should breath this aire
W*hi*ch hath been such a villaine ; thrusts him on 3478
To worke his owne death & confusion.

made a coward
of him,

He, though he had *th*e murderous hand to spill
Anothers blood, himselfe yet durst not kill,
And was afraide of others.   What e're stirres   3482
He iudgeth to be men & officers
Come to attache him, & his sight vnstable

Takes every bush to be a constable.[1]

Thus plagud & torturde with dispaire & feare,   3486

Out must the fact, he can noe more forbeare;

For which according to the course of lawe

Deaths heavy sentence one him he doth drawe;

And being brought vnto the place of death,   3490

There in dispaire yeildes vp his latest breath.

   Thus each affection like a tyrant raignes

Over mans soule, which letteth loose the reines

Vnto selfe will, in which soe slavish state,   3494

Mans sence captivd'e, his reason subiugate,

Makes the soule clogd, a massie lump of sinne,

Which following his creation should have been

Like his Creator pure;—soules were made free,   3498

Not to be held in base captivitie

By every passion, but with reasons bitte

To checke affections from all things vnfitt.

He therfore that intends to live vpright

Let him in time curbe hedstrong appetite.   3503

      [1] See 3 Hen. VI., v. 6.

Side notes:

and he fears every bush is a constable;

till he yields himself to justice.

So every passion reigns over man's soul.

He that would live upright must curb his appetites.

[END OF THE SATIRES.]

[Certaine Poems.]

[PART II.]

[leaf 39, back]

Certaine Poems, comprising Things
Naturall, Morrall, & Theologicall,
written by R. C., Gent.

E dulci virus contractat aranea flore,
Quando ex vrtica mella leguntur ape.

Ad Lectorem.

I did not intend to place these Poems before you,

I had not thought (courteous reader) to have pre-
tended thus conspicuously in thy sight this rude &
indigested chaos of conceites (the abortive iss[u]e of
my vnfertile braine) & to have set before thee this
immature & vnpleasing fruit, collected only for my
private recreation, & not for thy publique satisfaction
& delight ; but *th*e vehement importunity & instiga-

had not my friends per- suaded me to do so.

tion of certaine friends, w*i*th whom I did com*m*unicate
my moste private studies, prevailing above mine owne
determination, enforced me (otherwise vnwilling) to
com*m*it this piece of poetry alsoe to thy curteous

They were so suddenly put to press, that I

acceptaunce & kinde censure.   It was soe sodainlie
thrust into *th*e presse, *that* I had noe competencie of

time, with *th*e bear, to lick over this whealp, & with a pray you excuse errors. more diligent p*er*vsall to correct any easily overslipped erro*u*r. Wherfore I desire thee, if thou finde any, to think it is rather a lapsus pennæ then an error[1] mentis. As for *th*e crabbed & criticall interpretation of many, *tha*t would seeme moste iudicious Catoes, & As for judicious Catos, I care but little. yet are indeed most censorious coxcombes, I waigh it litle, and lesse *th*e detracting speeches of barking Momists ; & yet let them both know *tha*t it is easier to reprove then reforme, & a good word is as soone spoken as a bad. But least I seeme to begge their favo*u*rs, or distrust mine owne fancies, I will leaue them as I found them, & returne to thee, gentle reader (because thou shalt be both *th*e protasis & catastrophe of my epistle). If thou canst with *th*e bee. sucke honie out If you, gentle reader, can suck honey from this hemlock, of this hemlock, I hope, when *th*e garden of my wit shalbe throughly watered w*i*th *th*e spring of Helicon, to I may at a future time present you with flowers. present thee w*i*th flowers. In *th*e meantime, thy present kinde acceptation of this wilbe a great animation to my subsequent endeavo*u*rs.

Farwell.

[1] erro*u*r in MS.

112

[Certaine Poems.]

Vera quid hominis forma.

[leaf 40] What makes a perfect man? My Muse declare.

External qualities do not make a perfect man. Externall qualities? Their force is much
I doe confesse; but beastes excell vs farre   3
In them; our stepdame Natures will is such,
    The lions strength mans force doth overquell;
    The hare in swiftnesse doth vs all excell.   6

The brutes excel him in senses. In sences likewise brutes doe vs exceed;
Hartes in quicke hearing, eagles in sharp sight;
Spiders in touching; apes when as they feed,   9
Have daintier palates to procure delight:
    Tender-nosd houndes, & vultures, senting prey,
    In smelling doe surpasse vs every waie.   12

In his form, man excels all beasts. Neither doth mans essentiall forme consist
In lineaments of body well contr[i]vde;
Although heerin of force I must insist   15
He doth excell all beastes that ever livde;
    Since beastes aspect is downeward as they passe,
    And man the heavens hath for his looking-glasse. 18

Wealth cannot make him perfect. What then? Doth wealth mans perfect forme compose?
Noe, though thy wealth doe Crœsus wealth exceed;
Though many miles thy land cannot enclose,   21
Though all things to thine owne desire succeed:
    Yet this (if thou the matter rightly scanne)
    Is of noe force to make the perfect man.   24

There is a soule, not generate, but infusde,

Immortall therfore, w*hi*ch conjoyntly knit

With [the] corriptible bodie, & diffusde   27

By vertue through each member, as is fit,

 Informes each part, & animates *th*e same,

 And this mans true essentiall forme doth frame.   30

De quatuor anni partibus.

Apollo to his flaming carre adrest

Taking his dayly, never ceasing course,

His fiery head in Thetis watry brest,   3

Three hundred sixty & five times doth source :

 As many times Aurora doth appear

 Ere there be made a full & per*f*ect year.   6

This year equally doth it selfe distribute

Into 4 partes, w*hi*ch we doe quarters call,

Each having his peculiar attribute   9

Of name, & severall qualitie w*i*th all :

 Spring ever plesaunt, Sum*m*er hot & dusty,

 Fruit-ripening Autumne, Winter colde & frosty.   12

Sweet smelling Spring, *that* ever chearfull season,

Clad w*i*th *th*e verdure of fresh hearbes & flowers,

Renewes *th*e year & makes it alwaies geason   15

By distillation of his fruitfull showers :

 This quarter doth (for soe it is assignde)

 Refresh *th*e sence & recreate *th*e minde.   18

No sooner doth *th*e blazing bright beamd starre,

Sol, enter Cancer *that* signe tropicall,

But Sum*m*er in his progresse doth declare   21

A hot ensuing season *that* must fall :

 Now Ceres, goddesse of all corne & tillage,

 Begins her harvest in each country village.   24

When day & night are in equalitie,

Autumn, when
Bacchus treads
the vine.

Autumne doth then beginne his course to take,

Whom aires temp*e*rate serenity   27

A pleasaunt quarter evermore doth make :

    Now Bacchus treadeth[1] downe *th*e fruitfull vine,

    And doth compose the spirit quickning wine.   30

When longest night doth make *th*e shortest day,

Frostie-facde Winter Autumne doth succeede,

Winter when
nipping cold
breeds disease.

In boysterous stormes his force he doth display,   33

Whose nipping colde doth ofte diseases breed :

    Yet man to please this quarter doth present

    Domesticke sportes & homebred merriment.   36

Planet*arum* energia.

Astronomers
have found
seven planets.

Astronomers, w*i*th their heaven searching eyes,

Seven planets in their severall orbs have found,

Whose influence, they say, descends the skies,   3

And in o*ur* mortall bodies doe abound :

    Whose force is great, or else they greatlie lye

    That calculate mans fatall destinie.   6

Saturn is mounted in the highest sphear,

Vnder w*hi*ch planet if man life receive,

The morose and
melancholy are
born under
Saturn.

He shalbe subject to dispairefull feare,   9

Dull melancholy to his minde shall cleave :

    His stupid braine, his frowning looke, shall bear

    A crabbèd nature & a life austere.   12

Next vnto lumpish Saturn, sprightlie Iove

The honoured and
liberal under
Jupiter.

Moves in his orbe.   Who vnder his aspect

Shall breathe this aire (w*hi*ch doth him mortall prove)

He alwaies shalbe held in good respect :

    Pleasing his looke shalbe, comely his feature,

    Bounteous his minde, and ever kinde his nature.   18

          [1] MS. treading.

After Ioue, Mars assumes his proper seat,   [leaf 41]
Whom poets faine to be *th*e god of warre ;
That man in battell shall his foes defeate   21
W*hi*ch vnder Mars is borne, *that* warlike starre :   Soldiers under
    He will (for of his nature hath been tride)   Mars.
    Be quicklie angrie & soone pacifide.   24

In midle of *th*e planet*tes* regiment,
Bright Sol, that heauenlie ever burning lamp,
Himselfe doth in his glorious orbe present.   27 The skilful and
                                        religious under
Who vnder him receives his native stampe,   the Sun.
    Shalbe well skild in artes, in conference wise,
    Religious in heart, in life precise.   30

After bright Sol, the beauteous queen of love
Faire Citherean Venus takes her place :
Who vnder her aspect is borne, shall prove   33 The skilful in
                                        love under
Skilfull in love ; & w*i*th a blushlesse face   Venus.
    He shall vnto his lawlesse lust allure
    Many that are of thoughts & life impure.   36

Next Venus, in his sphear is Maiaes sonne,
Ioues messenger, wing-footed Mercurie :
Who vnder his aspect his life begunne   39 The deceitful
                                        under Mercury.
Shalbe endue w*i*th craft & subtilty ;
    He wilbe (soe his state thereby may mend)
    Apt to deceive even his most trusty friend.   42

Lowest of all *th*e planets placèd is
Selfe-chaunging Luna : vnder whose aspect
If man be borne, he never shall have misse   45 Women under
                                        the Moon.
Of an inconstant heart, w*hi*ch doth detect
    A p*er*verse nature, & a peevish minde :
    Vnder this starre are borne most women kinde.   48

Every man hath his constellation   Every man has
Vnder one of these planets influence   his star.

Stars rule man.   Predominating, & *th*e calculation   51
                   O[f] his ensuing fortunes comes from hence,
                        Be he to labo*ur* borne, to art, or warres :
                        Thus starres rule man, & God doth rule *th*e starres.

De quatuor elementis.

Earthly bodies   Each sublunarie bodie is composde
are composed of
the four elements.   Of *th*e fower element*es*, w*h*ich are proposde
                     By Nature to *tha*t end, a worke t' admire
                     That aire should meet w*i*th earth, water w*i*th fire,   4
                     And in one bodie friendlie sympathize,
                     Being soe manifestlie contraries.
                     These elements apparent to *th*e eye
                     Are mixt, & not of simple puritie ;   8
[leaf 41, back]   Pure simple ones ther are, but wher they be
Ther e are simple
elements,   Passes *th*e skill of o*ur* philosophie.
                     Wheither earths purer elementall part
                     Reside w*i*thin Thessalian Tempes heart ;   12
                     Wheither Arabia Fœlix it containes,
                     Or Edens garden, or th' Elizian plaines ;
but where can   Olympus hill, or mountaine Appenine,
they be found?
                     Our Albion heer, or fertill Palestine,   16
                     I rashly in opinion dare not enter.
                     Who shall finde out earth[s] yet vnheard of center ?
Where purest   Where purest water is, declare who can,
water ?
                     Whether in midst of *th*e vast ocean,   20
In Tagus or in   Or where rich Tagus workes vp golden sand ;
Ganges ?
                     Whether in some clear rivelet on land,
                     As in *th*e spring vpon Parnassus hill,
                     Where the nine Muses dip their learned quill ; 24
                     In silver Ganges, or that fountaine rather
                     Where faire Diana w*i*th her nymphs doth bath her?
Where purest   Art thou per*h*aps *tha*t purest breathing aire,
air ?
                     Sweet Zephirus, wh*i*ch wonst to make repaire   28

To amarous Psyche, when for Cupids love,
She fearlesse lept downe from *th*e rocke above.
If thou be *that* pure aire w*i*thout all doubte,
Shew me thy dwelling, & I'le seeke thee out,   32
And having found thee, then my next desire

Having found air, fire must next be sought.

Shalbe for purest elementall fire ;
Be it w*i*thin the moones concavity
Or above all the heavens convexity,   36
Doe it w*i*thin *that* fornace closely lurke,
Where Vulcan & his Cyclopes doe worke,
Or be it *that* celestiall fire above
Wh*i*ch wise Prometheus stole away from Iove.   40
    But I leave these pure elements alone,

Each body takes its existence from the elements.

To speake of these amongst vs better knowne.
This quadruplicity, these elements,
From whom each body takes his existence,   44
Have qualities calde elementarie,
Knowne by *th*e names of first & secundarie.
Earth is *th*e driest in his first degree,
Then coldnesse is his second quality.   48

And each has its particular quality,

Coldest is water in first quality,
Then moysture is his second propertie.
Moistenesse in aire hould*es* principality,
And heat is secundarie quality.   52
Fire doth predominate in calidity.
And then *th*e next degree is siccity.
Fire hot & dry, aire moyst & hot we call,

[leaf 42]
as hot and dry, dry and cold.

Seas colde & moist, earth dry & colde w*i*th all.   56
These elements, although they doe agree
In *th*e composure of mortalitie,
Yet in each body one it selfe doth vaunt,
And is above *th*e rest predominant.   60
In man complexions plainly doe dilate
What element is moste predominate.
In cholerick bodies, fire doth govern moste ;

In choleric bodies is most fire;

In sanguine, aire doth chiefly rule *th*e rost ;   64

in phlegmatic most water.

In flegmatick, hath water greatest sway,
Dull melancholy seemes to be of clay.
      It is recorded by some antiquaries,
Nor doe I see *th*at it from truth much varies,   68
That each before recited element
Gives to a bruit his onlie nutriment.
I speake not this of those we purest call,
For they, I know, cannot sustaine at all.   72

The mole lives in the earth, the herring in the sea.

The earth vnto *th*e mole her essence gives,
The herring only in *th*e water lives;

The chameleon lives in air, the salamander in fire.

Aire only *th*e camelion doth suffice,
And salamander from *th*e fire dies.   76
To these 4 brutes, living in this estate,
Fowre kindes of men we may assimilate.
Like to *th*e mole *th*e worldly minded man
Workes in *th*e earth, as if he headlong ran   80
Into her bowels; for some paltry gaine,

Man searches the earth for gold.

He digs, & delves, & toiels himselfe w*i*th paine.
His avaritious minde is wholy bent
Vpon *th*e purchase of this element;   84
Blind like *th*e mole in 's intellectuall eye
That should direct him to felicity.
The second kinde from water doth alone
Produce his lifes best sustentation,   88

Pirates live by sea-robbery;

And such are they w*hi*ch vse damnd piracie,
And live vpon *th*e sea by robberie,
These w*i*th *th*e herring make *th*e sea their friend
Till some of them at Wopping take their end.   92
Ambitious men doe one *th*e ayer feed;
Like *th*e camelion they are pleasde indeed

ambitious men on praise.

W*i*th meer aeriall praise; good word*es* (I think)
Fattens them better then their meat & drinke.   96
Some of this kinde build castles in *th*e aire,
Thinking themselues instald in hono*u*rs chaire
In their selfe pleasing mindes, when such promotion
Is as farre from them as they from devotion.   100

But they think soe ; & he should doe them wrong   [leaf 42, back]
That puts them by this their conceit soe strong.
Lust is *th*e fire that doth maintaine the life   Lust consumes
                                                       the life of the
Of the venereous man (but sets at strife   104   venerious.
The soule & body).   Did I say maintaine ?
I should haue saide consume, for soe 'tis plaine.
Yet can he live noe more *wi*thout desire,
Then can the salamandra *wi*thout fire.   108

De quatuor virtutibus cardinalibus.

What may the reason be that we doe call   Are these virtues
                                               called cardinal
Our fower excellent vertues cardinall ?   because Cardinals
                                               use them ?
Is it because Romes Cardinals moste vse them,
And other men doe more then they refuse them ?   4
No truely, for each severall vertue trie,
And you shall finde that they one few relie.
For wisedome first, what wisdome can ther be
In them, who, given supe*r*stitiouslie,   8
For the true God doe images adore,
And in necessity their healpe implore ?
Yet why should I their wisdome thus defie,
Whose crafty witt and damnèd pollicie   12   Their policy is to
                                                  enrich them-
Is to enrich themselves, though their soules have   selves.
Perdition, whom true wisdome seekes to save ?
For iustice next, doth iustice *wi*th them live
Who absolution to each sinne doe give   16
For a corrupting bribe ?   The sonne may kill   They do not
                                                     excel in justice,
His aged parent*es* ; man the blood may spill
Of his deepe foe & 'scape ; for a large fee
Wrong shall take place, & right pe*r*verted be.   20
If these thing*es* we may iustice iustly call,
Iustice is vsde by every Cardinall.
      But it may be in temperance they excell,   perhaps they do
                                                      in temperance,
And therin doe all only bear the bell.   24

if to be Epicures
is to be temper-
ate ;

If to be Epicures, and live at ease,
Swallowing vp pleasures when & how they please,
We doe account a temperat sober life,
Then these are they we graunt withouten strife.   28

and chastity, if
the keeping of
concubines is
chastity.

Their chastety is soe immaculate
That they doe alwaies live in virgin state,
Marriage they nill admitt by any meanes,
Yet doe allowe of concubins & queanes.   32

Lastly to speake of manlie fortitude,
Therin their calling shews them to be rude ;

[leaf 43]

Full ill (we know, & every man may see)
A steely helme, & Cardnals cap agree ;   36
As for their fortitude of minde, 'tis small,

They are proud
in power.

Proud in their height, dejected in their fall.
I, but their power 's great great; in oppression,

They tread down
virtue.

Treding downe vertue, raising vp transgression.   40
These are their cardinall vertues of cheife fame,
Which we may trulie cardnall vices name.
But now at last a reason shew I shall,
Why we these vertues doe name cardinall :   44

These virtues are
called cardinal
because they
embrace all the
rest.

Cardinall iustly may derived be
From cardo, which a hinge doth signifie ;
Soe these 4 vertues, all the rest enfolde,
Even as the hinges doe the dore vpholde.   48

Scilicet vt fulvum spectatur in ignibus aurum,
Tempore sic duro est inspicienda fides.

A rich young
man to prove his
friends

A certaine man which great possessions had,
Had likewise store of friendes ; as who 's so mad
To think that friendship doth not wealth pursue,
Though for the moste part fainèd & vntrue ?   4
This man of wealth (though seld it soe be found
In a young man) in iudgement did abound,

And him bethought a way his friend*es* to trie,
How they would serve him in extremity.   8
He kills a calfe & ties him in a sacke,   killed a calf, and
Whom vp he takes & carries one his backe ;   put it into a sack.
And then straightwaies vnto his friend*es* he goes,
And in this manner doth his minde disclose.   12
" My friend*es*," quoth he, " yo*ur* loves I now must trie,   He told his
                                                                 friends he had
For friend*es* are truly prov'de in misery ;   killed a man,
Vnlesse yo*ur* succo*ur*s doe my life defend,
I am in danger of a shamefull end.   16
Knowe, in my rage I have slaine a man this day,
And knowe not where his body to conveigh
And hide it from the searchers inquisition,   and wished them
                                                                 to hide the body.
My house being subject to no mean suspition.   20
Healp me, good S*i*rs, in my distressèd state,
Since thus to you my griefs I doe dilate."
" Depart," quoth they, " from vs, you are a stranger !
We mean not for yo*ur* love to bring in danger   24
Our good*es* & lives ; should we a murder hide
'Twould even by sencelesse creatures be descride.
Yo*ur* friendship thus distainde w*i*th innocent blood   They would have
                                                                 nothing to do
We doe disclaime.   While yo*ur* estate was good,   28 with him in his
And yo*ur* selfe free from danger of the lawe,   trouble.
The fatnesse of yo*ur* purse had power to drawe
Our wealth-p*ur*suing loves ; but you must knowe,   [leaf 43, back]
Our friendships w*i*th your fortunes ebbe or flowe."   32
   Thus severally he all his friend*es* did trie,
And had from them this or the like replie ;
At last he cals to minde a man of fashion,
W*i*th whom his father held much conversation   36
Whilome he livde, & oft had heard him praise   Then he tried his
His friendship, prov'de in divers hard assaies.   "father's friend,"
To this as to the rest the young man hies,
And in like manner his fainde griefe discries ;   40
He for his fathers sake, wh*i*ch was his friend,
Sweares he will doe his best his life to shend.

The body then he takes, & meanes to hide ;
Vowes secrecie, what euer doe betide.   44

who at once promised to help him.
"And if," quoth he, " you 'le on my faith relie,
I 'le keep you safe from the world searching eye,
Vntill this gust of danger be o're blowne,
Which threatens death, if that the fact be knowne."
The man reioycing in his friends firme love,   49
Sayes how he did it but his faith to prove,
"And now," quoth he, " by giving of false fire,

Having found a friend, he told him the trick.
I have found out the thing I doe desire,   52
A faithfull friend, vpon whose trust I may
My life, my landes, & all my substance lay."

A compact of never-dying friendship was made between the two.
Then vp & tels him all the project plaine,
How the dead body was a calfe yslaine.   56
The other, wondring at his pollicie,
Resolvèd straight a knot with him to tie
Of never-dying friendship to their end,
Thus each to other was a perfect friend.   60
Mean while the other from him he removde,
Whose fainèd love sufficientlie was prov'de.

Somnium.

About the dead time of the silent night,
Disquiet thought debarring sounder sleepe,

I had a dream about the choice of a wife.
A dreame I had that did me much delight,   3
Wherof my minde doth yet impression keepe,
 Because it chiefly touchèd single life,
 In good or bad election of a wife.   6

Three virgins introduced themselves to my notice.
Methought 3 virgins did appear vnto me,
In their attyer all full seemly clad,
Which saide they came on purpose for to wooe me,   9
To know to which I moste affection had :
 " But first (said they) before this thing thou shew
 Thou each of vs shalt severally knowe."   12

Then first gan say *th*e fairest of the three,   [leaf 44]
" I Beawty am ; if me thou list to take,   Beauty was poor
Thy fancy shall receiue content in me,   15   and faithful.
And I will never thy true love forsake :
    But I am poore, & have no meanes at all
    Reliefe to give, if want should thee befall."   18

The second then begann, " I Wealth am hight ;   Wealth promised
If me thou chuse thou never shalt have lacke ;   plenty,
Aboundance thee to give is in my might,   21
To fill thy belly, or to clothe thy backe :
    Only I am (as thou maist well beholde)   but she was ugly
    Deformde, hard-favo*u*rd, crabbed, wringkled, olde."   and deformed.

Then quoth the third & last, " My name is Witt ;
If me thou chuse to give thy minde content,
I can discourse, w*i*th wordes moste apt & fitt,   27   Wit was pleasing,
Of nature, heaven, & every element :   but wanton.
    But this be sure, a wanton I will prove,
    And not be tyed vnto on[e] only love."   30

" And now," quoth they, " thine answeare we request,
For we of purpose come the same to knowe ;
Tell whether of vs thou canst fancy best."—   33
And heer me thought they left to speake ; when loe !   I awoke before I
    I framèd me an answear them to make,   made up my
    But forc'd my selfe, & thus I did awake.   36   mind.

Brevis Allegoria.

Out from the depth[1] of Griefes infernall cave   Melancholy and
Sad Melancholie rose w*i*th weeping eyes ;   Discontent
Company had she none, ne would she have,   proceed from
But ne're pleasd Discontent, w*i*th whom she hies   4   Grief.
    W*i*th as swift feet as Griefe to her had lent,
    Vnto *th*e surging billowes of Lament,
To be washt[2] o're into *th*e desert Languishment.   7

    [1] MS. depht.   [2] MS. waste.

Despair is their
Ferryman over
Lament.

The ferriman, or boatswaine of *th*e lake,
Incredulous, all doubting, hight Dispaire,
Would none conduct *tha*t did not aye forsake
To draw *th*e breath of *tha*t halfe killing ayre   11
   Issuing from Hope, his still profess*è*d foe,
   W*hi*ch makes men constant in abiding woe,
Expecting still at length their trouble to forgoe.   14

The boat was a
fearful hulk,

The boat wherin this Ferriman of hell
Dischargde his office, was a fearfull hulke
Framd' of a guilty conscience (worst of ill) ;   17
The sailes com'posde of sinne, whose monstrous bulke
   Swelling w*i*th sighs, w*hi*ch were *th*e gales of winde
   Made *th*e barke seeme to flie ; a fearfull minde   20
Was the maine-mast, & doubt for anchor was assignde.

[leaf 44, back]

in which
passengers are
carried

Thus rigd & trimd, it floteth vp & downe,
To ferry passengers vnto *th*e shore
Of *tha*t inhospitable desert, where no towne,
Ne humane wight inhabited of yore ;   25
   Yet gins it now w*i*th people to abound,
   W*hi*ch daylie passe o're to *tha*t hatefull ground,
Although they know it will at length them quite con-
   found.   28

to the shores
of death.

For whie, w*i*thin that desert lyes a cave,
Where horrid Murder, Death[s] sterne sire, doth dwell ;
Him that Dispaire doth hither bring, this slave
Doth straight encounter, leads him to his cell,   32
   Presenting him w*i*th cordes to stop his breath,
   Poyson to kill him, or else doth vnsheath
Swordes, ponyards, knives, all instruments of curs*è*d
   death.   35

Hope met
Melancholy on
her way and
cheered her up

As Melancholie posted to the shore,
To be conducted to this balefull place,
Hope met w*i*th her & never gave her o're,
Till she had staide her rash vnsteady pace.   39

And with wise wordes, diverting her intent   with wise words.
From seeking out the desert Languishment,
At last she brought her to the house of Merriment.   42

De Fortuna.

Well have the poetes fainde the queen of chance,   The poets
Dame Fortune, blinde, & fixd vpon a wheele,   represent
                                       Fortune
The swiftnesse of whose motion may entrance   3 as blind and
                                       fixed on a wheel.
A dull spectatours eye ; at whose feet kneele
   Great potentates, & kinges that sue for grace,
   Whom as she list she spurns or doth embrace.   6

Sometimes she rayseth to emperiall throne   Sometimes she
An abject peasant & base cuntry swaine,   raises a beggar to
Who from the ycie to the torrid zone   9   the throne.
Boundeth the frontiers of monarchall raigne :
   Then downe she thrustes from their supernall seat
   Princes & kings, & makes them begg their meat.   12

O could she see, she would not be soe mad   Could she see she
(As now she is) in honour to advaunce   would not
(Vertue despisde, & art but meanlie clad)   15 promote the
                                       vicious.
Vnmatchèd vice, & worthlesse ignoraunce :
   But blinde she is, & seeth no mans fall ;
   Deafe, & can harken vnto no mans call.   18

Homo Arbor.

Like as a tree from forth the earth doth spring,   As a tree springs
So from the earth doth man his essence take ;[1]   from earth, so
                                       man takes his
The tree shootes forth & doth faire blossoms bring,   3 essence from it.
So man, till youth his mansion doth forsake :
   The tree growing crooked, if you 'l have it mended,
   Whilst that it is a twigg it must be bended.   6

[1] *Secundum corpus* written at the end of this line in the MS.

[leaf 45] Right soe it fares with man, whose infant age

"Just as the twig is bent the tree's inclined." Is apt of any forme to take impression,

Following advice & reason or else rage,   9

According as his youths frame takes succession :

If green he be not bended, but let grow,

When he is olde hee'l breake before hee'l bowe.   12

In spring trees put forth leaves; When lusty Ver approcheth, he doth bring

Fresh vigour to the tree & liveries gay ;

so man, and both die for want of nourishment. Soe man doth reassume new health i' th' spring ;   15

The tree when moysture failes will fade away :

And man will quickly perish like a plant,

If he that *humidum radicale* want.   18

The tree falls at last, and as it falls so it lies. Looke how at length the tree to ground doth fall,

Though long it stand fast fixèd in the earth ;

Soe man, thoug[h] long he live, yet die he shall ;   21

No helpe there is in honour, wealth, or birth :

The tree what way it falls, that way doth lye ;

Even so shall man be iudgde as he doth die.   24

Mundus Theatrum.

The world is by some compared to a theatre, the gods being spectators, men the players. The world by some, & that not much amisse,

Vnto a Theater comparèd is,

Vpon which stage the goddes spectatours sitt,

And mortals act their partes as best doth fitt.   4

One acts a king, another a poore swaine ;

One idely lives, another taketh paine ;

One, like Orestes, becomes mad with rage,

Another seeks his furie to asswage.   8

And as i' th' play that man which acts the king,

(Though many he to his obeisaunce bring)

In the end he who plays king and he who acts I' th' end is of no more account then he,

Which represents the beggers misery,   12

So is't i' th' world, when every man by death
Has his last exit, which doth stop his breath.
The king for all his crowne shall reape noe grace,
Nor beggers meannesse shall his cause embase. 16
    But to my thinking, in this saide compare,
Though many iump, yet some things differing are.
In our stage-plaies ther 's but one foole at most
And sometimes none at all ; we cannot boast 20
So much, farre otherwise with vs it is ;
We act the same part all, not one doth misse.
    They shew awhile in iest their foppery,
    We still in seriousnesse our foolery. 24

Sidenote lines 1–2: the beggar are alike

Sidenote lines 19–20: In plays there 's only one fool, in the world many.

Armat spina rosas.

Hard is it for the patient which is ill,
Fulsome or bitter potions to disgest,
Yet must he swallow many a bitter pill, 3
E're he regaine his former health & rest :
    To keep the body safe is mans desire,
    Though it be done through water, sword, & fire. 6

Sidenote: Physic is bitter, but man must keep himself in health.

Sidenote: [leaf 45, back]

The hardy soldier, with death-threatning sword,
To kill his hostile enemy procures,
In hope the conquest will rich spoiles afford, 9
He mortall strokes & bloody woundes endures :
    Victorious tryumph ther doth never grow,
    But by the adverse parties overthrowe. 12

Sidenote: The soldier endures wounds, hoping for conquest.

The silly bee his hony doth defend,
And from his hive doth chase the drone away ;
Yea oftentimes with man it doth contend 15
And 'gainst him doth his threatning sting display :
    Loth is it his mellifluous meat forgoe,
    Which with such paine it gathers too & froe. 18

Sidenote: The bee protects its honey with its sting.

The odoriferous & fragrant rose,
Which in the spring tide shewes his blushing hiewe,
The rose is fenced about with thorns. For fence it selfe with prick*es* doth round enclose,   21
Which make the gatherer oftentimes to rue,
 And wish, with his prickt fingers making mone,
 That he had let *th*e verdant rose alone.   24

T[h]e amorous lover, ere he can enioy
The lover undergoes many hardships. His wishèd end, doth many paines endure ;
Sometime his love disdainfull is & coy,   27
And will not stoop vnto his gentle lure ;
 Sometime he feares she will vnconstant prove,
 And not reward him faithfull love for love.   30

Straight is *th*e passage vertue to attaine,
And steep the hill that vnto hono*ur* leads ;
Things valuable are difficult of attainment. Art is not had w*i*thout industrious paine,   33
Nor wealth possest by praying vpon beads :
 Things of great prise are not atchiev'de with ease,
 But once attaind, they doe for ever please.   36

Comparatio mortis & Hyenæ.

The hyena has the shape of several beasts. A monstrous beast ther is Hyena namde,
Whose shape of sundry formes composèd is ;
Like to a wolfe her visage is iframde,   3
A vipers swelling neck she hath, I wis ;
 An elepha[n]ts huge backe, voice like a man,
 And Proteous-like, transforme her selfe she can.   6

Death is like it in many respects. Death like this monster is in each respect :
First like a wolfe that ravenous is of prey,
Whose very looke his rapine doth detect,   9
Ne spareth he ought commeth in his way ;
 So death is cruell, suffering none escape ;
 Olde, young, rich, poore, of all he makes his rape.   12

Next as a viper swelleth on *the* ground,
And glideth to & fro to many a place,
Yet wher he was no print there can be found,   15
So nimble is he & so quick of pace ;
 Soe death is heer & yonder in one stound,   *Death is subtle as*
 And kills & sleas, yet no man sees him wound.   18   *a viper :*

The elephant in strength to him doth yeild,   *strong like*
Though he 'mongst beast*es* the strongest be accounted,   *the elephant ;*
And castles carries on his back in field,   21
Where fighting men, as on a tower mounted,
 Safegard themselves & doe their foes annoy ;
 But death whole townes & countries doth destroy.   24

A man he is in craft & pollicy,
Lurking full closely to devo*ur* his prey ;
So death is full of craft & subtilty,   27   *crafty as man,*
And vnawares doth many take away ;
 As w*i*th sweet sleep he closeth oft the sight,
 Yet shutt*es* the eyes in an eternall night.   30

Lastly as Proteus into sundry shapes   *and can trans-*
(When as him list himselfe transforme) could change,   *form himself*
      like Protæus.
Or male or female he could be *per*haps   33
Nor male nor female ; soe doth death estrange
 Himselfe into each sexe when as him will,
 That is, both male & female he can kill.   36

Vesper exornat diem.

What proffits it the well built ship to ride   *What good is it*
Vpon the surging billowes of the maine,   *for a ship to*
      have a prosperous
Drivne w*i*th a pleasant gale & a calme tide,   3   *voyage, if it is*
If, ere it iornies end it doth attaine,   *wrecked in the*
      end ?
 By boysterous stormes, wh*i*ch cannot be w*i*thstood,
 Sea wrackt it p*er*ish in the raging floud ?   6

The learned artist*es* much admired skill

The old wife's medicine cannot cure grief. In life-preserving phisicke is then tride,

When some strange cure is wrought; not every pill   9

Or olde wifes medecine to the sick applide

> Can griefe recure ; 'tis arts all knowing lore
>
> Must man vnto his wonted health restore.   12

He who has fought and conquered may claim the crown. He that w*i*th trenchaunt blade in bloody fight,

Singlie opposde, & clad in equal armes,

Hath slaine his foe, or forcd him vnto flight,   15

Vsing noe witch-craft, sorcery, nor charmes,

> May worthely crowne his victorious brow
>
> W*i*th oken leaves of Ioues tryumphant bow.   18

[leaf 46, back] Who truely can affirme the day will prove

Pleasant & faire, e're even doth appeare,

The result praises or dispraises every man's work. When sodeinly[1] o'recast, the heauens remove   21

Oft times their beawty w*hi*ch our sight doth chear ;

> *Suçcesse by the event is knowne, the end
>
> Doth every action praise, or discom*m*end.[2]   24

Virtus persequenda.

He who pursues virtue in youth shall be famous in age. He that in youth doth vertues path way tread,

When age vpon his wrinkled front shall sitt,

A crowne of honour shall enguirt his head,   3

And though he dye, his praise shall never flitt :

> With her shrill trumpet never dying Fame,
>
> Vnto the world shall still resound his name.   6

He that despises virtue shall be forgotten, But he that vertue in his youth disdaines,

And like a lozell run*n*eth out his race,

---

[1] I cannot tell whether this was intended to be *sodeinly* or *sodainly*. The MS looks more like *sodæinly*.

[2] *——Careat successibus opto
     Quisquis ab eventu facta notanda putat.*
Written in the margin of the MS, with the asterisk as above. Ovid. Epp. 2. 86.

Shame & not honour in his age attaines,   9
And after death on earth shall have noe place :
  Lethe shall drowne his ill deserving name,   *and drowned by Lethe.*
  But vertuous acts are still enrolde by Fame.   12

Cur Venus orta mari.

The poet*es* faine (for soe I know I read)   *Venus, they say, was born of the sea-foam.*
That Venus of the seas white foame was bred,
And therfore Aphrodite doe her call,
W*h*ich name doth signifie as much to all   4
That know the word ; but wherfore she should be
Deriv*è*d from the froath of Neptunes sea
I know noe reason, since, as I doe gather,
Neptune her vnckle was & not her father ;   8
Vnlesse that we, against true logicks lawes,
From the effect produce th' efficient cause ;
And that too by comparison must be   *Perhaps so: we all know how*
As thus :—we all know that the foaming sea   12   *bitter her followers find her.*
Is salt & bitter to o*u*r tasting sence ;
So lustfull Venus, w*h*ich is saide from thence
To issue forth, proves salt & bitter still,
To them that follow her disordered will.   16

Medio tutissimus ibis.

Climenes brat, aspiring Pha*ë*ton,   *When Phaeton drove the chariot of the Sun*
Dryving the fierie horses of the sunne
Out of the midle way, vp to the seat
Of Iupiter, & scorching w*i*th the heat   4   *Jupiter sent him headlong into the sea.*
Of his bright flaming charriot all the godd*es*,
Was by incens*è*d Iove whipt downe w*i*th rodd*es*
Of thundering lightning to the raging wave   *[leaf 47]*
O' the vast ocean, his vntimely grave.   8

Icarus, soaring too high, fell into the sea.

Fond Icarus, proud of his waxen wings
Soaring to high, is drenchèd in the maine,
When Dædalus his plumèd bodie brings
Safe to the shore.   Ambition is a traine   12
That life entraps ; a golden mean the way
To live securely ; for we often see
Men of most honor soonest doe decay,
When meaner men live in tranquillity.   16

If you would not fall, don't climb.

Wilt thow be safe ? strive not to climbe at all ;
Low shrubs stand fast, when statelier okes doe fall.

Scribimus indocti docti*que* epigra*m*mata passim.[1]

Jonson, they say, has turned Epigrammatist. I don't believe it.

Iohnson they say 's turnd Epigra*m*matist,
Soe think not I, believe it they that list.
Peruse his booke, thou shalt not find a dram
Of witt befitting a true Epigram.   ·   4
Perhaps some scraps of play-bookes thou maist see,
Collected heer & there confusedlie,
W*h*ich piece his broken stuffe ; if thou but note,
Iust like soe many patches on a cote.   8

He has put Cato at the beginning of his book!

And yet his intret Cato sta[n]ds before,
Even at *th*e portall of his pamphlets dore ;
As who should say, this booke is fit for none
But Catoes, learned men, to looke vpon :   12
Or else, let Cato censure if he will,
My booke deserves the best of iudgement still.[2]
When every gull may see his booke 's vntwitten,

The epigrams are as bad as any written.

And Epigrams as bad as e're were written.   16
Iohnson, this worke thy other doth distaine,
And makes the world imagine that thy vein

---

[1] Scribimus indocti doctique poëmata passim.
                                    Hor. Ep. ii. 1, 117.
[2] *skill* in MS.—? iudgement[s] skill.

Is not true bred but of some bastard race.
Then write no more, or write w*i*th better grace ; 20
Turne thee to plaies, & therin write thy fill ;
Leave Epigrams to artists of more skill. 22

He had better confine himself to plays and leave Epigrams to better men.

In Madama*m* quandam.

A country lasse of silly parents bred,
In London was for service entertainde,
And being of a wealthy master sped 3
She w*i*th her luring lookes so farre him trainde,
    That he embr*a*c'd her in a marriage bed,
    But first she pawnd to him her maydenhead. 6

A country lass induced her rich master to marry her.

What plotte*s* she had, what tricks she then did vse,
To bring her matter to soe good effect,
I list not now repeat ; lest for the stewes 9
New stratagems I plainlie doe detect :
    But such they were, that from a scullians life
    Made her a wealthy marcheante*s* second wife. 12

[leaf 47, back] Her contrivances to bring this about need not be named.

Then gan she trip it proudlie one the toe,
And mince it finely vpon London stree*tes*.
She lady-like in her attire did goe, 15
Bought w*i*th the purchase of vnlawfull sheets ;
    At last, her of her husband death bereft,
    Who dying, her a wealthy widow left. 18

Then she tripped it finely till he died.

Ambition now began to swell her minde,
All her desire was to be ladifide ;
And w*i*th a knight at len[g]th she was combinde, 21
W*hi*ch made her think herselfe halfe deifide :
    But well she might, in Edens plot she lies,
    And all men know that place is paradise. 24

Afterwards she was married to a knight.

Long liv'de she not in Edens fruitfull soile,
For her aspiring minde straight drave her thence ;

But pride ruined her.

That serpent pride did her soe far beguile,   27
Eden she banisht was for her offence :
   Iudge, was not woman very much vnwise
   That thus by pride hath twice lost paradise ?   30

· In Neandrem.[1]

Neander, appointed to dispute before the king,

Neander, held a great cevillian
(Let me not say a Machiavillian)
Appointed to dispute before the king,

could not say a word,

Struck mute with fear, could not say anything   4
Save 'twas ill luck ; for if he had done well,
As we expected he would bear the bell
From the whole Academie for the test,
'Tis certaine he had been a knight a[t] lest,   8

so he lost the reward he expected.

And made his wife (what she hath lookt for long)
A Madame.   Fortune, thou hast done her wrong
To hinder his once dubbing of his wife,
Which hath dubde him soe often in her life.   12

In Asinium.

Asinius what I speake straight overhears ;

Asses have long ears.

Will you know why ?   Asses have longest eares.

In Balbutia*m*.[2]

[leaf 48]

Balbutia has induced a gentleman to leave his wife and family for her,

Balbutia, which hath all the tricks of art
That doe belong vnto a whorish part,
Wholly bewitchd a gentleman to leave
His wife & children vnto her to cleave   4

---

[1] This and the next poem but one have been so thoroughly ·
obliterated by means of a thick pen that at first I was tempted
to omit them. I have been at some pains to read them, but
I am by no means sure that my readings are absolutely correct.

[2] I cannot ascertain whether this was Bacbutia or Balbutia.
I am more inclined to think the former.

Even to his end, &, though God did him blesse

With a faire issue, clean to dispossesse

His children of his goode*s* & give her all

By his last dying testimoniall.   8

But how dost thrive w*i*th her? Exceeding well;

She is the likelyst still to goe to hell.

But heer she doth not w*i*thout crosses goe,

Those in her children, sonnes & daughters too. 12

Her eldest sonne is hangd or drownd i' th' seas,

Her other is as good in forwardnesse.

Her eldest daughter's married to her griefe,

Whose husband lives a prisoner & a theefe. 16

Her other daughters would fain married be,

But moste that knowe doe hate this progenie.

    Thus she w*hi*ch made mothers fare *th*e worse

    In her owne seed hath this deservèd curse. 20

Margin notes: and give her his property. / How does she prosper? / Her eldest son is hanged or drowned. / Her eldest daughter is married to a thief.

In adulantes Aulicos.

Base sycophante*s*, crumbe-catching parasites,

Obsequious slaves, w*hi*ch bend at every nod;

Insatiate harpies, gormandizing kites, 3

Epicures, at[h]eists, w*hi*ch adore no God

    But yo*u*r owne bellies & yo*u*r private gaine,

    Got by yo*u*r oily tongues bewitching traine! 6

O how my Muse, armde w*i*th Rhamnusiaes whip,

Desires to scourge yo*u*r hell[1]-bred villanie,

And w*i*th Astræas sharp edgd sword t' vnrip 9

The hatefull cloke of yo*u*r deformity;

    Whose naked view soe odious would appear,

    That we should hate what now is held full deare. 12

Yo*u*r sly deceits dissimulation hides,

Yo*u*r false intent faire wordes obnubilate;

Margin notes: Sycophants, / harpies, kites, / epicures, / how my Muse desires to scourge you! / Your deceits hide dissimulation,

        [1] *lell* in MS.

as grass hides serpents.

So 'mongst the greenest grasse the serpent glides,   15
And freshest flowers foule toad*es* coinquinate :
 All is not golde that hath a glistering hiew,
 But what the touchstone tries & findeth true.   18

You cause dissensions between friends.

Dissentions, & twixt friends vnfriendly jarres,
Your base tale-carr[y]ing tongues doe sett abroch,
Intestine broyles, cyvill vncivill warres,   21

[leaf 48, back]

W*hi*ch end in death or infamous reproch,
 Are causd' by yo*ur* insinuating wordes,
 Whose poysnous breath wounds deeper then keen
  sword*es*.   24

Leave the Court, and no longer flatter greatness.

Avaunt, ye fauning curres, & leave *th*e Court !
Flatter not greatnesse w*ith* yo*ur* scurrill praise.
Dare flies approach where eagles doe resort ?   27
And shall the cuckoe in [a] cove[r]t[1] chaunt his laies ?
 For ye, like cuckoes, all one note doe sing,
 And like to flies doe buzze about o*ur* king.   30

The king scorns the whole of you.

But he, the princely Eagle, scornes such flies,
Such butter-flies, such gnat*es*, whose hum*m*ing sound
Relisheth not his eare ; nor doe his eyes   33
Affect yo*ur* gaudy outside, w*hi*ch abound
 More in queint speach & gorgeous attire,
 Then in yo*ur* loves, w*hi*ch ought to be entyre.   36

Ye Aristippian zanies, Albions ill,

Leave off your flattery.

Leave off at last yo*ur* poysning honnied speach ;
Let not your sugred word*es* be traines to kill,   39
Iust like *th*e foxe when he to geese doth preach :
 And ye rich men, w*hi*ch selfe-conceit doe love,
 Be not such geese, foxe-flattering praise to prove.   42

And you rich men, remember Æsop's crow

So Aesops crow whom crafty rainard spide
W*i*th prey in bill, was earst by him deceivde ;

     [1] ? For *Court*.

" O thou faire bird " (a lowd lie !) then he cride,   45
" Why singst thou not, whose musick hath bereavd
  The nightingale of that respect she held,
  Since thy sweet voice a sweeter note doth yield ? " 48

which was deceived by the crafty fox

The silly crow, bewitchd with flattering praise,
Addrest herselfe to give the foxe a song,
When opening wide her bill to chaunt her laies,   51
Downe fell the prey she held ! The foxe ere long
  It quite devoured had, gan her deride ;
  Then, all too late, his cunning she espide.   54

and cheated out of her prey.

Such crowes are they whom flatterers beguile ;
Such foxes they which flatter, faune, & cog :
Brittans, let them no more sucke vp your oyle ;   57
Be Aesops crow noe more, but Aesops dog.
  Chace hence these foxes, which at your mercy stand,
  For our then happy made Eutopian land.   60

Men beguiled by flatterers are just like this crow.

Somnium.

About that time when as the chearfull spring
Bedeckes the earth with her sweet smelling flowers,
When pretty birds with their sweet caroling,   3
Record their ditties in Silvanus bowers,
  I fortunde, envited by the aire,
  Vnto a pleasant grove to make repaire.   6

In the spring I wandered into a grove,

Quite through the thicket ran a pleasant spring,
Whose gentle gliding a sweet murmure made ;
The place (sufficient to content a king)   9
Allurde me to repose vnder the shade
  Of a broad beech, the aptnesse of which seat
  Preservde me from the sunnes annoying heat.   12

[leaf 49]

and sat down under a broad beech,

Not many minutes did I there repose,
Ere gentle Morpheus, powerfull god of sleep,

where I soon
fell asleep,

With his compelling charmes mine eyes did close. 15
Such harmony the chirping birdes did keep
    Coniointly with the sweetly warbling streame,
    That my long slumber did begett this dreame : 18

and dreamed an
amazing dream.

Me thought it was about the dead of night,
What time there was presented to my view
A spectacle that did me much affright,   21
And all my sences in amazement drew ;
    Till manly courage, putting fear to flight,
    Made me expect the issue of the sight.   24

The fearfull obiect of my wandring eye,

A woman
appeared to me in
costly robes and
crowned.

In shew appeard to be a womans shape ;
Her looke was heavy, & did well descrie   27
She had been subiect to noe mean mishappe :
    Her robes were costly, crownèd was her head,
    Which did foretell she was not basely bred. 30

In one hand a
sword, in the
other she held a
torch.

One of her handes a bloody sword did graspe,
Wherwith had been transfixd her tender heart ;
The other hand a burning torch did claspe,   33
By light wherof I might descrie each part
    Of her well featured body, whose sad plight
    Drew forth salt teares from my relenting sight. 36

I would have
questioned her,
but was too
frightened.

I would have questiond whence, or who, she was,
But admiration such amasement bred,
That not one word from forth my lips could passe, 39
My voice had lost his office & was dead,—
    Buried in silence lay ; when loe, ere long
    The apparition thus let lose her tongue :—   42

"Young man " (quoth she) "thy spirites recollect ;
Be not amazde mine vncouth shape to see ;

She spoke and
commanded me
to listen.

Such peevish fear doth shew a minde deiect,   45
Or guilty conscience, which are farre from thee :
    Give ear vnto me, & I will relate
    A true sad story of my passèd fate.   48

"I am by birth of most divine discent;
For I am daughter to immortall Iove,
From whom into the world I first was sent   51
As witnesse of his reconcilèd love
    With mortall man; for which effect I came
    From heaven, & True Religion is my name.   54

    She said she was the daughter of Jove, True Religion by name.

"First went I to the vnbeleeving Iewes;
But there I could smale entertainment finde:
The greater part did vtterlie refuse   57
To lodge me in their heartes, & wilfull blinde
    Did cast me from them; though alone by me
    Man can attaine to true felicity.   60

    [leaf 49, back] She went first to the Jews, who refused her.

"By them reiected thus, I did intend
Vnto the Gentiles next to bend my course,
To see if they would greater favour lend: 63
With these I had indeed somewhile great force,
    And purchasde a large kingdome with this crowne,
    Till the ten persecutions put me downe.   66

    Then to the Gentiles, who listened to her.

"But noe oppression could me quite suppresse;
Nay, persecutions made me flourish more;
I still was slaine, yet still I did increase,   69
And growing lesse, grew greater then before:
    Cammomill trodden doth the farther spred,
    And the palme prest, the higher lifts his head.   72

    No oppressions could put her down.

"Rome was of yore my place of residence,
Where as a soveraigne I long time did sitt,
Till antichristian prelats drave me thence;   75
Then did I flie to Brittaine, & in it
    I have till now, & ever will remaine,
    Till the world shall to chaos turne againe.   78

    She was driven from Rome to Britain,

"With this sharp sword, which in my hand I holde,
A cruell Lady peared me to the heart;
The wound is fresh to see, the blood scarce colde,—   81
Her name was Mary that did act this parte:

    where Mary pierced her to the heart.

But e're she kilde me she was slaine by death,
And I revivd'e by young Elizabeth.   84

"Forty-fower yeares this far renownèd queen,

Honord of all, me above all did honor ;
But fates her, graie in yeares, in vertues green,   87
Cald to a worthier place, death seazd vpon her,
        And for this world, w*hi*ch nought but sorrow yeilds,
        Carried Eliza to th' Elizian fields.   90

"After her death the good Iosiah came,
When the land feard some sodaine innovation,
And, for the propagation of my name,   93
Contracts a league w*i*th many a neighbo*u*r nation ;
        Wisely foreseeing that by such a peace,
        My crowne should flourish & my power encrease. 96

"Vnder this monarch, or above him, rather,
I rule this Britaine Empire & doe bring
Many a soule vnto my heavenly Father,   99
In spite of Rome, w*hi*ch for me hates the king :
        But God will blesse him, & vnto *th*e end
        He and his issue shall my cause defend.   102

"If thou wouldst know whie this bright burning light
Mine other hand doth bear, I will thee tell ;
I have an enemie as darke as night,   105
Cald Error (I to heaven, she lead*es* to hell)
        Whose blacknesse to obscure me doth endevo*u*r,
        But that this light doth her false mists dissever. 108

"The reason why I looke thus heavily,
Is 'cause of late my power gins decay ;
That hellish monster, damnd hypocrisie,   111
Doth carry in the land far greater sway ;
        Enters my temples &, in spite of me,
        Vsurps my place & titles soveraigntie.   114

" There is a sort of purest seeming men,
That aide this monster in her wrongfull cause,
Those the world nameth—Puritanes I meane—   117   of the sancti-
monious
Sent to supplant me from the very iawes   Puritans,
    Of hell, I think ; by whose apparant shew
    Of sanctity doe greatest evils grow.   120

" Vnless the hand of wise authority
Doe reinstall me in my former place,
And punish them & their hypocrisie,   123   who must be put
down.
They will ere long mine honour quite deface.
    And so I prethee, tell him gentle youth,—
    Be not afraide, 'tis nothing but the truth."   126

This saide, methought she vanishd from my sight,   Then she
vanished,
And left me much perplexèd in my thought.
I musde a Puritan should be a wight   129   and I mused on
Puritans till I
So seeming good, & yet soe passing naught ;   awoke.
    Till thinking long vpon so strange a theame,
    At last I wakd, & then I writ my dreame.   132

In curiosos theologos.

You high aspiring wittes, which seeke to prie   Is it not enough
to know what is
Into the secretes of the Diety,   revealed, but
some would know
Is 't not enough to know his will reveald,   the Divine
secrets ?
But you must aime at that which is conceald ?   4
By curious inquisition, too much light
Hath made you lose the perfect vse of sight.
Saint Austines saying may you well befitt,   [leaf 50, back]
Which vnto one would know (without all witt)   8
By curious interrogation,
Remember the
What God did ere he layd the worldes foundation,   saying of
Augustine to one
Replide, " I think, or rather know full well,   of these in-
quisitors.
He made for such as thee infernall hell."   12

Hell is the place for them.

A place most meet for them that dare adventure
Into Godes secret cabbinet to enter.
O, strive not then to know his secret will,
W*h*ich art can never compasse w*i*th her skill !   16

Gratia peccatum superat.

Mounted on wing*es* of high aspiring thought,
I soar to the throne of grace,
I soare a loft vp to the throne of grace ;
My heart*es* repent, by true contrition wrought,
I there present before th' Almighties face.   4
and there seek pardon of my sins.
The spotlesse Lambe w*h*ich for my guilt was slaine,
I offer vp a ransome for my sinne :
W*i*th sighs, praiers, tear*es*, I begge release of paine,
Of him that ever mercifull hath been.   8
My soule thus seated in divine desires,
Selfe-love allurs me vnto vaine delight,
Then quench*è*d are my former heavenly fires,
Till grace doth once againe put sinne to flight.   12
Sin and grace strive together.
Thus sinne w*i*th grace, & grace w*i*th sinne doth strive,
Till sin lie dead, & grace doe sinne survive.   14

Christianus Agnus.

A Christian must be like a Lamb
Like a young tender lambe that man must be
W*h*ich doth professe true Chr*j*stianity
W*i*th sincere heart, in imitation
First of that spotlesse Lambe, whose Passion   4
Brought sinfull man from endlesse misery
To the true center of felicity.
in innocence, gentleness, quietness,
Next, as a lambe is harmlesse, innocent,
Meek, gentle, humble, quiet, patient,   8
So must a Christian be ; his harmlesse life
Must be devoide of all malicious strife.
Revilde, he must not once revile againe,
But must doe good for ill, must suffer paine   12

And persecution with an humble heart
And patient minde ; yea, though it doe impart
The bodies death ; such martirdome shalbe
A glorious crowne of immortality. 16
Lastly, in this respect (if I not erre)
A lamb is a true Christians charecter :
The infant lambe among a thousand sheep,
Whose frequent bleatings a loude murmere keepe, 20
Knowes his owne damme when he but heares her voice,
And to sucke her milke onlie doth reioyce :
So must a Christian know the Church his mother
By her owne voice, the word of God, from other 24
Which are but stepdames :—Popish congregations,
Brownisme, & Puritannicke invocation[s],
Which bleat false doctrine & damnd heresies,
He must distinguish from true misteries ; 28
And like an infant lambe, the childe of grace,
Sucke only from her breastes, which flow apace
With the sincere milke of Godes holie word,
His soules nutrition. Thus ther is accord 32
In these respectes & more, which I 'le not trace,
Twixt lambes of nature & the lambes of grace. 34

Margin notes:
patience in suffering,
[leaf 51]
and in knowing his own Mother
from all others by whom she is surrounded.
There are lambs of nature, and lambs of grace.

Christianus Navis.

A ship vnto a certaine haven bent,
Turmoilde in Neptunes watry element,
With longing expectation doth attend
To make arrivall to his wishèd end. 4
This ship thus troubled is a Christiane
Tost vp and downe in the vast ocean
Of this terrestriall orbe, of which even all
We fitlie by the name of sea may call ; 8
For 'tis a place of perturbation,
Of anguish, sorrowe & vexation,

Margin note:
The Christian is like a ship tossed upon the ocean,

Like the tempestuous sea ; & is to vs

For rockes, quicksand*es*, & gulf*es*, as dangerous.   12

Vpon this ocean terrestriall,

This ship, this vessell allegoricall,

A Christian, floating vp & downe, doth strive

To heaven his safest haven to arrive.   16

Wh*i*ch harbo*ur* ere he can entirely winne,

He must first passe by rockes & gulf*es* of sinne,

And therfore need*es* good preparation

To make a prosp*er*ous navigation.   20

Assist me Phœbus, & I will recite

How he must rigg**è**d be to saile vpright.

The earthly stuffe wherof this ship 's composde

Is flesh & bones in order well disposde.   24

Ships have their sid*es* or ribb*es*, & soe hath man

All tacklings else, soe must a Christian.

The maine-mast must be love o' th' Diety ;

The lesser ones, meeke heart & charity ;   28

The sailes strong faith, hope anchor is assignde,

And fervent prayer is the gentle winde

That blowes it forward ; other tacklings be

Good thought*es*, good word*es*, good work*es*, which trinity

Must all conioyne in one to holde the sailes,

For when these string*es* slip, faith then quicklie failes.

The pilote w*hi*ch must alway be aborde

To steere *th*e right way, is God*es* holy worde ;   36

The sences must the com*m*on sailers be,

Affections, slaves restrainde of libertie,

Kept only to take paines, their actions

Must still be ordered by directions   40

Given by reason, wh*i*ch must have some sway

In this same voyage ; but all must obey

The counsell of the pilot, & still stand

Prest at his service, when he doth com*m*and.   44

Now, 'cause this voyage cannot welbe made

Free from all danger, but ther will invade

Some hostile foe or other ; be ther placd
A prospective vpon the top o' th' mast,   48   A sharp outlook must be kept to discover enemies ;
Wherin 'tis fitt that carefull diligence
Keep evermore his watchfull residence,
And straight give notice, when he doth descrie
The force & comming of the enemie.   52
For Sathan, that leviathan, that whale,
Who is an enemie & ever shall
To Christian man, doth wat[c]h occasion
When he may make his best invasion.   56
Wherfore against this foe, which seekes to kill,   weapons offensive and defensive must always be ready,
Offensive & defensive weapons still
This ship must carrie, & himselfe prepare
To fight it out like a strong man of warre.   60
First at his beake-head he must fasten on
Th' impenetrable helme salvation,
And then the breastplate of true righteousnes
Which will resist the devill, & represse   64
His furious rage.   Then faith his sheild must be   and faith will, as a shield, "quench the balls of wild-fire."
To quench the balles of wilde-fyer presentlie ;
But the sword of the spirit Sathan quailes,
And to attaine the conquest never failes :   68
This is the weapon that the pirate woundes,
This is the sword-fish which the whale confounds.
    Thus if vnto the end he doe endure
Like a brave champion, then he shalbe sure   72
The fiend will like a coward run away,   [leaf 52]
And he, a happy victour, gett the day.   Enduring unto the end he will arrive safe in port.
Then having once attaind the victorie,
He may advance his flag trivmphantly,   76
And saile with ioy, till he the port attaine,
Where in perpetuall blisse he shall remaine.   78

Deum nescire est nihil scire, ipsum rectè scire, omnia.

Philosophers may search into all things,

Philosophers, which search the cause of things
As farre as nature gives their knowledge winges
To soar vnto ; whose quicke & ready witt
A definition to each thing can fitt ;   4
Though they can sillogize with arguments
Of all thinges, from the heavens circumference
To the earths center, & true reason give
Of natures power, which makes thinges move & live ; 8
Yet if they want faiths intellectuall eye

but if they are ignorant of God they are but fools.

First to believe ther is a Diety,
In Godhead one alone, in Persons three,
By whom all creatures are, & cease to be,   12
They are but fooles, & they 'r still blinde, not seeing
The Cause of causes, which gives all their being.

Astronomers can foretell many things,

Astronomers that can foretell eventes
By the celestiall creatures influence,   16
By errant planettes & by fixèd starres,
Can pre-divine of famines, plagues, & warres ;
And of their contraries pre-indicate,
Which come by an inevetable fate ;   20
Can shew th' ecclipses of the sunne & moone,
And how the planettes make coniunction ;
Which have found out, & will maintaine it true,
Three orbes, which Aristotle never knew.   24

yet all their knowledge is vain, and they are in ignorance.

Yet all this knowledge, though it reach as farre
As is the Articke from th' Antarticke starre,
Is nothing, if they know not God above,
That Primus Motor, which all orbes doth move ; 28
Their art wherin they doe themselves advaunce,
Lives still ecclipsèd in black ignorance.
    Phisitions which prescribe a remedy
To each disease & bodies maladie ;   32

That know what is nocivous, & what good,   [leaf 52, back]
When it is fit to bath, to purge, let bloode ;
Although they know the nature & the power   Physicians
                                              know the virtues
Of every simple, every hearbe, & flower,   36 of herbs,
With Solomon, which from the cedar tall
Vnto the hisope spreading on the wall,
Knew every growing plant, flower, hearbe, or tree,
With their true vse & proper qualitie ;   40
Yet all their skill as follie I deride,   yet if they are
                                           ignorant of
Vnlesse they rightly know Christ crucified.   Christ, their
                                               skill is but folly.
He, he it is, which truly is alone
The soules best physicke & Physition.   44
    All artes, as well those we call liberall
As other sciences mechanicall,
What e're they be, & howsoever lov'de,
And worthily by mortall man approv'de,   48
If the best knowledge theologicall,
Be not conioynèd with their rationall,—
What e're they may vnto the world professe—
All their best wisdome is starke foolishnesse.   52
He is the only wise & prudent man   The Christian is
                                     the only wise
Whose knowledge makes him the best Christian.   man.
For practise must agree with speculation,
Belief & knowledge must guide operation ;   56
Man may believe & yet he may dissemble,
For even the divels doe beleeve & tremble.   The devils
                                              believe and
'Tis not enough that we beleeve a God,   tremble.
For this will all confesse that feele his rod ;   60
But we must alsoe in this God beleeve,
And in our actions not the Spirit grieve.
We must beleeve that it was he alone   We must believe
                                        that God created
Which gave to man his first creation,   64 and redeemed us.
And that from him alone comes our redemption,
Which is from everlasting death exemption ;
That we in him alone are iustifide,
And by him only shall be glorifide.   68

This we must trow & (though it passe *our* sence)
Repose in this assurde confidence,
W*hi*ch how we must *per*forme in each respect
The Scripture plainly doth vs all direct.   72

The man who knows these things,

He that knowes this (although *the* poorest worme)
And to this knowledge doth his life conforme,

[leaf 53]

Want he the *giftes* of nature, education,
Speake he the tongue but of one only nation ;   76

though a fool in men's eyes,

Be he a foole in the esteeme of man,
In worldly thin*ges* a meer simplician ;
Yet for all this, I boldly dare averre

has a knowledge to be prefeired befoie that of physicians, lawyeis, astionomers.

His knowledge great, & will it farre preferre   80
Before the skill of wise philosophers,
Phisitions, lawyers, & astronomers,
W*hi*ch either want the knowledge of the Diety,
And live in sinne & damnd impiety,   84
Or, if they know a God, doe fear him rather
As a just Iudge then as a loving Father.
He that doth truly know Christ crucifide,
Doth know enough, though he know nought[1] beside ;
But he that knowes him not doth only rave,
Though all the skill else in the world he have.   90

Ternarius numerus perfectissimus.

The numbei Three is the principal number.

Of all the numbers arithmeticall,
The number three is heald for principall,
As well in naturall philosophy
As super*n*aturall theologie.   4
Philosophers, in causes naturall,
Holde that all thin*ges* have their originall

Three chief causes.

From three chief causes, or principia,
And therfor say tria sunt omnia,   8
From three all essence & existence growe,
Materia, forma, & privatio.

[1] Perhaps *naught* in MS.

The body three dimensions doth include,

And they are these, length, bredth, profunditude.   12

In mathematique bodies three thinge*s* please,

their punctum, linea, superficies.

Bodies have three dimensions.

The soule, that breath of life, we threefold call,

Vegitive, sensitive, & rationall.   16

The soul is three-fold.

Time doth his three divisive partes endure,

That w*h*ich is past, the present, & future.

So is time.

There are three graces ; ther be vertues three,

Theologicall, faith, hope, & charity.   20

Three Graces.

The father of the faithfull, Abraham,

Receivde three Angels w*h*ich vnto him came.

Three angels appeared to Abraham.

From the fierce flames of Nebuchadnezar

God was the three childrens Deliverer.   24

[leaf 53, back]
Three children.

Ionah, whose flight God*es* mandat had opposde,

In the whales belly three dayes was enclosde.

Jonah three days in the whale

Christ, to give man a new regenerate birth,

Was three dayes in the bowels of the earth ;   28

Christ three days in the grave.

When he from death & hell a Victo*u*r rose,

Did three times visible himselfe disclose

To his disciples ; thrice bad Peter keepe

And nourish well his flock of lambs & sheepe.   32

Thrice was let downe to Peter in a dreame

A sheet, w*i*th beast*es*, bird*es*, creeping things vncleane,

And he thrice bidden eat, denide consent,

Whilest three men sought him, from Cornelius sent.   36

The sheet was let down to Peter three times.

The heavenly kingdome, that celestiall bower,

A leaven is, hid in three peck*es* of flower.

Lastly, but principallie, above all

The Diety in P*er*sons three we call ;   40

This Trinity it is[1] indeed alone

W*h*ich gives this number best p*er*fection.

Three Persons in the Trinity.

   Thrice happy is that man, w*i*th ioy shall see

This P*er*fect Number, this Thrice Glorious Three.   44

---

[1] MS. *is is.*

De duplici adventu Christi.

As soon as man had sinned,

When sinfull man in Edens garden plac'd,
By stubborne disobedience had defac'd
The true idæa of his happinesse,
And had deservde, for soe great wickednesse,　　4
Eternall death, loe, mercy then began
To mitigate the punnishment of man.

mercy began to mitigate his punishment.

Though earth was cursde, & man must by the sweat
Of his owne labour make it yeild him meat ;　　8
Though woman, whom the serpent had beguilde,
In paine & sorrowe must bring forth her childe ;
Yet from eternall death the promisde seed
Put them in comfort that they should be freed.　　12
To which effect the only Son of Ioue,
Out of the infinitenesse of his loue

[leaf 54]

To his own likenesse man, came downe from heaven,

Christ made satisfaction for him.

Toke flesh vpon him, was of life bereaven,　　16
And made full satisfaction by his death
For all their sinnes, which by a lively fayth
Lay holde vpon his meritorious Passion,
The perfect path that leads vnto salvation.　　20

Christ's first comming was in the flesh.

This Christes first comming was, which we doe name
A comming vnto vs in grace ; to frame
Mans soule to come to him, he first began
To come him selfe in grace to sinfull man,　　24
From a pure Virgin to take incarnation,
From impure Iewes, his patient Passion.
　　His first Advent yeilds a quaternall section,
His birth, his life, his death, his resurrection.　　28

His birth was poor.

His birth was poore, that by his poverty
We might be made rich in eternity.
Borne in a cratch 'mongst beastes (yet for our gaine)
That in heavens kingdome we with saintes might raigne.

He lived despised of man,

He livd despisde of man, to get vs grace　　33
With God the Father ; meekly did embrace

(Sole sinne excepted) each infirmity

Coincident to fraile humanity,   36

That he might put vs in a better state,

And in his weaknesse vs corroborate.

As he was man he yeilded vp his breath   *and gave His life for man,*

To save vs men from an eternall death,   40

Which death was full of agonie & paine,

That our life purchasd, might in joy remaine.

Lastly, as God he subdued death & hell,

And rose againe from the infernall cell   44

Of conquerd Sathan, to prepare the way

For vs to follow him ; and now this day

Sitting in maiesty at Gods right hand,   *and is now his Mediator in heaven.*

Sole Mediatour for our cause doth stand,   48

And till his second comming, shall doe still

To plead their cause which doe obey his will ;

Which second comming shall in glory be,

And in vnvtterable maiestie.   52

    The generall resurrection shalbe then,   *[leaf 54, back]*

And dust & wormes returne to living men.

Then shall our corruptible[1] flesh put on

Immortalnesse & incorruption.   56

Then shall we see Christ comming in the cloudes,   *His second coming will be in clouds and majesty.*

When some will wish whole mountaines were their

    shroudes.

Then he the sheep from goates shall separate,

The iust & godly from the reprobate,   60

And sheepe have blisse ; the other for their hire

Perpetuall paines & everlasting fire.

    Thus shall his second powerfull comming be   *It will be joy to the godly, misery to the wicked.*

The godlies ioy, the wickedes misery.   64

Twixt his first comming & his latter one

There wilbe found much discrepation.

First did he come in all humility,

Then shall he come in splendant royalty ;   68

            [1] May be *corroptible* in MS.

First to be iudgèd by *th*e world he came,
Then shall he come as Lord to iudge the same ;
In his first com*m*ing he for man did die,
In this he shall give 's lifes eternity.   72

May we the first advent of Christ emploie
So to o*u*r good that at the latter day,
His second com*m*ing, when he shall appeare,
Before o*u*r Iudge we may w*i*thout all feare   76
Expect that happy sentence, " Come ye blest,
And enter into everlasting rest."   78

May we use the first to prepare us for the second!

In Momum.

Momus, that foulmouthd slave, my verse derides ;
Sayes they are plaine, bald balladstuffe ; besides
They want invention, poetrie, & witt,
And are farre worse then ever Bavius writt.   4
Dost not thou like 'em, Momus ?   Why I 'me glad ;
That w*hi*ch thou likst, I 'me sure must needs be bad.
But be they soe, as worse thou canst not prove them,
I tell thee they like me, & I will love them.   8
As for thy scoffes, I neither doubt nor fear them,
Thou hast wrongd better, therfore I may beare them.[1]

Momus derides my verse,

but he has wronged better men than I.

[End.]

[1] The Poems end here without any horizontal line.   The
next leaf of the volume is the fly-leaf of another MS.

GLOSSARIAL INDEX

(INCLUDING PROPER NAMES).

Note. For the extracts from Marlowe I have used Mr Dyce's ed. 1858 ; from Greene and Peele, his ed. 1861. For those from John Taylor, the Water-Poet, I have used the Spenser Society's reprint of the Folio ed. of 1630. Where not otherwise stated the reference is to the page. H. = Halliwell's Archaic Dict. P. = Kersey's Phillips, 1708.

A, a nightes, 90/2852.

A, a safe, 60/1813, very safe.
To steal sands from the shore he loves *a-life*. *Marlowe*, 337.

Abie, 23/613, pay for, expiate.
Thou shalt dear *aby* this blow.
Greene, 259.

Abraham, 39/1158, 149/21.

Abroach, new-set-abroach-fantastique fashion, 85/2706. Fantastic fashions, newly invented, or introduced.

Adon[is], 37/1101.

Adrus, 105/3352, Dives, rich.

Advantageous, 107/3429.
Advantageous care
Withdrew me from the odds of multitude. *Troil. & Cress.* v. 4.

Æsculapius, 69/2163.

Æsop, 136/43.

Aflaunt, 86/2726, showily dressed.
Al *aflaunt* now vaunt it ;
Brave wench, cast away care ;
With layes of love chaunt it,
For no cost see thou spare.
Promos and Cassandra, i. 2. H.

A forehand, 83/2609, before.

After-clap, 68/2126, the punishment which follows an unlawful act.

Ahab, 50/1501.

Alcheron, 9/188, Alcoran, the Koran.

Alehouse, 60/1821.
Farewell my Cowslippe sweete,
Pray lets a Sunday at the *Alehouse* meet. Sam. Rowlands,
The Letting of Hvmovrs Blood,
etc. Sat. 4.

Alehouse-haunter, 60/1813, a frequenter of the ale-house.

Alexander VI., 78/2436, Pope.
Died, 1503.

Allegant, 63/1919, wine from Alicant.
Sweet *Allegant*, and the concocted Cute. *Taylor*, 549.
Boxt *Alligant* with Sugar and Eggs. *Heywood's Philocoth.* p. 48.
Sweet wines . . . Tent, *Halligant*.
Ib.

Alston, 107/3442.

Camelion, 118/75, chameleon.

Can, 59/1800, a vessel.
Canne follow'd Canne, and Pot succeeded Pot. Taylor, 136.

Canarie, 62/1916. "From the Spaniard . . . Malligo . . . sherry, Canary, Moscatell." Heywood's Philocoth. p. 48.

Cancer, 113/20.

Canckered, 91/2887. Eaten with the Canker or with Rust. P. See Anat. of Abuses, p. 111 : "There are three canckers, whiche, in processe of time, wil eate vpp the whole common wealth," where caterpillar is meant, as in Two Gent. Ver. i. 1.

Captivde, 109/3495, held in captivity, enslaved.

Carrier, Dr, 52/1583. See note, p. x.

Cashier, 87/2744.
Maymed cassiered Soldiers and Mariners. Taylor, 87.

Cast, 61/1851, to vomit.

Cast office, 27/781, cast off, despised, abandoned.
While thread-bare Martiall turns his merry note,
To beg of Rufus a cast wintercoat. Hall's Satires, vi. 1.

Castles in the air, to build, 118/97.

Catastrophe, 111, end.

Cates, 56/1683, 87/2774, dainty victuals.

Cato, 29/824, 132/9.

Ceres, 87/2763, 113/23.

Cervisius, 59/1799, 61/1887, Cervisia, a Gallic word, meaning Beer.

Cevillian, 134/1, one versed in civil law. See p. xvi.

Chalk from cheese, phrase, 28/794.
Tom is no more like thee, then Chalks like cheese. S. Rowlands, The Letting of Hvmovrs Blood, etc., Sat. 6.

Chalkd out, 9/181, pointed out.
For it is you that have chalk'd forth the way
Which brought us hither.
Tempest, v. 1.

Channell, 105/3367, kennell, gutter. See quotation under Iustled.

Chapmen, 43/1282, dealers, customers.

Charles V., 25/685. Died, 1558.

Charnico, 62/1916, a kind of sweet wine.
Well, happy is the man doth rightly know
The vertue of three cuppes of Charnico.
S Rowlands, The Letting of Hvmovrs Blood, etc., Sat. 6.
And here, neighbour, here's a cup of charneco. 2 Hen. VI. ii. 3.
Peter-se-mea, or head strong charnico. Taylor, 549.
It is called charnio by Heywood, Philocoth. p. 8.

Charon, 72/2267.

Charret, 63/1921, claret.
Claret, Red nor White,
Graues nor High-Country could our hearts delight. Taylor, 549.

Cheap, phrase, good cheap, 65/2014.

Checke, 52/1576, restraint ; censure, reproof, or reproach.
Rebuke and check was the reward of valour. 2 Hen. IV. iv. 3.

Child, prov., "The burnt child dreads the fire," 102/3243.

Chinck, 61/1872, 104/3341, money.
Both lybertie and Chinck ynough himselfe he will allow.
Newes out of Powles, Sat. 5.
Some of their pockets are oft stor'd with chink. Taylor, 197.

Chockt, 14/343, choked.

Chremes, 103/3289, the name of an avaricious old man in the Andria of Terence.

Chuffe, 26/749, a reproachful term often applied to an old miser.

> Mizer *chuffes* who charitie doe banish. *Taylor*, 398.
> If he but steale a sheepe from out the fold,
> The *chuffe* would hang him for it if he could. *Ib.* 494.

Circe, 23/617.

Civet, 34/979, a perfume obtained from the civet-cat.

> Is not this a sweet pride, to haue *ciuet? Anat. of Abuses*, p. 73.
> And though they were perfum'd with *Ciuet* hot
> Yet wanting these things they would stinke and rot.
> *Taylor*, 549.

Clap, 80/2530, caught a clap = met with a mishap.

Claudia, 80/2530.

Cleopatra, 59/1779.

Climenes, 131/1(2).

Clogd, 109/3496, burdened.

Clogging, 92/2918, loading, or burthening. The noun is used in the following passage:—"I'll hang a *clog* about your neck for running away again." *Marlowe*, 59.

Closely, 85/2691, secretly.

> Now every man put off his burgonet,
> And so convey him *closely* to his bed. *Marlowe*, 234.

Cloy, 85/2674.

Cocus, 48/1433, a cook.

Codpiece, 27/758, an artificial protuberance to the breeches.

Codrus, 49/1481, proper name.

Cog, 137/56, to lie, to cheat.

Coinquinate, 136/16. "To coinquinate, staine, or defile." *Minsh.* 1627.

Cold comfort, phr. 57/1704, no relief, no sympathy.

Collation, 88/2785.

Collier—devil, prov., "Like to like, the collier and the devil," 98/3097.

Comines, Philip de, 28/814.

Commaculate, 71/2216, 96/3046, to spot, pollute.

Commerce, 51/1537, to trade with, deal with.

Comprisde, 85/2682, comprised to act, etc., in which the "villany" was to be acted.

Consubstantiation, 17/473.

Convented, 49/1472, convened, summoned.

> The king hath commanded
> To-morrow morning to the council-board
> He be *convented. Hen. VIII.* v. 1.

Convertites, 77/2413, converts.

> No, governor, I will be no *con vertite. Marlowe*, 149.

See *As You Like It*, v. 4.

Coram, 46/1382, "Justice of peace and coram." Coram, "an ignorant mistake for Quorum."

> "Robert Shallow, esquire . . . . . justice of peace and '*Coram*.'" *Merry W. of W.* i. 1.

Cornelius, 149/36.

Corrivals, 35/1024, rivals.

> So he that doth redeem her thence might wear
> Without *corrival* all her dignities. 1 *Hen. IV.* i. 3.

Corroborate, 151/38, to strengthen. "Meates (moderately taken) *coroborate* the body, refreshe the arteries, and reuiue the spirits." *Anat. of Abuses*, 114.

Coryate, 26/721, "was bepraised and abused as much as any man." See *Taylor's Works, Corbet's Poems*, etc. He died in 1617.

Cosens, 43/1282, cheats.

> To lye, to *couzen*, to forsweare, and sweare. *Taylor*, 536.

Cote, 13/316, 16/408, quote, speak about, "make a note of.'

> "He sayeth moreover that he hath

coated a number of contrarieties out of the Scriptures." (*Bame's Note*), *Marlowe*, 390.

Cotten, 62/1883, to cotton, to succeed or prosper; to go right. Why, so; now it *cottens*, now the game begins. *Geo. Peele*, 396.

Course, 26/718, coarse.
Her with your *course* wives compare. Taylor, *A Pedlar and a Romish Priest*, p. 8.

Cow, 26/731, coward. Cf. cowish, *K. Lear*, iv. 2.

Coy, 59/1804, shy.

Crasis, 24/647. " In a *Physical-Sense*, a proper Constitution, Temperature, or Mixture of Humours in an Animal Body." *P.*

Crassus, 46/1393, proper name.

Cratch, 150/31, a manger. " And she broght forth her fyrst begotten sonne, and wrapped him in swadlyng clothes, and layd him in a *cretche*, because there was no rowme for them with in y° ynne." *Luke* ii. 7, *Gen. New. Test.* 1557.

Cronologers, 100/3167.

Cronologized, 72/2253, chronicled.

Crosse-barre, 39/1151, an obstacle. There is probably a reference to the cross-bar, or cross-beam of the gallows.
Out of the water shall appeare one dead,
A halter and *a crosse-barre* o'r his head. *Taylor*, 316.

Crumbe-catching, 135/1.

Cue, 66/2038, 90/2879. " Cue, a terme vsed by Stage-players." *Minsh.* 1627.
His Buckram-bearer, one that knowes his *ku*,
Can write with one hand and receive with two." *Taylor*, 495.

Cuffe, 43/1255, same as chuffe, *q. v.*

Cupid, 45/1339, 93/2927.

Curry favour, 48/1434, to flatter, gain favour.

Cyclops, 117/38.

Cynick-dog, 99/3143.

Cynthia, 41/1214.

Cytheræa, 37/1102.

Dabbes, 77/2402, ? deceives. Perhaps the same as *dub*. See 134/11, 134/12.

Dad, 78/2448, father.
Thy body is the *Dad*, thy minde the Mam. *Taylor*, 232.
The names used for food in Northamptonshire sometimes show the different classes of society :
Dad, mam, and porridge ;
Father, mother, and broth ;
Pa, ma, and soup.

Dædalus, 132/11.

Dagon, 51/1559.

Damon, 24/654, a Pythagorean philosopher, the intimate friend of Pythias. When Damon was sentenced to death, and had obtained leave to go and settle his domestic affairs, Pythias pledged himself to undergo the punishment if Damon should not return in time.

Danae, 42/1252.

Dance, phr., " goe dance for," 39/1164, to wait for, obsequiously, perhaps. Cf. " Danced attendance on," 2 *Hen. VI.* i. 3 ; and " I dance attendance here," *K. Rich. III.* iii. 7.

Dareling, 37/1102, darling.

Daunce, a Scottish daunce, 86/2716. Cf. The Galliæ Morbus, and the *Scottish fleas* (*Taylor*, 549), which were the result of indulging in the " Scottish dance."

Daw, 46/1380, a foolish fellow, a slattern, or sluggard. *H.* A daw to a solicitor probably means what we now understand by a " lawyer's clerk."

Day, phr., " dying day," 62/1900, day of death.

Day, phr., "happie day," 12/275, happiness, prosperity.

Dealing trade. *See* Trade.

Debaush, 58/1759, debauched, dissolute. "A *Debosht* Drunkard." *Taylor*, 335.

Defame, 51/1541, 1556, to render infamous.

Deianira, 66/2059.

Demosthenes, 42/1237.

Descride, 121/26, descried.

Detect, 82/2569, 133/10, to accuse.
> These fishers tell the infirmities of men:
> And from their watery empire recollect
> All that may men approve or men *detect! Pericles*, ii. 1.

Devil, blew devill, 107/3443. "Blue devils," the "horrors," or the remorse which frequently follows an ill course of life.

Devil, prov., "Goe they must because the devill drives," 52/1582; "Needs must when the devil drives."

Diana, 93/2943, 116/26.

Dilate, 117/61, 121/22, to show, declare, open.

Diogenes, 99/3137.

Dioscorides, 29/821, flourished in 2nd century A.D.

Dirges, 13/336, dirge, corrupted from *Dirige*, the commencing word of *Dirige nos, Domine*.

Discrepation, 151/66, discrepancy, difference.

Distaine, 121/27, 132/17, to sully by contrast.
> Her beauty glancing on the waves
> *Distains* the cheek of fair Proserpina. *George Peele*, 430.

Distast, 100/3193, disgust, disagree with.

Divisive, 149/17, divisible.

Dog, phr., "A hair of the same

dog," 61/1860, the homœopathy of the period.

Dores, keep the doors, 86/2724, 2742.
> A Pander (Hostler like) that walks a whore,
> And for a Fee securely *keeps the doore. Taylor*, 215.

Drabbes, 80/2525.
> The Deuils deere *drab* must be the Church of Rome.
> That Church .. is ... the devils whore. *Taylor*, 503.

Draco, 57/1728.

Drivell, 98/3098.

Drugo, 78/2459.

Drusus, 37/1077, proper name.

Dubbing, 134/11 ⎱ *See* Dabbes,
Dubde, 134/12 ⎰ *supra*.

Ducke, 85/2699, an endearing term often applied to a child or young girl.
> Will you buy any tape,
> Or lace for your cape,
> My dainty *duck*, my dear-a?
> *Winter's T*. iv. 4.

"Eat to live, not live to eate," 56/1672. "The olde adage saith .. .. *we must not liue to eat, but we must eate to liue!" Stubbs's Anat.*, ed. 1836, p. 109.

Effeminize, 34/972, to effeminate, to make womanish or wanton, to soften by voluptuousness. *P.*

Elizabeth, 140/84.

Elohim, 7/112, God.

Elpinas, 106/3410, hopeful.

Embase, 127/16, debase.

Emilia, 90/2877, Emily.

Eminent, 101/3231, imminent.

Emperie, 35/1024, empire.
> Measuring the limits of his *empery*
> By east and west, as Phœbus doth his course. *Marlowe*, 10.

Enable, 12/272, to encourage, to make firm, to strengthen.

Enact, 39/1156, commit.

Enditers, 28/816, inditers, composers, writers. Cp. "My heart is *inditing of* a good matter." *Psalm* xlv. *P. B. Vers.*

Epainnutus, 37/1085, praise.

Equipage, 58/1764.

Eringoes, 87/2773. Eringo, sea-holly, the roots of which, being candied, made excellent sweat-meats : they were considered provocatives.

Errant, 146/17.

Estrange, 129/35

Eulalius, 76/2385, eloquent.

Eve, 32/915.

Except, 9/164, accept.

Exoration, 80/2511, a prayer, a desire or wish.

Extenuate, 96/3042.

Eyen, 56/1686, eyes.
> His angry *eyne* look all so glaring
> bright. *Hall's Satires*, v. 1.

Fact, 48/1451, act, deed.
> And praise his gentle soule and
> wish it well,
> And of his friendly *facts* full often
> tell. *Hall's Satires*, iv. 2.

Families of Love, 9/196, sometimes called Familists. See *Note*, p. xxix.

Fatuo, 44/1311, a fool.

Faune, 137/56, fawn.

Faustus, 53/1625. Marlowe's *Doctor Faustus* first appeared about 1590. It was published in quarto in 1604, and again in 1616.

Fawkes, 12/291.

Fees, 27/780, rewards.

Felt, 27/751, a hat.

Figs of Spaine, 39/1153, a kind of poison.

Fire, phr., "to give false fire," 122/51, to raise a false alarm.

Flat, "that's flat," 39/1166, that is certain, or clear. "The boy hath sold him a bargain, a goose, *that's flat." Love's L. L.* iii. 1.

Flavia, 45/1331.

Fleece, 86/2718, to rob, plunder, strip.
> To *fleese* and flea the simple
> wretche,
> to pylfer and to powle.
>   *Newes out of Powles*, Sat. 2.

Flincher, 59/1801, one who gives over.

Fond, 13/329, foolish.

Foulmouthd, 152/1.

Fox, 58/1762, 59/1806, 1807, to make drunk. "No man must call a Good-fellow Drunkard . . . but say . . . He is *foxt.*" 1635. *Hey-wood, Philocothonista*, p. 60. "The liquor . . . . would *fox* a dry Tra-veller, before he had half quencht his thirst." 1639. *J. Taylor, Tra-vels*, p. 8. "You were never so *fox'd* but you knew the way home." *Ib.* p. 46.

Fox, 64/1985, crafty fox, a clever rogue.

Frenchifide, 80/2518, made like a Frenchman. See Ladifide, *in-fra.*

Frie, "the yoonger frie," 15/386, the younger children.
> Thither went the doctors,
> And sattin-sleev'd proctors,
> With the rest of the learned *fry.*
>   *Bp. Corbet's Poems*, ed. 1807,
>   Intro. xxiii.

Fucata, 24/661, painted.

Fucus, 34/973, a red dye, rouge.

Fulsome, 127/1, nauseous.

Fume, 105/3368, angry humour.

Fumoso, 72/2237, well-smoked, smoke-dried, smoky.

Furder, 12/270, further.

Gabrina, 85/2699.

Galen, 29/822. Claudius Galen, d. A.D. 200; M. Galen in 1573.

Galla, 82/2581, proper name.

Gallicus morbus, 80/2519.
The Spanish Pip, or else the *Gallian Morbus*,
Bone-bred diseases, mainly doe disturbe vs. *Taylor*, 178.
The *Galliæ Morbus* or the Scottish fleas,
Or English Poxe, for all's but one disease. *Ib.* 549.

Ganymede, 79/2470.

Garnet, 12, *note*.

Geason, 113/15, this word generally means scarce, rare; as,
Base Death, that took away a man so *geason*,
That measur'd every thought by time and season. *Greene*, 279.
Good men are scarce, and honest men are *geason*. *Taylor*, 404.

George, 60/1814, 61/1879.

Gives, 95/3019, shackles, or fetters.
Manacles, and Bolts, and *Giues*,
Which fetter vs in bondage all our liues. *Taylor*, 291.

Glabria, 82/2567, one who loves a beardless youth.

Gogle, 98/3099, goggle.

Golde, King Harries golde, 61/1876. See *Note*, p. xxxv.

Grandams, 29/836, grandmothers.
If our Grand-fathers and *Granddams* should
Rise from the dead. *Taylor*, 488.

Gray-beard, 66/2038, 69/2135.

Grease . . . . in the fist, phrase, 43/1269, 48/1442. "If you have argent, or rather *rubrum unguentum*, I dare not saie gold, but red ointment *to grease them in the fist* withall, then your sute shall want no furtheraunce." *Stubbs's Anat.*, ed. 1836, p. 129.
Would now that Matho were the Satyrist,

That some fat bribe might *grease him in the fist.*
Hall's Satires, iv. 5.

Greece of Amber, 36/978. *See* Amber.

Guld, 29/838, cheated, deceived.
"But my Gowne-brother promised mee good stuffe . . . . and verily did *gull* mee." Sam. Rowlands, *Diogenes Lanthorne*, sig. B. 1628.

Gull, 29/843, a cheat, a deceiver.

Gulles, 13/320, people easily deceived.

Hackny, 86/2720, hackney women, women who let out, etc., as explained in ll. 2720-1.

Had I wist, 40/1194, a proverbial phrase = had I known; an expression of regret.
When dede is doun, hit ys to lat; be ware of *had-y-wyst.*
Qu. Eliz. Achad. p. 42.
Clad in a Gowne of mourning *had I wist. Taylor*, 165.
See also *Marlowe*, 201, and *Gower's Conf. Amant.* i. 105, ed. 1857.

Haire, phr., "unto a hair," 72/2244, 80/2520, to a nicety.

Hannibal, 99/3163.

Hard-favourd, 123/24.

Harry (Henry VIII.), 61/1876.

Heliogabalus, 59/1786.

Hell-bread, 45/1342, hell-bred.
Cp. *hell-borne* (*Taylor*, 511), and *hell-begot* (*Ib.* 535).

Hell-hatched, 37/1079, 58/1741.
For ther's no habite of *hell-hatchéd* sinne,
That we delight not to be clothéd in. Sam. Rowlands, *The Letting of Hvmovrs Blood*, etc., sig. A. 2.
Down must tumble
The Nimrods proud cloud-piercing Babylon
Like *hell-hatch'd* pride.
Taylor, 500.
Hell-hatcht plots. *Ib.* 501.

Hell-hound, 42/1249.
> Yet all their liues here they with
> cares are vext,
> Slaues in this world, and *Hell-hounds* in the next.
> *Taylor*, 489.

Helottes, 58/1755, Spartan serfs or bondmen.

Hercules, 66/2057.

Herod, 36/1059.

Hiew, 7/98, hue.

Hight, 123/19, 124/9, called, named.

Hippocras, 62/1918, a beverage composed of wine, with spices and sugar, strained through a cloth. It is said to have taken its name from *Hippocrates' sleeve*, the term apothecaries gave to a strainer. *H.*

Hippolytus, 69/2164.

Histriographers, 100/3168, historiographers.

Hobnol, 22/604, ? a countryman. "Hobbinol, as most readers are aware, was the poetic name of Gabriel Harvey." *George Peele*, 583, note by Ed. G. Harvey died about 1630.

Hoggishlie, 14/344, hoglike.

Homebred, 114/36.

Home-spun.
> Home-spun medley of my mottley braines. *Taylor*, 387.

Honorius, 98/3120, pertaining to honour.

Horace, 28/815.

Horn, give him not the horn, 78/2444, don't make him a cuckold.

Houreglasse, 53/1627.

Hunger-starved, 57/1705.
> Meanwhile the *hunger-starv'd* appurtenance
> Must bide the brunt, whatever ill mischance.
> *Hall's Satires*, v. 2.

Hutch, 60/1817, like lord within a "hutch;" hutch means a chest.

Here the sense seems to be "like a lord standing among his riches."

Hypocrates, 29/822, Hippocrates, d. B.C. 357.

Hypolitus, 98/3110, Hippolytus, a son of Theseus and of Hippolyte. The story of Hippolytus and Phædra is well known.

I, 46/1388, and elsewhere, Aye. "The motion was hotly canvas'd in the house of Peers, and like to pass, when the Lord Paget rose up and said, '*I*, but who shall sue the king's bond?' so the business was dasht." *Howel's Fam. Letters*, ed. 1678, p. 135.

Icarus, 132/9.

Ice, 3/38, phr., "To break the ice," to open or commence a subject, or conversation.

Ies, 41/1207, ? eyes, searches, examines.

Iet, phr., "jet it," 86/2726, struts.
> And, Midas-like, he *jets* it in the court,
> With base outlandish cullions at his heels. *Marlowe, Ed. Sec.* (Works, ed. Dyce, p. 193).

Iet, 72/2248, a stream of water. Fr. *jet*.

Iezebel, 34/965.

Iframde, 128/3, framed.

"Ignorance is the mother of devotion," phr., 11/244.
> The woman, musing little at the motion,
> Said, *ignorance is the Mother of Devotion*.
> If Ignorance be mother then (said he)
> Sure darknesse must her onely daughter be. Taylor's *Pedlar and Priest*, p. 21.

Immediatly, 6/89, without the intervention of anything.

Imp, 46/1363, child. "An *impe* of Sathan, and a limme of th deuill." *Stubbs's Anat.*, ed. 1836, p. 119.

Impostume, 2/12.
The Common wealths *Impostum* hee doth cut,
And the corruption in his purse doth put. *Taylor*, 495.

Inchoation, 3/56, a beginning of any work. *P.*

Index, phr., "The face is index to the heart," 23/631-2.

Inly, 99/3159.

Innocuous, 64/1955, harmless.

Intend, 56/1696, fix the mind on, aim at.
...... Men intend,
But God it is that consummates the end. 17/467-8.
Paraphrase of "Man proposes, but God disposes."

Intret, 132/7, introit, preface.

Invitement, 104/3308, invitation.

Iöle, 67/1961.

Ionah, 149/25.

Ionson, 132/1, 17.

Iosiah (James I.), 140/91.

Iot, 15/401, jot, small space of time.

Iove (Jupiter, *planet*), 114/13.

Irefull, 105/3376.

Irus, 102/3241, the name of a beggar in the house of Ulysses at Ithica.

It, 129/4, its.
It's

Iudas, 20/567, 44/1291.

Iump, phr., "many jump," 127/18, coincide, agree.
Master, for my hand,
Both our inventions meet and *jump* in one.
Taming of the Shr. i. 1.

Iuno, 38/1122, 93/2942.

Iupiter, 131/4.

Iustled, 105/3366. "A Gallant

iustled him from the wall almost into the kennell." *Taylor*, 352.

Keepen, 33/962, keep.

Kembe, 34/979, to comb.

Knights of the post, 49/1475, professional perjurers.
A *post-knight* that for fiue groats gaine
Would sweare & for foure groats foreswear't againe.
Taylor, 557.

Lacklattin, Sir John, 43/1267, a term of contempt applied to an ignorant parson.
This *sir Iohn Lacklatine*, true course doth keepe,
To preach the Vestry men all fast asleepe. *Taylor*, 493.

Ladifide, 133/20, made a lady.
Because his Landlords daughters (deckt with pride)
With ill-got portions may be *Ladyfide. Taylor*, 42.
Thy Female faire, adorn'd and turpifide,
Should, for thy services be *Ladifide. Aqua-Musæ*, 11.

Landresses, 89/2838, laundresses.

Latro, 108/3462, an assassin.

Lazarus, 56/1703.

Let, 18/503, a hindrance, an obstacle.

Let, 78/2435, to hinder, prevent.

Lethe, 131/11(1).

Letia, 102/3238, delighting, or taking pleasure in.

Levi, 76/2371.

Levie, the tribe of, phr., 76/2371, the clergy.
Cease to Abuse the Bishops, and the *Tribe of sacred Levi.*
Aqua-Musæ, p. 9.

Lidian, 88/2800, the Lydian stone.

Liew, 9/164, lieu.

Lightly come, lightly go, prov., 89/2828.

Lightsome, 85/2681, cheerful.

Linceus, 81/2563, Lynceus. See *note*, p. 81.

Linne, 91/2893, lin, to cease, to stop.

Forth then shotten these children 2, and they did neuer *lin* Vntill they came to merry church-lees, to Merry churchlee with-in. *Percy Fo.*, ed. Hales and Furnivall, i. 55.

Lip-labour, 102/3252.

Littleton, 46/1380.

Loaf, prov., "'Tis safest gutting at a loaf begun," 76/2393, may be for "*cutting* at," etc.

Lockram band, 27/755, a band or collar to the shirt made of *lockram*, which was of a finer texture than the shirt itself.

Hempseed doth yeeld or else it doth allow Lawne, Cambricke, Holland, Canuase, Callico, Normandy, Hambrough, strong poledanis, *Lockram*. *Taylor*, 549.

Loose, 17/452, to lose.

Lop, 88/2809, to lop off, cut away.

Lot, 75/2347.

Loutish, 58/1756, clownish.

Lovelock, 34/971, a pendant lock of hair, falling near or over the ear, and cut in a variety of fashions.

Lozell, 130/8, a worthless fellow. Sot, I say, *losel*, lewdest of all swains. *George Peele*, 561.

Lucius, 36/1063, proper name.

Luctantia, 100/3187, L. *luctans*, struggling, reluctant.

Luna, 115/44.

Lunacy, 51/1549. The MS. reads *lunary*. Mr Halliwell's note on the latter word is :—"The herb moon-wort. This herb was formerly believed to open the locks of horses' feet. See Harrison, p. 131. Some

of our early dramatists refer to it as opening locks in a more literal sense."

Lurch, 46/1364, to evade, neglect. There's a crue of Thieues that prie and *lurch*, And steale and share the liuings of the Church. *Taylor*, 279.

Lusco, 82/2571, one who is deprived of something.

Ly, 34/977, lye. "Will Backstead the Plaier cast his *Chamber-lye* out of his window." *Taylor*, 342. *See* 1 Hen. IV. ii. 1.

Machivillian, 49/1467, 94/2963. Thou . . hast beene a *Machiuilian*, For damned sleights, conceits, and policie. *Taylor*, 510. Hee's no state-plotting *Machiuilian*. *Ib.* 535.

Mahomet, 51/1561.

Maiæ, 115/37.

Malago, 62/1915, Malaga wine. Little were your gaine, By *Mallegoes*, Canaries Sacke from Spaine. *Taylor*, 549.

Malicing, 94/2956, maligning, envying. I willingly receive th' imperial crown, And vow to wear it for my country's good, In spite of them shall *malice* my estate. *Marlowe*, 9.

Manlius, 106/3398, proper name.

Marchpaine stuffe, 87/2773. "Marchpanes are made of verie little flower, but with addition of greater quantitie of filberds, pine nuts, pistaces, almonds, and rosed sugar." *Markham's Country Farme*, 1616, p. 585, quoted in H. They sell so deare and take such gaine, that well they may afoorde To set fine *Marchpanes* and such like vpon their seruaunts boorde. *Newes out of Powles Churchyarde*, Sat. 4.

Marle, 68/2130, marvel. " I *marle* in what dull cold nook he found this lady out." *Ev. Man Out of H.* ii. 1.

Marmalade, 87/2772, a confection commonly made of quinces.
Greeneginger, Sucket, Suger Plate, and *Marmaladie* fine.
Newes out of Powles Church-yarde, Sat. 4.

Mars, 26/732, 82/2590, 115/19.

Mary (Queen), 139/82.

Massie, 47/1422, massive.
To make a Globe to serue this *massie* earth. *Taylor,* 236.

Maudline, 64/1959, corruption of Magdalene. " With *Maudlin* sorrow . . . . they have wept with very griefe." Taylor, *Apology for P. Preaching,* p. 7.

Maw, 101/3226, stomach.

May, 65/2010, the blossom of the white or haw-thorn.

Meacocke, 27/783, a silly effeminate fellow. " Some are suche peasantes and such *maicokes,* that either they will not, or . . . . they dare not, reproue them for it." *Stubbs's Anat.,* ed. 1836, p. 105. " He (The Great Eater of Kent) is no puling *Meacocke,* nor in all his life time the queasinesse of his stomacke needed any sawcy spurre or switch of sowre Veriuice." *Taylor,* 156.

Mechanico, 24/655, mechanic, wright.

Mediocrity, 71/2210, moderation.

Medusa, 23/623.

Mercury, 115/38.

Messalina, 77/2424, the name of the profligate wife of Claudius.

Messe, 60/1826, number.

Microcosme, 8/145, 92/2908.
" *Microcosme,* or little world, Man." *Minsh.* 1627.
I haue a heart doth like a Monarch raigne,

Who in my *Microcosme* doth lawes ordaine. *Taylor,* 208.

Midas, 45/1351.

Mirre-breathing, 38/1112, having sweet breath.

Mirrha, 82/2595, Myrrha.

Misotochus, 99/3129, man-hater.

Misthink, 67/2086, think amiss.

Mollified, 45/1327, softened.

Momists, 111, fault-finders, carping critics, so named from Momus.

Momus, 152/1.

Moncking-stock, 5/23, perhaps for mocking-stock. " One that doth purpose to make this towne a iesting *mocking stocke* throughout the whole Kingdome." *Taylor,* 356. Cf. *laughing-stock.*

Montaigne, 28/813.

Mony-taker, 48/1442, a receiver of bribes.

Mopsa, 100/3181. " Mopsey, a term of endearment." *H.* See the *Anatomie of Abuses,* p. 169. "Handekercheifes . . . borrowed for the moste parte of their *pretie mopsies* and loouyng bessies, for bussyng them in the darcke."

Moros, 28/789, L. *mos,* manners.

Morpheus, 137/14.

Muskadine, 62/1918, 88/2778, a rich wine; muscadel.
The wind no *Muskadine* could hither bandy,
Or sprightly Malmesey out of fruitfull Candy. *Taylor,* 549.

Mutius, 100/3199, changed in circumstances.

Nænius, 99/3153, a heaping up of praise, or commendation.

Nappy ale, 71/2224, strong ale.

Narcissus, 34/984.

Nathlesse, 23/624, nevertheless.

Neandrem, 134, ? Newman.

Nebuchadnezar, 149/23.

Necessity, that hath no law, 46/1379, a quibble on the phrase, "Necessity has, or knows, no law."

Nectar, 62/1913, the drink of the gods; hence, a delicious or inspiring beverage.
What god soever holds thee in his arms,
Giving thee *nectar* and ambrosia.
　　　　　　　　　Marlowe, 53.

Neighbour, 52/1594,　140/94, neighbouring.
The hope of Persia . . . . .
. . . .
That holds us up and foils our *neighbour* foes.
　　　　　　　1 *Tamburlaine*, i. 1.

Neotimus, 38/1121, an upstart.

Nepenthe, 62/1914, the name of an Egyptian drug which lulled sorrow for the day. Gr. νηπενθης, removing all sorrow.

Neptune, 75/2353, 131/6, 143/2.

Nessus, 66/2059.

Nill, 120/31, ne will, will not.
[I] left my mill to go with thee,
And *nill* repent that I have done.
　　　　　　　　　Greene, 264.

Nisus, 23/645, proper name.

Noble, 48/1443, the name of a coin. "A *Noble* in money . . . six shillings and eightpence in England, where there hath beene an old English coine of gold called an *Edward Noble* . . . . worth some fifteene shillings sterling, and is the Rose *Noble* . . . as I take it, now worth seuen shillings, and six pence." *Minsh.* 1627.

Nocivous, 147/33, hurtful.

Nonce, 60/1831, occasion.

Nothus, 80/2513, spurious, illegitimate.

Obeisaunce, 25/703, obedience.

Obnubilate, 135/14, darken, confound, cloud over. "Immoderate slepe . . . doth obfuske and doth

obnebulate the memory." *Andrew Boorde's Dyetary*, p. 244, ed. Furnivall.
Mans vnderstanding 's so *obnubilate*,
That when thereon I doe excogitate,
Intrinsicall and querimonious paines,
Doe puluerise the concaue of my braines. *Taylor*, 404.

Observancie, 89/2830, respect, obsequiousness.

Occasion, as occasion serves, 97/3062, as opportunity offers, or presents.

Occurrentes,　104/3307,　occurrences.

Oddes, phr., "by odds," 11/259, 62/1914. "The *ods* is, my Cormorants appetite is limited, but most of theirs is vnsatiable." *Taylor*, 483.

Oldcorn, 12, *note*.

On, on 's, 94/2976, 2986, of his.
Look how his brains drop out *on 's* nose. *Jew of Malta*, iv.

One, 4/9, on. This form is not common in other writers of this period.

One, phrase, "all one with," 30/866, equivalent to.

Opifice, 7/104, workmanship, L. *opificium*, from *opifex*.

Orestes, 126/7(2).

Orgia, 106/3380.

Orleance, 62/1917, wine from Orleans. "From France Red, White, claret, *Orleance.*" Heywood's *Philocoth.* p. 48.

Orpheus, 93/2934.

Ougly, 23/638, 37/1100, ugly.

Overquell, 112/5, overcome.

Oxe, phr., "A right ox," 64/1986.

Pact, 39/1166, packed, sent; often "be off," as,

'Tis time, I think, to trudge, *pack* and be gone. *Com. of Er.* iii. 2.

Pallas, 93/2940.

Pamphila, 98/3105, all-loving.

Pamphlet, 29/842. " Should I write all that I am truely informed, my Booke would out-swell the limits of a *Pamphlet.*" *Taylor,* 74.

Pandarus, 50/1529. *See* Troilus and Cressida.

Papistrie, 4/16.
Yea, and a church, unspotted, pure, From dregs of *papistry* secure.
A Poem on New England, Ined. Misc. 1870.
I may be mannerly In Gods House, and be free from *Papistrie.*
Taylor, *Mad Fashions,* p. 7.

Pasiphæ, 82/2593.

Passion, " void of passion, void of good," phr., 96/3038.

Pelt, 27/752, a skin. " The Lord ... gaue them *peltes,* felles, and skins of beastes to make them garments withall." *Anat. of Abuses,* p. 20.

Peppercorne, 65/2010.

Peter, S., 35/1014, 149/31.

Phaeton, 34/995, 76/2367, 131/1.

Phalerno, 62/1917, a wine now known as Falernian wine, from Mount Falernus, in Italy.

Philarchus, 39/1143, a lover of authority, or the power which comes of wealth.

Philautus, 97/3071, self-love. " Such as give themselves to *philautia* .... are choleric of complexion." *Greene,* 204.

Philogonous, 76/2391, loving his children ; here his flock is probably meant.

Phisicall, 71/2212, medicinal.

Phœbe, 41/1212, the moon-goddess, sister of Phœbus, or Sol.

Phœbus, 103/3295, 144/21.

Phœdra, 98/3109. *See* Hippolitus, *supra.*

Phorbus, 102/3255, fear.

Phrygian, 79/2470.

Pickle, 60/1841, condition of drunkenness.
Where should they Find this grand liquor that hath gilded 'em ?
How camest thou in this *pickle ?*
Temp. v. 1.

Pils of Italy, 39/1153, a kind of poison.

Pinne, 58/1742, phr., "not worth a pin," of no value.

Pistor, 53/1601, miller, baker.

Pithias, 24/654, Pythias. *See* Damon, *supra.*

Pixes, 13/333, pix, the sacred vessel in which the Host is kept.

Plato, 29/823.

Pluto, 99/3162.

Polte-foot, 98/3101, a club foot.

Polupragma, 103/3305, many matters, well rendered in the same line by " Tittle-tatle."

Poppæa, 36/1037, L. a cosmetic made of dough moistened with asses' milk.

Pot companion, 59/1795.

Poynts, 69/2135, tagged laces used in dress. *To truss a point* was to tie the laces which held the breeches ; *to untruss a point* was to untie them.

Praise, prov., " A man's praises in his own mouth stink," 37/1089.

Pratle, 103/3306, prattle.

Precisians, 10/213, persons who are over scrupulous in matters of religion. " I will set my countenance like a *precisian.*" *Marlowe,* 82. " Corbet was certainly no *precisian.*" *Gilchrist's Corbet,* xxxi.

Pre-devine, 146/18.

Pre-indicate, 146/19.

Pre-ordainde, 101/3216.

Profunditude, 149/12.

Promethean, 67/2078.

Prometheus, 117/40.

Prospective, 145/48.

Protasis, 111, beginning; protasis and catastrophe, commencement and ending.

Proteus, 128/6, 129/31.

Provocatives, 87/2765.

Psyche, 117/29.

Ptolomeus, 29/823, Ptolemy.

Put up all, phr., 105/3361, put up with all, endure all.

Putrefactious, 70/2178, putrifying.

Quadruplicity, 117/43.

Quailes, 145/67, quells, cows.

Quarrell, 61/1852, combat, bout.

Quaternall, 150/27, fourfold.

Quean, 36/1053.

Quintus, 82/2568.

Quite, 81/2537, requite.
> Lose more labour than the gain shall *quite. Marlowe*, 17.

Quoted, 63/1937, same as *cote, supra.*

Rafe (Ralph), 60/1814, 61/1880.

Rape, 128/12, prey. Cf. *rapine.*

Ravaillac, 12/283. See *n.* p. x.

Reassume, 126/15.

Recordation, 68/2108, the act of recording, mentioning, writing.

Recover, 100/3176, return to, reach. "I swam, ere I could *recover* the shore, five and thirty leagues off and on." *Tempest*, iii. 2.

Recure, 2/14, 130/11, to cure, heal.
> A smile *recures* the wounding of a frown. *Venus and Adonis*, 465.

And to *recure* me from this strange quandary,
Hence Vsquebaugh, and welcome sweet Canary. *Taylor*, 179.

Regiment, 99/3162, kingdom, rule.
> Four elements
> Warring within our breasts for *regiment. Marlowe*, 18.

Repent, 53/1628, 142/3, repentance.

Repurifide, 38/1118, purged, made pure.

Residence, monthly residence, 102/3245. Reference to Canons of Cathedral Churches being "in residence" one month in the year.

Rhamnusiæ, 135/7, Nemesis.

Rhamnusian, 2/1.

Rhenish, 62/1918.
> No . . . .
> . . *Rhenish* from the Rheine would be apparent.
> *Taylor*, p. 549.

Rising, prov., "A sudden rising hath a sudden fall," 39/1142.

Rivolet, 116/22, rivulet.

Romanus, 102/3245.

Roring boy, 47/1397, roring boyes, 62/1889, riotous fellows who took delight in annoying quiet people. "And many sat there [in the Parliament] that were more fit to have been among *roaringboys* than in that assembly." *Court & Times of James I.* i. 322.
> Like shamelesse double sex'd
> : Hermaphrodites,
> Virago *Roaring Girles. Taylor*, 43.
Sometimes these disturbers of the peace were called "roarers." See *News From Hell, Hull, and Hallifax, etc.*, p. 43.

Rost, phr., "to rule the rost," 117/64, to have most influence.

Roundly, 81/2556, vigorously, without fear.

Rushes, phr., "picking rushes," 90/2882, idling away the time.

Ruffino, 47/1397, It. *ruffiano*, a pimp. "She will . . . cause thy throate to be cut by her *Ruffiano*." *Coryate*, 264/4.

Salamander, 118/76, 119/108.

Sampson, 25/688.

Sanctimonious, 10/224, holy, full of sanctity; used in a *good* sense, as it is in

All *sanctimonious* ceremonies may With full and holy rite be minister'd. *Temp.* iv. 1.

Sardanapalus, 59/1785.

Saturn, 114/7.

Sawe, 37/1088, " Saw, saying," proverb.

Scanderbeg, 25/687. Died, 1467.

Scilla, 82/2575, Scylla.

Score, 81/2561, to cut, or mark.

Scotus, 27/767, Scott, probably a fling at one of James's courtiers.

Scullian, 133/11.

Scurrill, 136/26, scurrilous.

Sea, 51/1564, see. " And now I speake of Rome euen in her *Sea*." *Taylor*, 484.

Seld, 120/5, seldom, not often.

Seeld and seldome can they helpe to keepe the good from harme. *Newes out of Powles*, Sat. 2.

Seller, 60/1829, cellar.

Sempronia, 77/2417, proper name.

Separists, 15/375, separatists. See *note*, p. xxx.

Sharke, 85/2694, to cheat, to " sponge." Cf.

The *sharking* tricks Of cooz'ning Tradsmen. *Taylor*, 210.

Sheet, standing in a sheet, 104/3342, customary mode of punishment for a certain sin.

Shelfe, 43/1288, a ledge of rock.

Shend, 68/2103, 121/42, to protect, defend.

Give laud to him that loveth Israel, And sing his praise that *shendeth* David's fame.
George Peele, 471.

Sherry, 62/1916.

Gascoygne, Orleance, or the Chrystall *Sherrant*. *Taylor*, 549.

Ship, made a ship out, 106/3411, fitted out a ship.

Shoe, to tread the shoe awry, 81/2542, to leave the path of virtue. This is probably Taylor's meaning :
—" He bade me leave prating, for I hindred him from mending Alderman Pennington's shooes, (who had gone much aside,) and that his especiall care and charge was, to set him upright if it were possible." *Complaint of Christmas*, p. 3.

Shoes, prov., " He who waits for dead men's shoes goes barefoot," 106/3408.

Shoone, 27/754, *pl.* of shoe, shoes.

Shroudes, 151/58, coverings or a shelter. " They turne them [the poor] out of their *shrouds* as mice." *B. Gilpin's Sermon*, p. 33.

Siccity, 117/54, dryness.

Sillie, 25/710, seely, simple.

Silvanus, 137/4.

Silvius, 90/2851, proper name.

Simple, 147/36, simples, medicinal plants.

Simplician, 148/78, simpleton.

Simpring, 29/829, simpering.

Simula, 26/733, pretence.

Sir, 28/807, a scholastic title, the translation of *dominus* commonly applied to priests and curates.

Skip-iacke, 71/2219, a dandy, a puppy.

Iacke of Newbery I will not repeate, Nor Iacke of both sides, nor of *Skip-Iacke* neate. *Taylor*, 123.

Skin, leap out on's, 94/2976, to be beyond one's self with joy.

Skull, 71/2218.

Slavering, 43/1259.
> She mumbled and she *slavered*, and she spun. Taylor, *A Pedlar and a Romish Priest*, p. 20.

Sleas, 129/18, slays.

Sleeve, " pinned upon the," phr., 28/784.
> This gallant *pins* the wenches on his *sleeve*. *Love's L. L.* v. 2.

Snake, 71/2221, a poor wretch ; a term of reproach.

Snowt-faire, 34/975, contempt-ible, coxcombical.

Snuffe, 60/1833, a very small quantity. Cf.
> When as is spent his credit and chink,
> . And he quite wasted to a *snuffe*.
> *Taylor,* 214.

Sodomeo, 79/2467.

Sol, 113/19, 115/26.

Solomon, 147/37.

Solon, 38/1120.

Sordido, 26/749, sordid, dirty. See Ben Jonson, *Every Man out of H.*

Sorrow, phr., " drink down sor-row," 62/1894, " to drive dull care away " by drinking.

Source, 113/4, souse, dip. " This little barke of ours being *sourst* in cumbersome waves." *Optick glasse of Humors*, 1639, p. 161, quoted in *H.*

Spare, prov., " He harmes the good that doth the evill spare," 45/1350.

Spleenfull, 97/3070.

Spring, phr., " 'Tis sweetest drinking at the spring," 60/1830.

Spurio, 77/2421, false-one.

Spurt, 79/2494, probably an error for sport.

Stage-plaies, 127/19.

Starke, 147/52, mere, sheer.

Stationer, 28/806, a bookseller. See *Taylor,* 228.

Stint, 89/2808, stop.

Stolido, 45/1352, dunce.

Stones, 87/2769, *testes.*

Stound, 129/17, an instant of time.

Stow, 81/2544, bestow.

Straw, 5/21, phr., " Not to set a straw by," to hold in small esteem.

String, phr., " lead in a string," 76/2383.
> Following their Vickers steps in every thing,
> *He led the parish euen by a string.*
> Sam. Rowlands, *The Letting of Hvmovrs Blood, etc.,* Epi. 37.

String, a golden, 44/1307.

Stroke, phr., " bear the stroke," 92/2917.

Strouting, 89/2844, swelling out.

Sulpitia, 78/2441, proper name.

Sumner, 81/2538, summoner, ap-paritor.

Swinge, 71/2232, swing, bent, inclination.

Sword-fish, 145/70.

Tagus, the river, and its golden sand, 116/21.
> The sands of Tagus all of burnish'd gold. *Greene,* 90.

Take me e're, 72/2251, take me to any ; show me.

Tamburlaine, 25/686. Mar-lowe's *Tamburlaine the Great* was probably written before 1590. It was printed in 8vo in 1592, and in 4to, in 1605 and 1606.

Tane, 26/739, taken.

Taurus, 48/1449, bull.

Tellus, 41/1209, Earth, as a deity.

Temerus, 104/3318, rashness.

Tempe, 116/12.

Tender-nosd, 112/11.

Thersites, 43/1255. "Thersites, a deformed and scurrilous Grecian." *Troi. and Cres.*, Dram. Pers. It is probable that R. C. gained his idea of Thersites from seeing this Play performed.

Thetis, 113/3.

Thieues—receivers, prov., "No receivers no thieves," 89/2818.

Thrush, prov., "One thrush in the hand is worth two in the bush," 106/3406. "A bird in the hand," &c.

Timon of Athens, 94/2965.

Timophila, 103/3279, love-honour.

Title-tattle, 103/3305.

Tobacconist, 72/2239, a tobaccosmoker.
The smoakie black-lung puft *Tobacconist :*
Whose ioy doth in Tobacco sole consist. *Taylor*, 511.
See also *Ib.* 214.

Toiels, 118/82, toils, fatigues.

Trade, common trade, 83/2626 ; see next.

Trade, phr., "The dealing trade," 72/2258. "And why should not Whores haue a Mistris of their owne *dealing-trade ?*" *Taylor*, 261. A gentlewoman of the *dealing trade* Procur'd her owne sweet picture to be made. Sam. Rowlands, *The Letting of Hvmovrs Blood,* etc., Epi. 29.

Traine, 87/2761, trick, arrangement.

Trans, 17/473, trans[ubstantiation].

Trencher-scraper, 27/771, a menial who works for food. Cf. Trencher-man, trencher-fly (Ash.).

Trinity, 144/32, three things.

Troth, 2/21, tell-troth rimes. Tell truth, the phrase was a favourite

one at the time. "In 1600 John Lane published his *Tom Tel-troths Message,* and his *Pens Complaint."* Tom *tell-troth* is a foolish gull to thee. *Taylor*, 237.

Troynovant, 86/2725, London.
Like Minos, or iust iudging Rhadamant,
He walkes the darkesome streets of *Troynouant. Taylor*, 491.
See also *George Peele*, 543.

Tuffe, 27/752, tough.

Turnus, 49/1465, Latin name.
Come, now, as *Turnus* 'gainst Æneas did. *Marlowe*, 39.

Tyranness, 92/2917.

Veneria, 83/2622, Venus.

Venus, 77/2418, 87/2753, 93/2939, 97/3072, 115/32, 131/2.

Ver, 126/13, spring.

Vilde, 44/1321, 68/2120, vile.
Goe but to Spaine, and shew thy *vild* condition. Taylor, *A Pedlar and a Romish Priest,* p. 8.
This form is sometimes used in the folio *Shakespeare*, 1623.

Virgil, 28/815.

Vitellius, 89/2825.

Vixen, 106/3394.

Vncase, 82/2579, expose. In a literal sense—
Tranio, at once
Vncase thee ; take my coloured hat and cloak.
Taming of a Shr. i. 1.

Vndermining, 44/1317, undermining bribes, bribes which procure one to commit unlawful or dishonourable actions.
They . . . .
Have hired me to *undermine* the duchess,
And buz these conjurations in her brain. 2 *Hen. VI.* i. 2.

Vnkemd, 27/760, uncombed, untrimmed.

Her unkemb'd locks asunder tearing. *Marlowe*, 345.

Vntemperate, 58/1763, intemperate.

Vntrust, 69/2135, unfastened. See 'poynts,' *supra*.

Vntwitten, 132/15, ?

Votarius, 102/3271, wish, desire.

Vp, phr., "Up and tells," 122/55, tells without hesitation.

Vpsefreese, 60/1816, a kind of beer imported from Friesland. Cf. *upse - Dutch, upse - English.* "To drink upse-freeze," "to drink swinishly;" to drink all off at a swig.
    This valiant pot-leach, that vpon his knees
    Has drunk a thousand pottles *vp se freese. Taylor*, 487.
See also Heywood's *Philocothonista*, p. 45, where one of the names for a drunkard is "One that drinkes *Vpse-freeze.*"

Vulcan, 82/2588, 117/38.

Warrant, phr., "A warrant seald with butter," 12/276, an empty promise.

Warrantize, 12/275, to warrant, promise.

Whilome, 121/37, once, formerly.
    Thou Saint (quoth he) I *whilome* did adore. *Taylor*, 388.

Whipping-cheer, 13/332. "Nowe and then not a fewe haue *whipping cheare* to feede themselues withall." *Stubbs's Anat.* ed 1836, p. 111.

Whit, "ne're a whit," phr., 100/3190, not in the least.

Wilde-fyer, 145/66.

Wishers, prov., "Great wishers and common woulders seldom good householders," 103/3277.

Worser, 75/2358.

Wreck, 97/3070, wreak, inflict.

Ycie, 125/9, icy.

Yclad, 30/869, clothed.

Ycleped, 22/607, called, named.

Yslaine, 122/56, slain.

Yspread, 64/1988, spread.

Yspunne, 27/753, spun.

Zephyrus, 116/28.

GENERAL INDEX.

JOHN CHILDS AND SON, PRINTERS.

The manufacturer's authorised representative in the EU for product
safety is Oxford University Press España S.A. of El Parque Empresarial
San Fernando de Henares, Avenida de Castilla, 2 - 28830 Madrid
(www.oup.es/en or product.safety@oup.com). OUP España S.A. also acts
as importer into Spain of products made by the manufacturer.
Printed and bound by CPI Group (UK) Ltd, Croydon, CR0 4YY

05/05/2026

02102998-0004